OF SHEFFIELD

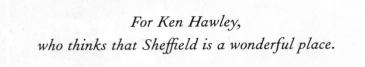

For Ken Hawley,
who thinks that Sheffield is a wonderful place.

A History of
Sheffield

David Hey

Carnegie Publishing

Also published by Carnegie:
Prof. David Hey, *'County of the Broad Acres': A History of Yorkshire* (2005)

Other town and city histories available from Carnegie:
Prof. John K. Walton, *Blackpool*
Peter Aughton, *Bristol: A People's History*
Dr John A. Hargreaves, *Halifax*
Dr Andrew White (ed.), *A History of Lancaster*
Peter Aughton, *Liverpool: A People's History*
Prof. Alan Kidd, *Manchester*
Dr Jeffrey Hill, *Nelson*

Forthcoming town and city histories:
Dr Graham Davis and Penny Bonsall, *Bath*
Prof. Carl Chinn, *Birmingham*
Dr Derek Beattie, *Blackburn*
Dr John Doran, *Chester*
Dr John A. Hargreaves, *Huddersfield*
Dr Andrew White, *Kendal*
Prof. Trevor Rowley, *A History of Oxford*
Dr Mark Freeman, *A History of St Albans*
Prof. Bill Sheils, *A History of York*

Full details on www.carnegiepublishing.com

© David Hey, 1998, 2005

First published in 1998 by Carnegie Publishing Ltd

This revised edition published in 2005 by
by Carnegie Publishing Ltd,
Chatsworth Road,
Lancaster LA1 4SL
www.carnegiepublishing.com

British Library Cataloguing-in-Publication data
A catalogue record for this book is available from the British Library

ISBN 10: 1-85936-110-2
ISBN 13: 978-1-85936-110-8

Designed, typeset and originated by Carnegie Publishing
Printed and bound by CPI, Bath Press

Contents

Preface

SHEFFIELD HAS BEEN FORTUNATE in its local historians. It has the early work of Joseph Hunter, Alfred Gatty, and the Leader brothers, and of numerous other scholars associated with the Hunter Archaeological Society on which

to build. In recent years, a fine series of academic studies (listed in the bibliography at the end of the book) have been published on many different aspects of local history, particularly industrial history. A joint enterprise to mark the city's centenary resulted in a huge, three-volume history covering the years 1843–1993. Sheffield might justly claim to have the best collection of local histories anywhere in Britain.

But no general history of Sheffield has appeared since Mary Walton wrote *Sheffield: Its Story and Its Achievements*

left Sheffield's coat of arms, granted to the new borough in 1843, displayed on the gates to Sheffield Manor. The sturdy figures are Thor and Woden, representing the metal industries. The sheaves of arrows and the sheaves of wheat are from the badges granted by Queen Mary Tudor to the Town Trustees and Church Burgesses, the successors of the medieval Burgery, and are puns on Sheffield's name, which was derived from the River Sheaf. The motto suggests that with God's help and hard work prosperity will flow.
PHOTOGRAPH: CARNEGIE

right Detail from the tomb of George, Sixth Earl of Shrewsbury, Sheffield Cathedral. The Order of the Garter surrounds his coat of arms under an earl's coronet. The talbot dogs are a pun on the family name.
PHOTOGRAPH: CARNEGIE

in 1948. There is no book that takes account of the modern researches of the city's local historians. I have often been asked by extramural students, school teachers and members of local history societies to write an introductory history that provides a general framework for further enquiry. Now that I am retired, the time has come to do just that.

A few years ago, I published a book that covered just 80 years of Sheffield's early history. It was much longer than the present book. Clearly, every paragraph that I have written here could have been extended. My intention has been simply to write a broad account into which more detailed studies might be fitted. A lot has had to be left out. Other writers would have had more to say about the Sheffield Flood, the Chartists, women's history, and so on, but in return they would have had to leave out a lot of the material that I have included. This book is *A History of Sheffield*, not *The History*.

I can claim to be a Sheffielder when it suits me, for I was born in Jessop's Hospital, some 300 yards from the office where I worked at the University of Sheffield. But Sheffielders know from my accent that I am not really one of them. I come from a distant place 15 miles to the north, just beyond the ancient boundaries of Hallamshire. I like to say that I therefore possess the necessary detachment to write about Sheffield and Sheffielders.

I joined the Department of Extramural Studies (now the Institute of Lifelong Learning) at the University of Sheffield in 1973. The material in the present book was largely gathered for use with classes or for lectures to local societies. Teaching adults is a two-way process, and I have learned a great deal from class members over the years. Some of my postgraduate students will recognise some facts and figures that have been taken from their dissertations. The Names Project group will smile at some familiar surnames that they have proved to be intensely local. It is impossible to list all those people who have provided me with information or have helped to widen my understanding over the years. I hope they will enjoy those parts of the book which are new to them. The study of local history is a co-operative venture. Here, I have drawn on the work of many people in order to present a new synthesis which I hope will provide the basis for future research.

David Hey

Introduction

THE EARLIEST SURVIVING PRINT of the town of Sheffield is Thomas Oughtibridge's view of 1737 from Pye Bank, on the hills north of the river Don, not far from the present ski-slope. It is not an expert drawing, for it gives undue prominence to the parish church (now the Cathedral), but it does give a good impression of how small the town was then compared with the city of today, with the houses clustered together on the ridge on the other side of the river. It gives the impression that Sheffield was little more than a large village before the Industrial Revolution.

But that impression is mistaken. Contemporaries thought of Sheffield as a town, and a busy, thriving one at that. Daniel Defoe wrote in his *A Tour through the Whole Island of Great Britain* (1724–26), 'The town of Sheffield is very populous and large, the streets narrow, and the houses dark and black, occasioned by the continued smoke of the forges, which are always at work.' Defoe was an informed commentator, who had travelled widely, so we must take his opinion seriously. It was similar to that of the Rev. Thomas Cox, who described Sheffield in 1720 as 'exceedingly large, populous and flourishing.'

In 1736, the year before Oughtibridge's view was drawn, the population of the town had been counted at 10,121. A further 4,410 people lived in the rural parts of the enormous parish of Sheffield, the whole of which was to be incorporated as the borough of Sheffield in 1843 and as the city fifty years later. These figures do indeed seem small compared with the half a million people who live in Sheffield today, but at that time the entire population of England was only between five and six millions. London was a colossus, with over half a million inhabitants, but the next largest city – Norwich – had only 30,000 or so. Sheffield was already in the second rank of towns and it was starting to grow rapidly. Soon, it was to overtake the ancient cathedral cities and county towns.

Like Manchester, Liverpool, Leeds, Birmingham, and most of the other great Victorian industrial cities, Sheffield had long been a market town, larger than the surrounding villages, and distinctly urban in character. From at least 1296, and probably from long before, the lords of Sheffield had the right to hold a weekly market. During the early Middle Ages the present web of streets in central Sheffield had been created around the market place. The medieval pattern was intact in 1736 when Ralph Gosling drew the earliest map of the town which has survived. The streets have been widened in modern times and the old buildings have gone, but the names have been preserved. Names such as High Street,

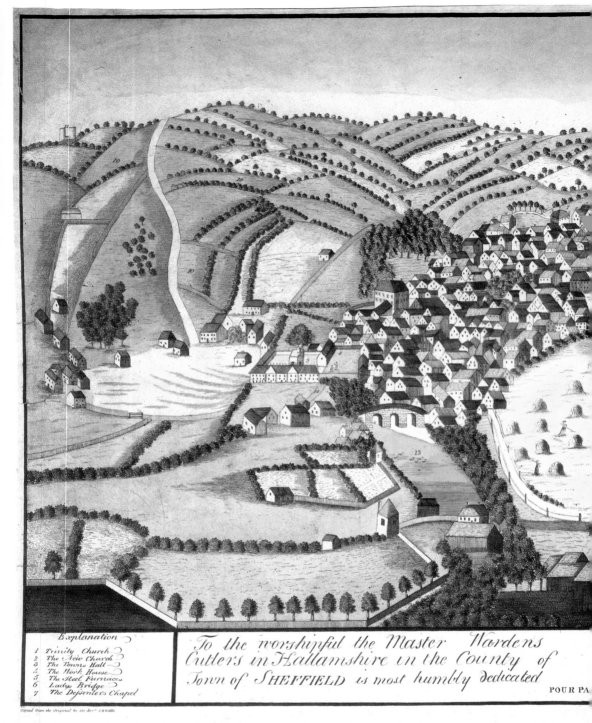

To the worshipful the Master Wardens Cutlers in Hallamshire in the County of Town of *SHEFFIELD* is most humbly dedicated

POUR PA

Thomas Oughtibridge's *View of Sheffield*, 1737 (1745 edition). The view, taken from Pye Bank on the northern side of the town, shows Sheffield just as it was beginning to expand beyond its medieval limits. The parish church is drawn to a larger scale than reality. Behind it is the new St Paul's. The Manor Lodge is shown at the far top left, alone in the former deer park. In the foreground the river Don curves to Lady's Bridge. The cutlers' grinding wheel

(bottom right) was leased by one Kellam Homer in the early seventeenth century. The goit which powered the wheel and then ran on to the corn mill in Millsands formed an island with the parallel river, hence the name of Kelham Island, where Sheffield's industrial museum is now situated.

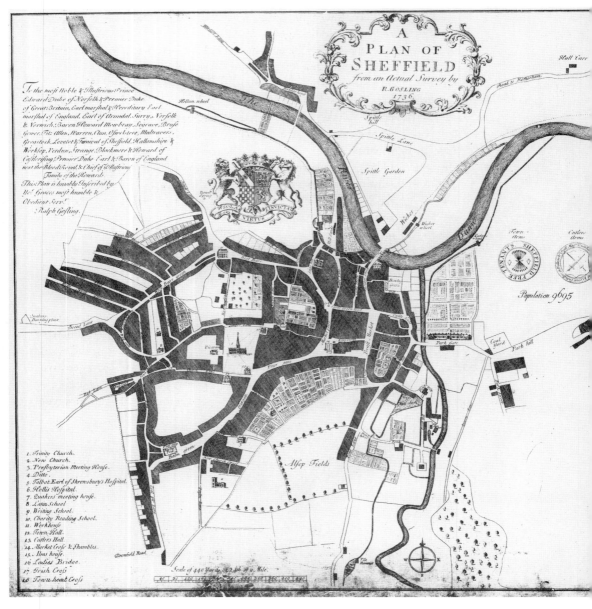

Ralph Gosling's *Map of Sheffield*, 1736. This earliest surviving map of the town was drawn the year before Oughtibridge's view. Together, they provide a clear picture of Sheffield before the era of rapid expansion. The rivers Don and Sheaf provide effective borders in the north and the east. The Market Place lies at the heart of the town. Much of the medieval street pattern survives to this day. The town was expanding over the former 'townfields' in the north-west, but many spaces within the town centre were occupied by gardens and orchards. The curving line of the park wall separates the 'burgage plots' to the south of 'Prior Gate' (High Street) from Alsop Fields. The new St Paul's church lies at the southern edge of the town.

A HISTORY OF SHEFFIELD

Far Gate, Market Place, Snig Hill, Barker's Pool, and the Wicker are as familiar now as they were in the Middle Ages.

Other aspects of the town's history can also be traced back to at least the thirteenth century. The present Church Burgesses and Town Trustees are the successors to the burgesses who were granted a charter outlining their privileges in 1297. By chance, the first documentary reference to a Sheffield cutler is from the same year. The industry which made Sheffield famous is at least seven hundred years old and no doubt stretches back much further to a time for which we have no information.

Many Sheffielders possess surnames which were coined locally in the Middle Ages. The most distinctive ones are derived from the names of small, surrounding settlements, such as Broomhead, Creswick, Crookes, Dungworth, Housley, Shirtcliffe, or Staniforth. Some names – such as Shemeld, which was first recorded in Handsworth in 1379 – have origins which defy explanation. Other Sheffielders who have common surnames such as Hall or Wilson are also descended from families that have been in the locality for centuries. Members of the Sheffield and District Family History Society can often identify ancestors who lived in Sheffield long before the Industrial Revolution.

The history of Sheffield must naturally be largely concerned with the great industrial changes of the last 250 years. They have made Sheffield the distinctive place that it is today. But the town is an old one and its early history has affected it in ways that are still evident on the ground and in how its inhabitants perceive themselves. That earlier history must also receive due attention, even though the evidence is thin and unsatisfactory, and sometimes open to different interpretations.

'The Population of Sheffield is, for so large a town, unique in its character, in fact it more closely resembles that of a village than of a town, for over wide areas each person appears to be acquainted with every other.'

FREDERICK BARRY, 1888

The earliest settlements

CHAPTER I

The evidence of archaeology and place-names

One of the objects on display in Weston Park Museum is a Bronze Age burial urn that was discovered in Crookes in 1887. The urn was made from baked coarse clay and contained the cremated remains of human bones, a small cup, and a bronze knife. It is similar in purpose and design to others that have been found on the moors to the west of Sheffield, where a great deal of physical evidence from the Bronze Age survives in the present landscape. The find is a reminder that prehistoric people probably occupied the same district as modern Sheffielders, but that the evidence of their activities has been obliterated by later housing and industrial development. In recent years archaeologists have come to recognise that the prehistoric population of the British Isles was far higher than they once believed and that much of the countryside had been cleared for farming long before the arrival of the Romans.

The most dramatic evidence of the pre-history of the district that now lies within the boundaries of the city of Sheffield is provided by the Iron Age fort which occupies a commanding position on the top of Wincobank Hill, high above the river Don. The fort was built to defend the local population, who for most of the time must have farmed peacefully nearby. Even now, a double rampart and an earth bank constructed over a stone wall enclose the summit of the hill. Material extracted from the ramparts

Bronze Age burial urn. In 1887 this urn was found in six to eight inches of soil by the roadside at Crookes. It contained the cremated remains of human bones, a small cup, and a bronze knife. The urn was made from coarse clay and is 9½ inches high and 26 inches round its largest circumference.

The linear earthwork known as the Roman Rig formed a boundary north of the River Don. It is seen here near Dyson's Plantation in Wentworth Park, on its way from Sheffield to Kilnhurst and Mexborough. Despite its name, it actually dates from the period after the withdrawal of the Romans.
HUNTER ARCHAEOLOGICAL SOCIETY

has been radio-carbon dated to about 500 BC. We do not know whether the fort was occupied continually until the Roman invasion or if it was brought back into use once the Roman threat became apparent, but it is remarkable that the earthwork has survived so intact within the city boundary, over two-and-a-half millennia. It is easily accessible by a public footpath and still provides the finest viewpoint for surveying the whole of eastern and north-eastern Sheffield.

The names of Britain's major rivers are amongst the oldest words in our language. The Don (or the Dun, as it was pronounced and spelt well into the eighteenth century) is one of the river names that is pre-Celtic in origin, going back far into the prehistoric period. The course of the river through Sheffield, beyond its confluence with the Sheaf, is thought to have marked the boundary between the British tribes, the Brigantes and the Corieltauvi. When the Romans arrived in the district in AD 54, they stopped at this frontier and erected a fort for 800 soldiers at Templeborough, on the opposite bank of the river to the hill fort at Wincobank. In AD 69 the Romans advanced north and defeated the Brigantes. Wincobank hill fort fell into disuse, while Templeborough was rebuilt twice before reaching its final form in the late third or early fourth century. After the withdrawal of the Romans, the ruined fort was known simply as Brough (the Anglo-Saxon word for a fort). It seems to have acquired the fanciful name of Templeborough in the sixteenth century. The site was excavated in 1916 before it was built over by the steelworks of Steel, Peech and Tozer, and the finds can now be viewed at Clifton Park Museum, Rotherham.

The Roman military road that headed west from Templeborough joined another route that came from Lincoln, via Littleborough (Notts), Bawtry and Catcliffe. The combined road is known to have proceeded along the line of the present Cricket Inn Lane and is thought to have crossed the river Sheaf into the modern city centre, then to have climbed past the Cathedral to Broad Lane and

A HISTORY OF SHEFFIELD

to have headed west towards Sandygate. In 1819 the Rev. Joseph Hunter wrote that it was 'the prevalent opinion at Sheffield' that the [Cathedral] churchyard was 'anciently a camp of the Romans.' Another reputable local historian, R. E. Leader, reported that during restoration work at the beginning of the eighteenth century the east end of the church was found to stand upon a vast bed of human bones, a discovery that prompted comparison with a similar find at Ilkley, where the church stands in a Roman fort. The Cathedral stands on a level platform high above the river valleys, on a site that might well have appealed to Roman military engineers, but although the evidence is tantalising, it is only circumstantial.

The destination of the Roman road through Sheffield was Brough (*Anavio*), the Roman fort near Hope. It was once believed that the Long Causeway to Stanage was Roman, and old Ordnance Survey maps mark it as such, but the paved track on the moor near Stanage Pole is now considered to have been a nineteenth-century road for transporting millstones. The Romans probably crossed Stanage Edge a little further to the north. The evidence for other Roman military roads in the Sheffield district is thin, but historians now realise that many of our present roads, lanes and tracks were probably in everyday use by the local farming population during the Roman occupation. The discovery at Stannington (long ago, in the eighteenth century) of a bronze diploma granting land to a retired Roman soldier suggests that the hills as well as the more sheltered sites around Sheffield were cultivated. Farming probably continued in the time-honoured way no matter who the rulers were.

After the withdrawal of the Romans in the early fifth century, the native population formed part of the British kingdom of Elmet, which covered much of West and South Yorkshire, as far east as the magnesian limestone belt. Elmet retained its independence from the Anglo-Saxons until 617, when it fell to the Northumbrians. The linear earthwork known as the Roman Rig may mark the southern border of Elmet, though it is equally possible that it may have been cast up to separate the Northumbrians from the Mercians. The inaccurately named Roman Rig was formerly known as Kemp Ditch, from an old name meaning warrior; it runs parallel to the Don to the north of the river, passing close to the fort at Wincobank, and stretches for ten miles from Sheffield to Mexborough and Kilnhurst. The most substantial remains can be seen in the fields between Wentworth Park and Abdy Farm, Swinton.

The centuries between the Roman withdrawal and the Norman Conquest were named the Dark Ages by earlier historians. The Sheffield district was a border zone between northern and midland England, just as it had been in the pre-Roman period. For much of the time this district lay within the southern limit of the Anglo-Saxon kingdom of Northumbria, but at other periods it was ruled by

Wincobank hill fort from the air. Modern housing has spread up both sides of the hill, but this dramatic site is still intact 2,500 years after it was constructed on the skyline above the River Don. The prominent trackway along the ridge and through the fort is likely to be ancient.

Mercia. The continued use of certain dialect words over the whole of the area that once was Elmet suggests that the Mercians held sway long enough for their forms of speech to become accepted. By the early ninth century the border between Northumbria and Mercia had become fixed, probably along the line of the later boundary between Yorkshire and Derbyshire. In 827–30, when the army of Egbert (or Ecgbert) of Wessex reached the Sheffield district, the Northumbrians symbolically crossed their frontier to Dore, in order to agree terms that prevented a Mercian invasion. The *Anglo-Saxon Chronicle* records also that in 942 Edmund, the son of Edward the Elder, conquered the Danes of Mercia, 'as far as where Dore divides.' The place-name literally means a door or 'narrow pass'. The Limb Brook, at the eastern limit of Dore, separated Mercia from Northumbria, and the border continued along the river Sheaf and the Meersbrook, both of whose names mean division or boundary. To the north of the Limb Brook the frontier was marked on the moors by Whirlow (whose name means 'boundary mound'), by what was described in 1574 as 'a great heape of stones called Ringinglowe', and by that ancient marker, Stanage Pole. In later centuries these rivers, mounds and pole separated Yorkshire from Derbyshire and the Archbishopric of York from that of Canterbury. Sheffield's border position has been a constant theme in its long history.

In the Anglo-Saxon period the district around Sheffield was known as Hallamshire, a name which is still in widespread use, though the limits of the original territory have expanded as Sheffield has grown. The meaning of the name is uncertain, for although it is most likely to have been derived from the rocky nature of the terrain, it could have arisen from Hallamshire's border position on the south-eastern edge of Northumbria. In 1642 a survey defined the

Hallamshire's border. Marked on a map of 1805 as 'Ancient Ditch', this medieval earthwork between Stanage End and Moscar separated Hallamshire from Hathersage, and Yorkshire from Derbyshire. It is mentioned in boundary disputes in 1559 and 1724.
PHOTOGRAPH: AUTHOR

A HISTORY OF SHEFFIELD

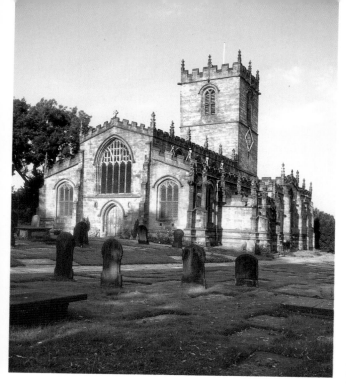

Ecclesfield church in late summer sunshine. This fine medieval building in Perpendicular Gothic style is the successor to an even older Romano-British church which served the whole of Hallamshire.

PHOTOGRAPH: CARNEGIE

lordship of Hallamshire as the 71,526 acres of the parishes of Sheffield and Ecclesfield and the chapelry of Bradfield. This definition confirms an earlier claim made in 1268 that only Sheffield, Ecclesfield and Bradfield lay within the 'metes of Hallamshire.' The kingdom of Northumbria contained numerous 'shires', for example Riponshire, Allertonshire, Sowerbyshire, Blackburnshire and Howdenshire. Each of these large estates had a focal point for military and administrative purposes and a separate religious centre. Thus, Hallamshire was administered from Sheffield Castle, but its ecclesiastical centre was at Ecclesfield, whose Celtic name indicates the presence of a church before the arrival of the Anglo-Saxons. All the 'eccles' names in historic Yorkshire are from within the territory of Elmet. (Ecclesall's name is derived from its position on the southern border of the original parish of Ecclesfield.) Not for nothing was Ecclesfield church described in 1619 as 'The Minster of the Moors'. Bradfield remained a chapel-of-ease within the parish of Ecclesfield until Victorian times. The parish church (now the Cathedral) at Sheffield had acquired its independence by the thirteenth century, but it had been described as a chapel of Ecclesfield in 1178 and its former dependency was acknowledged in 1376. The whole of Hallamshire originally formed one enormous parish, served by the church at Ecclesfield.

Ecclesfield Priory and Hall. The thirteenth-century Priory (*right*) was built for the Benedictine monks of the Abbey of St Wandrille in Normandy, the owners of the tithes and a large estate in Ecclesfield. After the Dissolution of the Monasteries in the sixteenth century, it was converted into a Tudor Hall. The Georgian extension was built in 1736.

PHOTOGRAPH: CARNEGIE

The earliest evidence of the establishment of the Christian religion in Sheffield is in the form of a ninth- or tenth-century cross, which is carved with grapes, vine scrolls and the figure of a man with a bow-and-arrow. The original stone is in the British Museum, but a cast is on display at Weston Park. The cross was discovered in the early nineteenth century in Sheffield Park, when it was in use as a cutler's hardening trough, with one side hollowed out. Perhaps it was the churchyard cross that was pulled down in 1570 as a result of the Reformation. The figure of the archer appears on several other Anglo-Saxon crosses and is thought to have symbolised the Christian attack on evil. The vine scrolls are so similar to those on the cross in Eyam churchyard as to suggest the work of the same craftsman. Artistically, the Sheffield cross is amongst a group of Derbyshire crosses which must be viewed in a Mercian context.

The Domesday Book

The first written record of Sheffield is in the Domesday Book of 1086, when the name was spelt in three different ways: Scafeld, Escafeld, and Sceuelt. The Norman clerks had difficulty with the English 'Sh' sound (which is why Shropshire became Salopshire and eventually Salop). Sheffield's name means the 'open country' by the Sheaf, open probably in the sense of having no trees. The names of Ecclesfield and Bradfield have a similar ending, and so do those of Huddersfield, Wakefield, Dronfield, Chesterfield and Mansfield. The terse entries in the Yorkshire folios of the Domesday Book are difficult to interpret. Before the Conquest, Sheffield and Attercliffe had belonged to Swen (a Scandinavian name), but by 1086 they were regarded as *inland*, farmed directly by the lord of Hallamshire, rather than land rented to tenants. Hallamshire was described in imprecise measurements as being ten leagues long and eight leagues broad. It contained sixteen unnamed *berewicks* or outlying farms. Earl Waltheof, the last Anglo-Saxon lord of Hallamshire, was said to have had a hall, which, as we shall see, was probably at the confluence of the Sheaf and the Don, on the site of the later castle. The Domesday Book also records six small manors at Ecclesfield, and other small manors at Grimeshou (near Grimesthorpe), Wadsley, Worrall, Ughill, Holdworth, and Onesacre. Places recorded just beyond Hallamshire included Handsworth, Tinsley, Rotherham, etc. Many other settlements, probably including Bradfield, were silently included amongst the unnamed *berewicks*. The Domesday Book is far from being a complete record of settlement at the time, but it does indicate that even some small settlements on the edges of the moors were in existence by the eleventh century. Some of them were probably already several centuries old, but we do not have the documentary evidence to prove it.

The Domesday Book entries enable us to classify certain groups of local place-names. For instance, the burial mounds of the leading Anglo-Saxon and Scandinavian inhabitants must have been prominent features of the landscape, particularly in the Lower Don Valley, where Grimeshou, Wincobank, Meadow Hall and Tinsley are all names that were derived from such (vanished) structures. The old minor names of the Sheffield district were formed by Anglo-Saxon settlers long before their first mention in the Domesday Book; Owlerton, Stannington, Dungworth, Hawksworth Head, Holdworth and Sugworth all have common Anglo-Saxon place-name endings. Some of the numerous Hallamshire names that end in -ley are also Anglo-Saxon, but others of this type may refer to post-Conquest clearings. The list includes Birley, Heeley, Walkley, Whiteley, Hartley, Longley, Wadsley, Brightholmlee, Loxley, Beeley, Cowley, Housley, Hesley, Mortomley, Whitley, and the lost place-names Hawley and Winkley.

Place-names derived from the Vikings or their descendants form a much smaller group. Sheffield has no names ending in -by (the common Danish element), but Crookes is an Old Norse name meaning 'a nook or corner of land', Onesacre is derived from a Viking personal name, and Butterthwaite is Old Norse for a clearing with rich pasture. The Danish word thorpe, meaning 'outlying farmstead', is found to the east and north of the city centre, sometimes in combination with a Viking personal name. Thus, Grimesthorpe, the lost Skinner-thorpe, and probably Renathorpe (now Hatfield House) are derived from Old Norse personal names, but the first element of Osgathorpe may be either Old Norse or Old English, and Upperthorpe (which was Hoperthorpe in 1383) was derived from a surname which was a Middle English name for a cooper. By the time that some of these settlements were founded, both Anglo-Saxon and Viking words had obviously become absorbed into local speech.

Other early names were derived from natural features in the landscape. The first element in Attercliffe seems to be from a shortened form of a personal name, such as Aethelred. The cliff has gone, for it was levelled in Victorian times when the river was diverted and Sanderson's steel works was built on the site. Carbrook meant 'the stream in the marsh', Darnall's name referred to 'secluded land in a nook on a boundary', and Brightside was a sixteenth-century attempt to make sense of the older name Brekesherth, which is recorded in a variety of spellings from the twelfth century onwards, and which combined an Old English personal name with 'hearth'. Pitsmoor was first recorded as Orepitts, for ironstone was mined there, Shirecliffe was 'the bright hillside', and Neepsend took its name from its position at the foot of this steep hill. In western Sheffield Broom Hall and Fulwood (the 'foul or dirty wood') are obvious topographical names. Wardsend is a corruption of World's End, a nickname which refers to its position on the border between the parishes of Sheffield and Ecclesfield.

Sheffield's Anglo-Saxon Cross. The cross is displayed in the section of the British Museum which is devoted to Anglo-Saxon England. The style is that of the ninth- or tenth-century Mercian sculptors who produced crosses such as the one that stands so prominently in Eyam churchyard.

I. Shaw, *Christ Church, Attercliffe* (*c*.1845). Christ Church was one of the new 'Million Act' churches of the 1820s which were intended to serve the rapidly growing industrial districts. It has been demolished. Shaw's view shows the cliff that gave Attercliffe its name. This, too, has disappeared under industrial development.
SHEFFIELD INDUSTRIAL MUSEUMS TRUST

The Lovetots and the Furnivals

The last Anglo-Saxon lord of Hallamshire, Waltheof, Earl of Northumberland, Huntingdon and Northampton, had large properties elsewhere in England and so would have resided in Sheffield only occasionally, if at all. The Domesday Book records that he had a hall in Hallamshire and that Earl Edwin of Mercia, another great Anglo-Saxon landowner, had a hall at Laughton-en-le-Morthen, a few miles to the east. Both of these halls were probably built on the same sites as the later Norman motte-and-bailey castles. The earthworks of the Norman castle at Laughton remain a prominent landscape feature to the west of the church; those at Sheffield were replaced by a later stone castle whose ruins lie beneath Castle Markets. After the Conquest, both earls were allowed to keep their estates, and Waltheof's reconciliation with the new regime was marked by his marriage to Judith, a niece of William the Conqueror. Further rebellions brought their downfall soon afterwards, however. Edwin was beheaded in 1070 and Waltheof suffered the same fate in 1076. The lordship of Hallamshire remained with Judith, but Roger de Busli, the powerful lord of the new castle at Tickhill, was her tenant by the time that the Domesday Book was compiled in 1086. Despite this tenurial arrangement, Hallamshire never became part of the great honour, or lordship, of Tickhill, whose manors covered large parts of South Yorkshire, Nottinghamshire and Derbyshire. It remained a distinct lordship and preserved its old name throughout the Middle Ages.

Roger de Busli had come from Bully-en-Brai in Normandy with the Conqueror. One of his tenants in Nottinghamshire was Roger de Lovetot, who took his surname from another small place in Normandy. This Roger was succeeded in turn by his son or nephew, Richard, who died about 1116 leaving a son, William. This William de Lovetot became lord of Hallamshire and was largely responsible (as far as we can tell) for building a castle there and for developing a market town alongside it. Remarkably, the lordship of Hallamshire was never sold or forfeited by later lords. The ownership passed through male and female lines from the Lovetots to the Furnivals, briefly to the Nevills, then to the Talbots (Earls of Shrewsbury) and finally to the Howards (Dukes of Norfolk) in unbroken descent into modern times. Few places in England experienced such continuity of ownership.

The location of Earl Waltheof's hall has excited much speculation. Many local historians in the past have advocated the claims of a site at Hallam Head, high in the Rivelin Valley, next to Burnt Stones Common, in the belief that it was destroyed at the Conquest. The arguments are slender and unconvincing. It is far more plausible that Earl Waltheof, or his predecessors, chose the same obvious defensive position at the confluence of the Sheaf and the Don for his stronghold, as did his Norman successors. The excavation of the Castle Markets site in 1927–29 revealed extensive remains of a late Anglo-Saxon (or Anglo-Scandinavian) building, which had been partly destroyed by fire, below the foundations of the Norman castle. These excavations also showed that after the Norman Conquest the site was left vacant for a time, until a new motte-and-bailey castle was built. This seems to have been the work of William de Lovetot. The rivers provided natural defence on the north and the east; the southern and western sides were defended by a wide and deep moat, filled with water. William's castle occupied a low-lying, but secure position.

William de Lovetot was probably the lord who founded the town of Sheffield alongside his residence. The market place which stretched up the hill from the castle may have been his creation, but as we have no evidence of market activities until the following century, we cannot be sure that he was responsible. Perhaps, too, it was William who set up bars at the entrances to the town? A thirteenth-century charter refers to land 'outside the bars of Sheffield', but only West Bar survived as a local place-name. We do know that he built a corn mill, which was called the Town Mill until well into the nineteenth century, in the area known as Millsands, and that this was supplied with water by a long goit fed by the river Don (see the detail of Fairbank's map of 1771 on page 20).

Nearby, he crossed the river with a wooden bridge, which was later named Lady's Bridge after the chapel of Our Lady which was built on the southern bank. This wooden bridge was replaced in 1486, when the townsmen paid William Hill, a local mason, to build a new one in stone. From Castlegate, the late fifteenth-century Gothic arches and ribs can still be glimpsed underneath the present Lady's Bridge, which has been widened on several occasions to take the present heavy traffic. On the hillside beyond his bridge, away from the town, William de Lovetot also founded the Hospital of St Leonard, an isolation hospital which survived until the reign of Henry VIII and whose site is commemorated by the name Spital Hill.

William also seems to have been responsible for building a new church and for making Sheffield an independent parish. A third of Sheffield's tithes were granted to the priory that he had founded in Worksop, and in return the prior and monks provided a vicar. Among the Sheffield properties of Worksop Priory were some houses that occupied a prime position on the north side of High Street. The memory of this ownership was so strong that, two hundred years after the dissolution of the priory, Ralph Gosling's map of 1736 still marked High Street as Prior Gate.

At the end of the twelfth century the Lovetots failed in the male line and an heiress, Maud, married Gerard de Furnival, whose ancestors had come from Fourneville in Normandy. Gerard died on crusade in 1219. His sons also took part in the crusades and seem to have been equally warlike and involved in national affairs. They were in Hallamshire for only a part of their time and were content to allow their favoured retainers to create sub-manors at Ecclesall, Shirecliffe, Darnall, Owlerton, Wadsley, and further out in Hallamshire at Cowley, Hesley, Bolsterstone and Midhope.

In 1266, during the Barons' War, William de Lovetot's old castle was destroyed. Four years later, Thomas de Furnival was rewarded for his loyalty to the crown by the receipt of a royal charter that allowed him to build a substantial new castle on the same site. This stronghold dominated Sheffield for the best part of four centuries. Unfortunately, no plans or illustrations survive, but it was clearly comparable in size with the castles that Edward I was soon to build in north Wales, such as those at Conway and Harlech. Something of its plan and size is known from excavation and from John Harrison's survey of Hallamshire in 1637, shortly before its demolition. Harrison described it as 'very spacious, built about an inward court. On the south side an outward court yard or fould, builded round with divers houses of officers, as an armoury, barns, stables, and divers lodgings'. It covered just over four acres. Close by were three orchards, a hop yard, a cock pit and nineteen acres of land that were farmed by the keeper of the castle. Ralph Gosling's map of 1736 shows the outline of the former barbican on the south side, preserved by a curving lane.

In 1281 another Thomas de Furnival was asked by a Quo Warranto enquiry to explain the grounds by which he claimed his rights as a lord. He said that rights to administer capital punishment, to hunt, to hold a market and to regulate the weight and price of bread had belonged to his ancestors since time immemorial. This statement is our first evidence for a market at Sheffield. Thomas subsequently decided to make his claims more certain and on 12 November 1296 he obtained a royal charter which allowed the holding of a market every Tuesday and of a fair on the eve, feast, and morrow of Holy Trinity (a movable feast in May or June). At the same time, he obtained another charter which formalised his rights to hunt in his park, and shortly afterwards he granted his townsmen a charter confirming their privileges. It seems that he was concerned to get everything down in writing instead of relying on oral memory.

The townsmen were granted their charter on 10 August 1297. Thomas called them 'my free tenants of the town of Sheffield' and he gave them and their heirs

Detail of Ralph Gosling's *Map of Sheffield* (1736) showing the market place and town centre. The northern entry to the town was via Lady's Bridge (16) and Bridge Street, which followed the line of the moat of the castle, and which was renamed Waingate later in the eighteenth century. Two street names mark the site of the castle, which had been dismantled in 1649–50. Beast Market was renamed Haymarket in 1784 when the livestock market was moved to the Wicker. The other limits of the market place are marked by the Market Cross (14) and the Irish Cross (17). Almshouses (15) occupy the site of the former bridge chapel. New Hall (6, top left) was a private house, then a dissenters' chapel, then the Hollis Hospital.

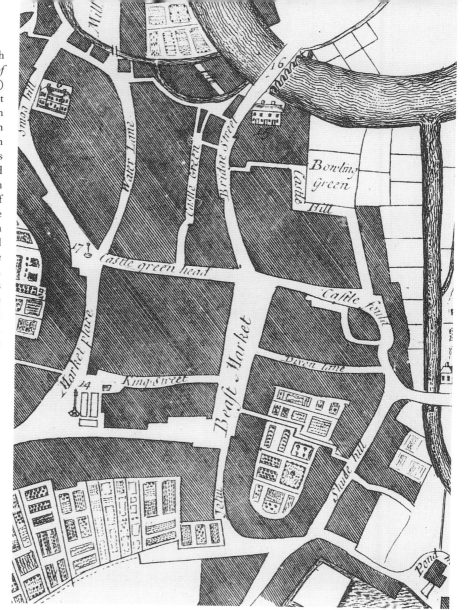

'all the tofts, lands and holdings which they hold of me' at the fixed annual rent of £3 8s. 9¼d., but reserving certain feudal dues, including the continued use of his manorial court. The townsmen were exempted from other feudal services and were not required to pay tolls at the lord's market. It is clear from the wording of the charter that the townsmen already held such privileges, which were now being confirmed in writing. Sheffield never became a fully fledged medieval borough with its own mayor and corporation, like Doncaster, but was what historians call a seigneurial borough, where the lord remained dominant but the townsmen had some measure of independence. Manorial records from 1441/42 include 'The Account of Richard Wode, bailiff of the borough there'. They also record '5s. 8d. received from the toll of the Market and Fairs of the borough.' In 1479 the

ARCUS, the Archaeological Research and Consultancy Unit at the University of Sheffield, have recently excavated part of Thomas de Furnival's castle, which was demolished after the Civil War in the late 1640s. The excavators believe that up to 75 per cent of the ground plan of the inner bailey may survive under Castle Markets as foundations, cellars, doors, floors and the lower course of walls.

ARCUS, UNIVERSITY OF SHEFFIELD

Burgery of Sheffield was recorded for the first time. As we shall see, this institution was later split into two bodies which still administer funds derived from the rents of the lands mentioned in 1297: the Church Burgesses and the Town Trustees.

Ralph Gosling's map of the town of Sheffield in 1736 marks the long gardens that stretched from the houses on the south side of the High Street as far as the wall of the lord's park. These property divisions are identical in appearance to the 'burgage plots' that historians have noted in medieval towns in many parts of western Europe. Demand for a frontage on the High Street or the Market Place produced these characteristic long, thin patterns. Gosling's map shows that decisions made by the Norman lords were reflected in the layout of the town several centuries later. Even now, the basic plan of the Norman borough is evident in the street pattern of the city centre. The importance of the Market Place at the heart of the medieval town is immediately obvious from Gosling's map. It was probably much larger originally, for the street names imply that it covered the whole of the large rectangular area on the slope between the castle and High Street.

The lord's hunting park stretched from the rear of the burgage plots across the river Sheaf as far as the fields of Attercliffe and Heeley and the boundary with the parish of Handsworth. The park had probably long been in existence by 1281, when Thomas de Furnival had claimed ancient hunting rights. Two fourteenth-century *Inquisitions Post Mortem* of the Lords Furnival mention the park; the first, in 1332, noting 'a certain park with deer ... [and] ... the underwood of the said park'. A subdivision known as the Little Park covered the area north of the Roman road (Cricket Inn Lane), as far as the Castle Orchards and the Nursery in the west. Harrison's survey in 1637 gave the size of the whole park as 2,461 acres and noted that the ring fence was eight miles in circumference. Part of the park wall was still standing near Newfield Green in the early nineteenth century, and short sections of the earthen boundary bank and ditch survive even now on the Manor Estate. From Heeley the park boundary curved in a northerly direction across the Sheaf, so as to enclose low-lying land known as The Pastures. It then crossed the Porter Brook and followed a course that marked the southern edge of the town of Sheffield, which in the eighteenth century was widened into a thoroughfare called Union Street and Norfolk Street. The inhabitants of Sheffield must have been very conscious of the presence of their medieval lords. By the late fifteenth century, and probably long before, a hunting lodge had been built on a high point within the park. During the sixteenth century this Manor Lodge was turned into a splendid country house.

The lords of Hallamshire also hunted in the woods and on the heather moors of Rivelin Chase and Loxley Firth. A hunting lodge was built in a prominent position on the gritstone escarpment, high above the Rivelin Valley, near the Long Causeway. A house called 'Rivelin Lodge' now occupies the site and the whole district is known as Lodge Moor. In the fourteenth century the lords of the sub-manors of Ecclesall and Shirecliffe also created parks close to their halls. In 1319 Sir Robert de Ecclesall, whose manor house stood near the top of Carter Knowle Road, obtained a licence to enclose a deer park on the hillside between Park Head and the River Sheaf, in the area now chiefly occupied by Ecclesall Woods. In 1392 Sir John de Mounteney obtained a royal charter to hunt throughout his lands at Cowley, Shirecliffe, Ecclesfield, Rotherham and Wath, and permission to enclose 200 acres of land, 200 acres of wood, and 20 acres of meadow into a park at Shirecliffe, on the steep hillside above the Don, now occupied by the ski-slope. The sub-manors of Darnall and Owlerton were smaller

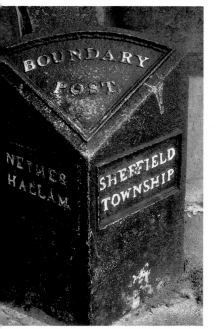

Township boundary post. This old boundary post separated the townships of Sheffield and Nether Hallam, outside the main buildings of the University of Sheffield. Townships were of medieval origin, but their roles as units of local government began to disappear when Sheffield was incorporated as a borough in 1843. Curiously, the University of Sheffield is in Hallam, but the University of Sheffield Hallam is not!
PHOTOGRAPH: AUTHOR

Detail of Fairbank's map of 1771 showing the castle site very close to the confluence of the Don and the Sheaf. Also the Town Mill (top left).

units which were never able to support a deer park, but in the northern parts of Hallamshire deer parks were created at Wadsley and Cowley, near modern Chapeltown.

The parish of Sheffield stretched far beyond the town and covered 22,370 acres, from Stanage Pole in the west to Carbrook in the east, and from Owlerton in the north to Ecclesall Woods and Heeley in the south. Two medieval chapels-of-ease provided services for the rural inhabitants. In the west, early in the thirteenth century, the lord of the sub-manor of Ecclesall granted the Premonstratensian canons of Beauchief Abbey (which lay just beyond Sheffield, in Derbyshire) a corn mill on the River Sheaf at Millhouses on the condition that they performed a daily service in the chapel near his manor house. This arrangement continued until 1536, when the abbey was dissolved. In the east, the early history of the chapel that stood on Beighton Green (later Oakes Green), Attercliffe, is obscure; it was dissolved under the Chantries Act of 1547. As we shall see, these old chapels at Ecclesall and Attercliffe were re-built by puritan landowners in the seventeenth century.

The parish was divided into six townships for civil purposes: Sheffield town and park, Attercliffe-cum-Darnall, Brightside, Ecclesall, Nether Hallam, and Upper Hallam. In many parts of England, townships, or vills, were the most ancient units of local government, but in Sheffield their origins are obscure. The townships of Ecclesall and Brightside were known by the Scandinavian word *bierlow*, so they were probably ancient, but on the other hand Ecclesall seems to have been carved out of Upper and Nether Hallam; in Crookes the township boundaries twisted in and out of the open-fields, following the divisions between the strips, and, curiously, Heeley remained part of the township of Nether Hallam until 1904. An old boundary stone separating the townships of Sheffield and Nether Hallam still stands at the roadside by Sheffield University on Western Bank.

etail of William Fairbank's *Map of the Parish of Sheffield* (1795) showing Attercliffe township. The long, narrow
rips of the open fields of Attercliffe and the separate system at Darnall, together with the commons in the east,
ere a survival from the Middle Ages. The regular arrangement of the village of Attercliffe around a triangular
reen suggests deliberate planning, in contrast to the irregular arrangement of houses and cottages which were built
ter alongside the Sheffield–Rotherham road. Forges and other industrial premises were powered by water drawn
om the River Don. Beyond lay the very different fields and coppice woods of Brightside bierlow and Sheffield Park.

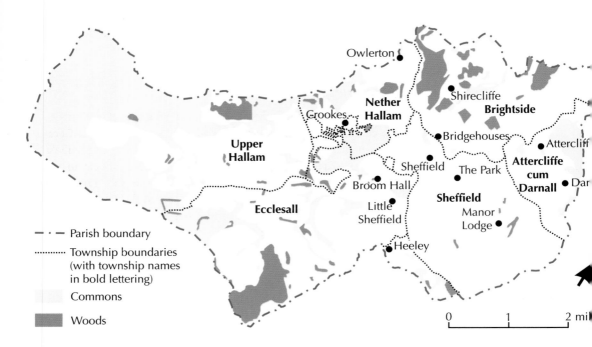

Map of the parish of Sheffield. For local government purposes the ancient parish was divided into six townships (Upper and Nether Hallam, Ecclesall, Sheffield, Brightside and Attercliffe-cum-Darnall). Heeley was a detached portion of Nether Hallam and the boundary between Ecclesall and Nether Hallam was far from straightforward. The whole parish was incorporated as the borough of Sheffield in 1843.

DRAWN BY ADAM GREGORY CARNEGIE

The map legend reads:

— · — Parish boundary

·········· Township boundaries (with township names in bold lettering)

Commons

Woods

0   1   2 mil

The Norman lords of Hallamshire may have re-planned the Anglo-Saxon settlements of Attercliffe and Darnall in the eastern part of the parish of Sheffield. William Fairbank's map of the parish in 1795 shows that the village of Attercliffe was arranged around a triangular green in a regular manner and was surrounded by three open-fields and a common in the fashion of Midland England. A reference in Harrison's survey of 1637 to 'Old Town' on the southern edge of Darnall's fields explains the relevance of the place-name, which means 'secluded nook of land on the parish boundary'. It looks as if the village of Darnall was re-sited alongside the road from Attercliffe to Handsworth, across the fields from 'Old Town'. A charter of c.1178 which refers to four acres in Darnall, divided equally between four furlongs in the open-fields, suggests a symmetry of layout that had been achieved by conscious planning.

The ancient parish of Sheffield contained few other villages; most of its medieval settlements were in the form of scattered farmsteads and hamlets. A tax return of 1297 mentions Crookes and Little Sheffield, both of which grew into villages. At Crookes the ancient pattern of the strips in the former open-fields is preserved by long, parallel rows of nineteenth-century terraced houses, and the name Crookesmoor commemorates the former common. The common pasture of the inhabitants of Little Sheffield was the present city-centre shopping district known simply as The Moor. The people of Little Sheffield and other nearby hamlets also had common rights on Sharrow Moor, whose name means 'the hill where the shared common land was'. Shire Ley (commemorated today by the name Shire Hill) was another shared open pasture at the edge of this moor. Further east, the strips of an open townfield descended the steep hill from Sharrow Head to Little Sheffield. The open-fields of the town of Sheffield stretched over the hill from Broad Lane on the north-western edge of the town, towards the common pasture of Shalesmoor.

The beginnings of industry

The history of industry in and around Sheffield no doubt goes back much further than the thirteenth century, when documentary evidence is first available. Coal, for example, was burned by Roman soldiers at Templeborough. The Sheffield manorial accounts of 1442–43 refer to coal-pits and to charcoal-making in the lord's park, and by then a few water mills had been erected on the rivers. We have seen that the manorial corn mill, known as the Town Mill, had been built in the twelfth century. Part of the revenues of another manorial corn mill, at Brekesherth (Brightside) were granted in 1328 to Worksop Priory. Next came the fulling mills, where the weavers took their cloth to be scoured with fullers' earth. These were often called Walk Mills from the earlier practice of trampling the earth into the cloth before fulling was performed by water power. In 1383 the possessions of the Furnivals included 'a certain fulling mill within the park'. This was probably the Walk Mill on the Don, just beyond the Wicker. The Sheaf Walk Mill, which was granted by Sir Ralph de Ecclesall to Beauchief Abbey about 1280, was on the site now occupied by Dore railway station. The canons of Beauchief Abbey also received a grant from the same lord of a corn mill at Millhouses. We do not have documentary evidence for cutlers' grinding wheels before the sixteenth century, though some are likely to have been in existence in earlier times.

Lord Furnival had forges or 'smithies' in his park by 1322 and probably long before. A John del Smithe is recorded in Sheffield in 1329, and fifty years later

Town Mill grinding wheel and goit. Two archaeologists from ARCUS struggle with adverse weather conditions on a very wet day in February 2000 in order to complete the excavation. The cutlers' grinding wheel was built next to the old Town corn mill in the 1740s by Thomas Ford. It was worked by the Vickers family from 1761 until the 1840s.
ARCUS, UNIVERSITY OF SHEFFIELD

the poll tax returns list several people in Sheffield with the surname 'del Smythe' or 'de Smethe'. At the beginning of the fifteenth century the constable of Chester Castle, faced with the threat of Owain Glyn Dwr's rebellion, began to order arrowheads from 'John del Smythy de Sheffeld'. Between 1401 and 1405 John supplied several thousands.

The history of the cutlery trades is probably much older than the naming of Robert the Cutler (Robertus le Cotelar) in a list of tax payers in 1297. Sheffield 'whittles' (multi-purpose knives which were carried in a sheath attached to a belt) were well enough known for Chaucer to refer to one in *The Reeve's Tale* in the late fourteenth century, and for one to be included among the king's possessions at the Tower of London in 1340. A fourteenth-century knife of this type, with a plain wooden handle hafted onto a pointed blade, was recovered from the excavations at Sheffield Castle. The cutlers of Hallamshire continued to make cheap wares of a simple design throughout the Middle Ages, under the jurisdiction of the manorial court of the lord of Hallamshire. John Leland, England's first topographer, who came this way about 1540, noted, 'Ther be many smiths and cutlers in Hallamshire'. Medieval Sheffield had acquired a distinctive character as a market town where cutlery was made. As we shall see, the town and its neighbourhood was soon to triumph over its provincial rivals, notably Thaxted and Salisbury. Its triumph over the London cutlers came much later.

'Ther be many smiths and cutlers in Hallamshire.'

JOHN LELAND, 1540

The people of Sheffield in the Middle Ages

We have no precise information on the size of the population of Sheffield in the Middle Ages, but it is unlikely that the inhabitants of the town exceeded one or two thousand, or that more than a few hundred people lived in the rural parts of the parish. As in the rest of England, the local population probably grew steadily in the thirteenth century but was checked in the second decade of the fourteenth century and declined dramatically at the time of the Black Death of 1349–50. The poll tax returns of 1379 record 177 married couples and 177 single persons in Sheffield, suspiciously regular numbers which nevertheless probably give an approximate idea of the size of the population at that time.

The wealthiest inhabitants whose names were recorded as taxpayers in 1297 were headed by Thomas de Furnival, the lord of the manor. Prominent amongst the next rank of landowners were Robert of Ecclesall, Elias of Midhope, Thomas of Mounteney, the Prior of Worksop, the Abbot of Beauchief, Daniel the chaplain, and Thomas of Fourness. Three of these men witnessed the grant of the town charter in the same year. The taxpayers also included William of Little Sheffield, Robert the miller, Robert of Crookes, Robert of Osgathorpe, Ralph of Grimesthorpe, Roger and Robert of 'Brikeserd' (later known as Brightside), John of Skinnerthorpe, Robert of Neepsend, Ralph of Wadsley, Robert the cutler, and others. The surnames Furnival and Mounteney were already hereditary, and it is possible that a few of the local place-names listed above had also been adopted as family names, but we cannot be sure. Most Sheffielders did not acquire hereditary surnames until well into the fourteenth century.

One of the clearest examples of the way that a surname originated is provided by the minor place-name Staniforth, a 'stony ford' over a stream. The place is now known as Low Wincobank. Matilda of Staniforth was named in the tax return for Ecclesfield in 1297. The connection between the place-name and the surname is made explicit by a manorial court roll of 1434, when Richard of Stannyford inherited land in 'Stanyford' from his father, John of Stannyford. The surname has become one of the most distinctive in Sheffield.

Some other well-known Sheffield names are amongst those listed in the poll tax returns of 1379. During the fourteenth century the Hattersleys had crossed the Pennines to Langsett and the Scargills had arrived from north Yorkshire. The Bullases had moved fifteen miles south from Bullhouse, near Penistone, the Creswicks lived close to the hamlet of that name near Ecclesfield, and other families had taken their surnames from places such as Bamford, Beighton, Crookes, Housley (near Chapeltown), Oxspring, and the lost place-name Ramsker (near the Dale Dyke reservoir). Surnames recorded in the Chapelry of Bradfield included some that were derived from minor place-names in that vicinity, such as Broomhead, Dungworth, Moorwood, Hawkesworth, Loxley, Ronksley and Worrall, while those recorded in Ecclesfield included Shirtcliffe and the occupational name Crapper (a cropper of iron or textiles). Most of these surnames are of a single-family origin.

Some surnames that were derived in ways other than from place-names and

Plan of Beauchief abbey.

DRAWN BY ADAM GREGORY,
CARNEGIE

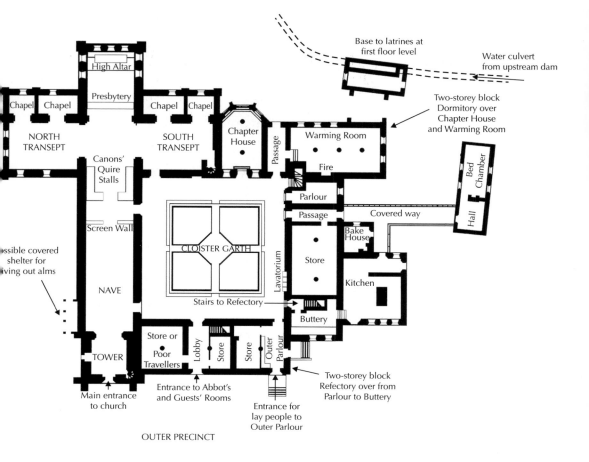

which became well established locally were also recorded in the Sheffield poll tax return of 1379. They include Rawson (son of Ralph), Base (meaning illegitimate, and later changed to Bayes), Revell (a nickname), and Trippett (either a dancer or a butcher). An intriguing local name whose meaning has so far not been discovered is that of Shemeld. The poll tax return of 1379 for Handsworth provides our first reference. In that year Robert Schemyld, a smith, and his wife Dionisia, paid 6d. tax and. Adam Schemyld paid 4d. Over the centuries the name acquired other forms: Shimild, then Shimmell, and finally Shimwell. A generation ago, Eddie Shimwell played right-back for Sheffield United and Ron Staniforth played full-back for Sheffield Wednesday. Their surnames were formed in Sheffield more than six centuries ago.

Beauchief Abbey was founded between 1173 and 1176 by Robert FitzRanulf, lord of Alfreton and Norton as a daughter establishment of Welbeck Abbey. The White Canons, as the Premonstratensians were popularly known, were a preaching order who shared a communal life. Beauchief is a Norman-French name for the 'beautiful headland' that lay on the edge of the parish of Norton, just beyond Sheffield. The canons received gifts of land, corr mills at Millhouses and Bradway, and water-powered industrial sites on the River Sheaf from the lords of Ecclesall, in return for taking services at their chapel. Gerard de Furnival gave them a grange at Fulwood. The abbey was dissolved in 1537 'without giving any trouble or opposition.' In the 1660s Edward Pegge of Beauchief Hall converted the ruins of the church into a private chapel, which is still furnished as he left it.

PHOTOGRAPH: CARNEGIE

right The tomb of George, Fourth Earl of Shrewsbury (1468–1538). This alabaster tomb i the Shrewsbury Chapel of Sheffield Cathedral provides a likeness of George Talbot and hi two wives. He was the first of the Talbots to make Sheffield his major residence and wa responsible for the Shrewsbury Chapel at the south-east corner of the cathedra

PHOTOGRAPH: CARNEG

A HISTORY OF SHEFFIELD

CHAPTER 2

Hallamshire under the Talbots, earls of Shrewsbury

The lords of the manor

In the late Middle Ages Hallamshire acquired new lords. The male line of the Furnivals came to an end during the late fourteenth century when the estate passed to Sir Thomas Nevill, who had married Joan de Furnival. Thomas and Joan had no sons and by 1410 the new lord of Hallamshire was John Talbot, who had married their daughter Maud. John was the first of a mighty line of Talbots who dominated Sheffield from their castle and their Manor Lodge over the next

two centuries. He was the Talbot of Shakespeare's history plays, the famous soldier who served in Ireland from 1414 to 1419 as Lord Lieutenant and who in 1428 was put in charge of the English army in France. Because of his military achievements he was made a Knight of the Garter and then in 1442 ennobled as the Earl of Shrewsbury, Shropshire being the centre of his considerable estates. He was killed in battle in France in 1453.

His son, the second earl, was killed at the battle of Northampton in 1460 and was buried at Worksop. The first three earls (all of whom were called John) did not have strong connections with Sheffield, but in time the family came to regard Hallamshire as their chief estate. George, the fourth earl, was born at Shifnal (Shropshire) in 1468 and died seventy years later at Wingfield Manor (Derbyshire). He was the first of the earls to make Sheffield their principal residence when they were not at Court. By the late fifteenth century Sheffield Castle was two hundred years old and (despite some later improvements) was decidedly unfashionable. Although it continued in use until the Civil War of the mid-seventeenth century, a more up-to-date residence was deemed necessary when George decided to move to Sheffield. The obvious solution was to upgrade the old Manor Lodge within the deer park. This was originally a hunting lodge, in use since at least 1479–80. George converted the lodge into a large country house. The conversion was sufficiently advanced by 1530 for Cardinal Wolsey to spend eighteen days in a 'goodlie tower with lodgings' there on his way south to face the wrath of Henry VIII; he died four days later at Leicester. Earl George had become a powerful figure in the land, the Lieutenant-General of the North, who with the Duke of Norfolk stopped the rebellion known as the Pilgrimage of Grace when the rebels reached Doncaster in 1536. Sheffield was a small seigneur-ial borough under George's control. Upon his death, his body was brought to Sheffield for burial in the chapel that he had built on the south-east side of the parish church (now the Cathedral), which is still known as the Shrewsbury Chapel. The large alabaster monument to George and his two wives (the second of whom was still living at the time of his death), was erected in the chapel shortly afterwards.

Francis, the fifth earl, was born at Sheffield Castle in 1500, and upon his death at Sheffield Manor Lodge in 1560 he too was buried in the Shrewsbury Chapel, with great pomp and ceremony. He was as important a national figure as his father had been, a pre-eminence which was acknowledged when he became President of the Council of the North, based at the King's Manor, York, and a member of Queen Elizabeth's Privy Council. An undated letter written before 1553 remarks that his 'building at Sheffield Lodge goes well', so he must have extended his father's work there. He benefited from the opportunities of acquiring other prop-erties at cheap rates upon the dissolution of the monasteries. His acquisitions included Worksop Priory and Rufford Abbey, a grange of Beauchief Abbey at Fulwood, and the tithes of Ecclesfield (including Bradfield) and Penistone parishes. The town of Sheffield benefited too from his influence at Court, for when the Burgery lands were confiscated by the Crown upon the dissolution of chantries in 1547 he was able to recover them. It is probably also significant that

George, Sixth Earl of Shrewsbury (c.1528–90). George's hard and gloomy nature is well captured in this portrait. He was the richest nobleman north of the Trent. His many properties included Sheffield Castle and the Manor Lodge, where he held Mary, Queen of Scots, in custody.

SHEFFIELD LIBRARIES, ARCHIVES AND INFORMATION: LOCAL STUDIES

The remains of Sheffield Manor Lodge. Once the impressive country house of the Earls of Shrewsbury in the midst of their deer park, it was abandoned by their successors, the Dukes of Norfolk and mostly demolished in the early eighteenth century.

PHOTOGRAPH: CARNEGIE

  A HISTORY OF SHEFFIELD

G Talbot earle of Shrewsbury

the first cutlers' marks that were recorded in the rolls of the manor court were awarded in 1554, during his lifetime. Francis was a powerful lord who took an interest in his lowly neighbours.

George, the sixth earl, became the most powerful of all the Talbots and eventually the richest nobleman in the north of England. He was a member of Queen Elizabeth's Privy Council, Lieutenant-General for Yorkshire, Nottingham-shire and Derbyshire, and after the execution of Thomas, Duke of Norfolk, in 1572, Earl Marshal of England. His first wife was Gertrude Manners of Haddon Hall, the second was the redoubtable Bess of Hardwick, one of whose previous husbands had been Sir William Cavendish of Chatsworth. The extensive estates of the Talbots and Cavendishes were brought together by a triple marriage on 9 February 1568, when George married Bess, her eldest son, Henry Cavendish, married George's daughter, Lady Grace Talbot, and her youngest daughter, Mary, married Gilbert Talbot, George's son and heir. George had large estates in York-shire, Nottinghamshire, Derbyshire and Shropshire, and other properties in Staffordshire, Herefordshire, Oxford-shire, Cheshire, Wiltshire, Leicestershire, Gloucestershire, and London. He owned castles at Sheffield, Pontefract and Tutbury, a large manor house at South Wingfield, hunting lodges at Sheffield, Tutbury and Worksop, the former Rufford Abbey, a house by the baths at Buxton, and a small lodge at Handsworth, beyond Sheffield Park. He rebuilt the lodge at Worksop into a fine country house, for a time he owned the new hall in the park at Tankersley, he converted the monastic buildings at Rufford into a desirable

Turret House, Manor Lodge. During the sixteenth century the Earls of Shrewsbury converted the old hunting lodge in their deer park into a splendid country house. Most of the house was dismantled in the early eighteenth century, but the Elizabethan turret house, which stood at the entrance to the grounds, still stands in much the same state as when it was built in the 1570s and 1580s. The style is reminiscent of the hunting tower at Chatsworth and the hall at North Lees, Hathersage, both of which were built about the same time, perhaps to designs by Robert Smythson, the architect of Hardwick Hall.

PHOTOGRAPH: CARNEGIE

MARIA REGINA

Bess of Hardwick. Born into a decaying gentry family, Bess took Sir William Cavendish as her second husband and George, Sixth Earl of Shrewsbury as her fourth. After George's death, she had the resources to build Hardwick Hall, whose skyline she adorned with coronets and her initials, ES, to signify that she had made it as Elizabeth, Countess of Shrewsbury. The portrait was once thought to be Mary, Queen of Scots, hence the MARIA REGINA inscription.

NATIONAL TRUST PHOTO LIBRARY / ANGELO HORNAK

right Tomb of George, Sixth Earl of Shrewsbury. This alabaster tomb is set against the south wall of the Shrewsbury Chapel in Sheffield Cathedral. George is depicted as a knight in armour, with his head resting on a rolled-up mat, as was usual then, and his feet on a talbot. A huge monument, inscribed with his virtues, honours and connections, rises above him. His wife, Bess of Hardwick, is buried in Derby Cathedral.

PHOTOGRAPH: CARNEGIE

CHRISTO OPT. MAX. ET POSTERITATI SACRVM.

IN SPEM CERTAM FVTVRÆ RESVRRECTIONIS ILLVSTRISS. CONDITVR HIC HEROS GEORGIVS SALOPIÆ COMES SVI NOBILISSIMI
GENERIS SEXTVS SERIE A NORMANORVM CONQVESTV DERIVATA INVIOLATA VNQVAM PERFIDIÆ LABECVLA ASPERSI, COMITVM
ORDINE SEXTVS, SVMMVS REGNI MARESCALLVS, DOMINVS INSVPER ET BARO TALBOTO, FVRNIVALL, VERDVN, LOVETOFT, EXTRANEOQ. DE BLACKMERE HOS
NOBILIS AMPLISSIMVS, FRANCISCI COMITIS VNICVS QVI SVPERERAT, OMNIVMQ. ORDINIS SANE PRÆCLARISSIMI,
PIETATE IN DEVM, AMORE IN PATRIAM, FIDE IN PRINCIPEM SVAMQ. DELLI DVCE BELLICAM ... VT ... MARIÆ REGINÆ TEMPORIBVS IN NOR-
THVMBRENSIS COMITIS SVCCVRSVM, ET IATER IN SVPERSTITE ... CVM LAVDE BELLICAM ... ILLAM PRÆFECTVRAM ADMINIS-
TRARAT, PARIQ. CVM LAVDE [IR]E IVSSVS, ETENNVE SVMMAC. PAVLO POST AD BERVICVM HOSTI IN OCCVRSVM MISSVS OVINGENS
RESB. AD LOVVICAM, CVM SCOTIAM [IRE] IVSSVS, COHORTE STIPATVS FVIT CONCOMITANTIVM TVM GERENTI WESTMARIO COMITE, DEVS
TERVM CATAPRACTORVM EQVITVM, AVLE ... PRINCIPATIVM. OMNIVM DIVERTIQTE ... DONEC IN VTRIVSQ. REGNI TERNILLEM.
DEINDE REGNANTE ELIZABETRA ANGLORVM GEMMA, CVN SCOTORVM REGINA MARIA PRÆLIO GERENTI DOMI SVPERATA, IN ANGLI-
AM COMPVLSA ESSET, ATQ. APVD SCOTICI LIMITIS PRÆFECTVM CVSTODIENDA TRADITVR, ANNO M.D.LXVIII. QVEM PENES
HONORE AC SPLENDIDI SATIS VRO, ANNO, AD M.D.LXXXIII. PER TREA AMPLIVS LVSTRA, HOSPITATA NON SINE
MAGNA IPSIVS SOMPTITIS IMPENSA, CVRAQ. ANXIA TAM ARDVA, CVIVS MAGNITVDO GRAVISSIMA VTILITAS PVBLICA FVIT TAM
LAVDATE AC PELICITER SE GESSIT, EVM VIRVM FIDELEM NON MINVS IN QVAM PROVIDVM ATQ. PRVDENTEM, IPSA INVIDIA INDICARE
DEBET, QVAMO SEMPER AB OMNI SVSPICIONE FIDEIS FVERAT ALIENVS, ILLVD DECLARAT, QVOD LICET A MALEVOLIS PROPTER
SVSPECTAM CVM CAPTIVA REGINA FAMILIARITATEM SÆPIVS MALE AVDIRET, CVM TAMEN MAGNATES QVI REATVS SVI IN TESTIMONIVM AC
VINDICIAM A PROCERIBVS IN ARCE NODRINGHAENSI CONVOCARI, DATO AD HOC DIPLOMATE REGIO, MAGNO SIGILLO ANGLIÆ COMMVNITO
IVSSI, EIVSDEM SENTENTIA, TRANSACTOREM CONSVTVIT, INTER MAGNATES VNVM ESSE VOLVIT; ILLVMQ. POST IVDICIVM
ETA VIII. GENERE CLARVS, GENERALIS ... APVD OMNES HONORIS, QVEM AD FATALEM NATVRÆ SENECTVTIS HORAM SINE FORTVNÆ LVDIBRIO
FERVIXERAT, ÆTERNO NVMNE SPIRITVM SVO ACCEPERAT, FIRMA IN NATVRÆ GESTIS ... CLARIOR, DOMI AC FORIS CLARISS.
XVIII MENSIS NOVEMBRIS ANNO REDEMPTORIS XTI M.D.XC. AD PATRIAM FIDEI SVÆ ... QVO IN XTVM FIDE PLACIDE ET TRANQVILLE REDDIDIT.
EX PRIORE CONIVGE D. GERTVRIÆ, THOMÆ ROTOLANDIÆ COMITIS NATA, VTRIVSQ. SEXVS PROLEM SVSCEPIT EGREGIAM:
FRANCISCVM SCILICET FRIMOGENITVM, EO SVPERSTITE, E VIVIS SVBLATVM; GILBERTVM HÆREDEM FVTVRVM; EDVARDVM:
HENRICVM; CATHERINAM HERBERTI REGVLO COPVLATAM AC SINE SOBOLE EXTINCTAM; MARIAM GEORGIO SAVILLO EQVITI
RESPONSANT: GRACIAM HENRICO CAVENDICHII EQVITIS HÆREDI, NVPTAM.

residence, and upon his marriage to Bess he acquired a life-interest in the great house at Chatsworth. Sheffield Manor Lodge remained his favourite seat, however, and he and Bess spent much time and money on enlarging it and in laying out new gardens. They erected an impressive entrance framed by two brick towers, and at the edge of the estate, between 1574 and 1584, built the Turret House, which still stands intact. This Turret House was not built as a prison for Mary, Queen of Scots, as is commonly believed, but served as a gatehouse, hunting tower, and banquet house. It is similar in style to the contemporary Hunting Lodge at Chatsworth and to the house built for one of the Talbots' principal officers at North Lees (Derbyshire). These buildings are compact and tall and contain sturdy stone fireplaces, decorated plaster ceilings, and staircases leading up to fine views from the roof. They may all have been designed by Robert Smythson, the great Elizabethan architect who was responsible for George and Bess's house at Worksop and, after George's death, Bess's splendid new hall at Hardwick.

The banqueting room within the Turret House. Sited on the top floor, this was the most important room in the house. The arms of George Talbot, Sixth Earl of Shrewsbury, are displayed over the fireplace. The elaborate plasterwork ceiling contains allusions to Bess of Hardwick and the captivity of Mary, Queen of Scots. Talbot dogs stand guard.
CARNEGIE COLLECTION

George Talbot was energetic in developing the mineral wealth of his estates. He brought Frenchmen, or men of French descent, from the Sussex Weald to erect charcoal blast furnaces and forges at Attercliffe, Kimberworth and Wadsley; he exploited his coal reserves under Sheffield Park; his officers managed his springwoods and built cutlers' wheels; and he tried to monopolise the Derbyshire lead export trade through his wharf on the River Idle at his manor of Bawtry. His surviving correspondence shows that he was a ruthless man, endlessly involved in squabbles. But even such a powerful figure as he was unable to get his own way all the time. He failed to stop the burgesses of his manor of Chesterfield when they successfully applied to become a corporate borough with their own mayor in 1598; he failed to destroy the rights of the Bawtry burgesses to use their own wharf; and he did not succeed in raising the rents of his Glossop tenants, despite a long and bitter dispute. But at the same time, Sheffield Manor Lodge reflected some of the culture of the Court in London. Musicians, actors, and craftsmen as varied as embroiderers and plasterers were provided with opportunities to practise their arts as members of the great household.

This was particularly true during the fourteen years from 1570 to 1584 when Mary, Queen of Scots was a prisoner at Sheffield. George's position as the leading nobleman in the North, and his family's long record of loyalty to the Crown, made him Queen Elizabeth's obvious choice as custodian when Mary was apprehended in 1569. She arrived at Sheffield accompanied by 39 persons, chiefly French and Scots. Sheffield Castle and Manor Lodge became her main prisons, but from time to time she was moved to Buxton or Chatsworth, and on one occasion to Worksop. George's dilemma was that he had to discharge his responsibility to Elizabeth, but if she died Mary would have been the successor

to the throne. He lived in constant fear of plots to release her and of armed rebellion. In 1584 Mary was removed to South Wingfield and then to Tutbury, before George was relieved of responsibility. Mary was executed at Fotheringhay (Northamptonshire) in 1587, the year before the thwarted invasion by the Spanish Armada. In Armada year George was active in rooting out possible dissidents in the area, notably the Catholic priests who were arrested at Padley Chapel, Hathersage, and executed at Derby. It was during this long, tense period of Mary's custody and the threat of armed conflict that George and Bess's marriage broke down. Their portraits at Hardwick Hall depict two stubborn, strong-willed people; a fiery Bess and a

Bawtry was a planned medieval town where the Great North Road passed the highest navigable point on the river Idle. Derbyshire lead and millstones and Sheffield cutlery and metalwares were brought down Wharf Street to the pool where the river wound past the church. In the early eighteenth century Defoe said that 'wrought iron and edge-tools, of all sorts' were exported from 'the country called Hallamshire'. The port declined under competition from the Don Navigation and the Chesterfield Canal later that century.

gloomy George. Bess moved to her birthplace at Hardwick and started to build. George moved across his park to Handsworth, where he lived openly with Eleanor Britton, 'a female domestic'. He died at Sheffield Manor in 1590, and was given a sumptuous funeral in Sheffield parish church on 10 January 1591. Bess lived another seventeen years and was buried at Derby.

Upon his death in 1590 at Sheffield Manor, George was succeeded by his son, Gilbert, the seventh earl (1553–1616), who had been educated at the University of Padua. Gilbert quarrelled bitterly with Bess after George's death. He became a Privy Councillor and a prominent figure at Court, but never achieved the distinction and honours accorded to his father and spent much of his time on his country estates. Other courtiers regarded Sheffield as a remote place, far from the centre of national affairs. In 1606 Viscount Lisle wrote from Hampton Court to say that he hoped Gilbert had returned safely to Sheffield, 'half way to the North Pole'. Two years later, Sir John Bentley wrote to say that he planned to see the Earl in Wingfield or Sheffield 'where I look to be half choked with town smoke'. Nevertheless, the surviving Talbot correspondence makes it clear that the Earl's household at Sheffield Castle and Manor Lodge were able to drink claret, sack, and other wines, and to enjoy imported groceries such as almonds and cinnamon. Gilbert seems to have taken as active a role in Sheffield's affairs as did his father. In particular, his manor court issued new regulations for the cutlery trades. He demonstrated his concern to continue the family's major role in the district when, in 1608, he paid the considerable sum of £12,000 for an estate in Hathersage.

Upon his death in London in 1616, Gilbert's body was brought back for burial in the Shrewsbury Chapel at Sheffield parish church. The heralds orchestrated a funeral in the same style as those provided for his father and grandfather. A long procession was led by four conductors with staves and 128 poor men in gowns, followed by yeomen and large numbers of the servants and retainers of gentry and noble families, friends of the Talbots. Behind them, at a suitable distance, came a group of notables, including Sir Thomas Fairfax, the bearer of a great banner, the Archbishop of York, the preacher of the funeral sermon, the knightly bearers of the coffin, and finally the heralds and the aristocratic chief mourners and their retinues. As Gilbert's body was laid to rest, Sheffield began to emerge from the feudal era. The great days of the Castle and the Manor Lodge were nearly over. The new lords did not live in Sheffield and most of them rarely visited the town.

As Gilbert had no sons and his brother, Edward, died soon afterwards, the title of Earl of Shrewsbury passed to a very distant relative. Gilbert's estates were shared between his three daughters. The Yorkshire and Derbyshire properties went to Alethea, his youngest daughter, the wife of Thomas Howard, Earl of Arundel and Surrey. In jtime, Alethea's grandson was created the fifth Duke of Norfolk, the title which the Howards had forfeited in 1572. The lordship of Hallamshire therefore descended in unbroken succession, through female lines, from the Lovetots, Furnivals, Nevills and Talbots to the Howards. This continuity of ownership of the manor over several centuries is remarkable.

In 1637 the Howards employed John Harrison, a Norfolk surveyor, to survey their estates in and around Hallamshire. He was suitably impressed by what he found. His concluding remarks summarised the great riches that the Howards had inherited:

Park: This parke is very well adorn'd with great store of very Stately Timber and not meanly furnished with fallow Deare, the number of them at this present is one Thousand, whereof Deare of Auntler is two hundred, if you look into the bowels of this Parke, you shall find the inside correspondent to the outside, being stored with very good coales and Iron stone in abundance.

Rivers: These Rivers are very profitable unto the Lord in regard of the Mills and Cutler wheeles that are turned by theire streames, which weeles are imployed for the grinding of knives by four or five hundred Master Workmen.

Timber: There are alsoe within this Mannor very stately Timber especially in Haw Parke, which for both straitness and bignesse there is not the like in any place that you can heare of being in length about 60 foot before you come to a knot or a bow [i.e. bough].

Quarries: Alsoe there are within this Mannor good stones for building, and slate stones for tyling or slateing of houses, and course grinding stones for knives and scithes, and alsoe very good Millnstones are hewen out in Rivelin or stone edge, there is likewise very good clay for pots and bricks.

Pleasure: This Mannor is not only profitable, but for pleasure alsoe, being furnished with red Deare and Fallow, with hares and some Rowes, with Phesants

and great store of Partridges, and moore Game in abundance both black and red, as moore Cockes, moore Hens and young pootes [half-grown birds] upon the moores, as also Mallard, Teale, Hearnshewes and Plover, the chiefest fishing within this Mannor is in the River that passeth through the same, wherein are great store of Salmon, Trouts, Chevens [chulm], Eles and other small fish.

Conclusion: There may be within this Mannor raised iron worke which would afford unto the Lord (as is thought) a thousand pounds yearly and all charges discharged and for the maintaineing of this worke, there are within this 2 thousand acres of wood and timber (besides Sheffeild Parke) whereof there are above 16 hundred acres of spring woods besides great store of old trees fit for noe other purpose but for the makeing of Charkehole. All these things considered (with many more which for brevity sake I omit) this Mannor is not inferior to any Mannor in England as I suppose.

The woodland round Sheffield has long been of economic importance, especially as a source of fuel for the metal industries. Ecclesall Woods occupy the site of the deer park of the medieval sub-manor. They became commercial springwoods during the sixteenth century. Charcoal platforms and the white-coal pits or kilns of the lead smelters can still be found, scattered around the woods.

PHOTOGRAPH: CARNEGIE

At the time of Harrison's survey the park had already been divided into large fields and leased to tenant farmers. The fields within the park had very different shapes from the neighbouring strips of the open fields of Attercliffe, Darnall and Heeley. Some were used for growing cereals, but most were laid down as pasture. The park also contained a coppice wood, which later became known as Clay Wood, and 'great store of very Stately Timber', in particular, a long, straight avenue of oaks and walnuts which led towards the Manor Lodge. In his famous work, *Silva or A Discourse of Forest-Trees* (1662), John Evelyn quoted a Sheffield correspondent, who claimed that in the park over a hundred trees, worth a thousand pounds, and including some of enormous girth, had been felled in recent years and that only in Hall Park, Stannington, did the famous oaks of the Rivelin Valley survive. When Gilbert Talbot died, the heyday of Sheffield Park was almost over, though a thousand deer still roamed there in 1637. The new lords rarely came to Sheffield, even though it was their principal source of revenue, and so the deer were eventually removed, and the Manor Lodge was allowed to fall into disrepair.

The springwoods noted by Harrison were carefully managed, with a regular cycle of coppicing. Several such woods – Burngreave, Wincobank, Roe, Cook, Hall Carr, and Shirecliffe Park – adorned the slopes of the township of Brightside

Sheffield in 1637, a reconstruction by Dr G. Scurfield based on John Harrison's survey of the manor. The boundary of the Great Park can be followed all the way round. The open-field strips and the commons of Attercliffe, Darnall and Heeley can be seen beyond.

G. SCURFIELD, *Yorkshire Archaeological Journal*, 58 (1986).

bierlow, north of the River Don. South of the river, by contrast, the township of Attercliffe-cum-Darnall had no trees other than those standing in hedgerows. A survey in 1642 reported that some local woods had been left for over three decades so as to allow the trees to grow to sufficient width for pit props or 'punch wood'. The chief customers for underwood, however, were the charcoal ironmasters. Greno Woods, Hall Wood, Beeley Wood, and other springwoods beyond Sheffield were used in this way. They also supplied bark for the tanners and underwood for hurdles, fences, broom handles, and so on. Ecclesall Woods, which (like Shirecliffe) had been converted from a deer park by the late sixteenth century, were also coppiced by rotation. A mid seventeenth-century map divided Ecclesall Woods into 21 sections, which were felled at intervals of up to sixteen years' growth. Some of the tenants were lead smelters, whose interest was in making 'white coal', the fuel which fired their smelting mills in the river valleys of north Derbyshire. The characteristic shallow pits where white coal was made can be seen in Ecclesall Woods and in most of the other deciduous woods that stretch from Sheffield and Chesterfield as far west as the River Derwent.

The town

One of the perquisites of the lord of Hallamshire was his right to collect market tolls. Sheffield had a growing reputation for its cutlery manufacture, but most visitors still regarded it first and foremost as a market town. In 1637 John Harrison noted that the town of Sheffield had weekly markets on Tuesdays and

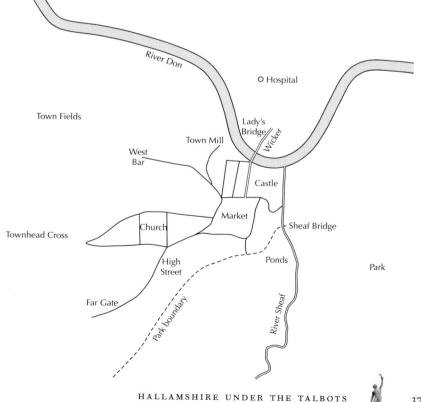

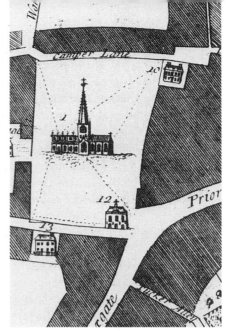

Thursdays and a one-day fair in November in addition to the ancient three-day fair at the feast of the Holy Trinity (the week after Whitsuntide). The scale of business was such that it spread beyond the Market Place. Eleven shops offered goods for sale under and around the modest Town Hall, at the entrance to the churchyard at the top of High Street. Judging by other town halls elsewhere, this building was probably a timber-framed structure with an open space on the ground floor where the stallholders could find shelter.

A document known as The Easter Book of 1571 divided the town into the following districts: 'Sheffield, The farsyde, The Kynges Streat and Market Place, The yreysche Crose, West Barre, The Newhaule, The Water Lane and Castellgrene, The Pryor Rowe'. These locations can readily be identified. 'Sheffield' contained that part of the centre of the town that was not included in the other districts. The 'farsyde' was probably Fargate. Prior Row was the name

Carvings from the
interior of the Old
Queen's Head.

of the five principal properties on the north side of High Street that had once belonged to Worksop Priory. King Street, which occupied the northern part of the Market Place, was otherwise known as Pudding Lane, for here was the common bakehouse. (The parallel with the bakery in Pudding Lane, London, where the great fire of 1666 started, was probably fresh in mind, for the alternative name was first recorded in Sheffield in 1672.) Water Lane, descending to the Don, was there by 1413 and seems always to have been a poor district. West Bar formed the

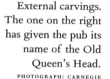

External carvings. The one on the right has given the pub its name of the Old Queen's Head.

north-west limit of the town. New Hall stood in Snig Hill, the little hill that climbed to the Irish Cross and the Market Place. The Irish Cross was recorded in 1499; the only explanation that can be offered for the derivation of the name is that the cross may have been erected during the time of John Talbot, the first Earl of Shrewsbury, who spent several years on military campaigns in Ireland. The names recorded in The Easter Book suggest that the Elizabethan town had much the same shape and size as that depicted by Ralph Gosling in 1736 on the first surviving map of Sheffield. It had probably not altered much in its layout since the time of the Norman lord, William de Lovetot, in the twelfth century.

The townspeople obtained their fresh water from pumps and public wells, and from Barker's Pool in Balm Green, at a high point on the western edge of the town. The pool lay just down the hill from the present City Hall. A man named 'Barker of Balm' was recorded in 1434, but the pool was not specifically mentioned until 1567. Five years later, it was enclosed by a stone wall and fitted with a shuttle or sluice gate. Perhaps this is when it was first used to cleanse the streets in the fashion which we shall describe in the next chapter?

An inventory of the contents of Sheffield Castle in 1582 goes on to list the furnishings 'in the hawle at the Pondes'. This is the timber-framed building by Pond Street bus station which has long served as a pub under the name of the

Watercolour by B. K. Dale of the Old Queen's Head (1815). A surprising survival in the city centre, this timber-framed building dates from c.1500. It was once known as 'The Hall in the Ponds', for it stood by the mill ponds that were fed by the River Sheaf, near the entrance to the lord's deer park. It is built in the usual style of the larger timber-framed buildings of the district.

Bishops' House. The home of the Blythe family, yeoman farmers and organisers of the scythe trade in the parish of Norton. The main body of the house (right) was erected about 1500; the wing in the centre of the picture was built half a century later; and the stone extension to the rear was added in the 1630s. The timber-framing is in the king-post style of the better houses of the district. It acquired the fanciful name of Bishops' House in Victorian times in the belief that two members of the Blythes who had become bishops in the early sixteenth century had been born here. It is now Sheffield's Folk Museum.

PHOTOGRAPH: L. NUTTALL

Queen's Head. The pub was named after one of the carved heads that act as corbels on the exterior of this high-quality building, which dates from *c.* 1500. Inside, the dining room is decorated to the same high standard. The original structure was larger, but a wing has been demolished. The Hall in the Ponds stood alongside the mill ponds (and possibly some artificial fish ponds) which have given this low-lying district its name. Perhaps the hall was built to entertain parties from the castle that were fishing and fowling in the ponds or starting a day's sport in the adjacent park?

All the other houses of the Tudor town were also timber-framed. That built by William Dickenson, the Earl's bailiff, in 1574 was still standing on the southern side of High Street, where Change Alley entered the Market Place, when it was photographed in 1886. Some derelict timber-framed houses in Snig Hill survived until their demolition in 1900. The Hall in the Ponds is the only timbered structure to remain standing in the centre of Sheffield, but further out, a wing of Broom Hall, hidden from public view, is contemporary and Bishops' House at

A timber-framed house at the corner of High Street and Change Alley. Photographed by F. Mottershaw in 1886 shortly before its demolition, the house was probably built for William Dickenson, the Elizabethan bailiff of Hallamshire. It was later converted into an inn and then into shops. It was one of the last surviving timber-framed houses in the centre of the town and one of the most substantial. All the properties shown here were dismantled when High Street was widened at the end of the nineteenth century.

Norton Lees (which was formerly in Derbyshire) has a main range of *c.* 1500 and a wing dating from about fifty years later. As Bishops' House is now a museum, it is the best building in the district for viewing the construction methods of Tudor carpenters. Otherwise, all that remains from the timber-framed tradition is a scattered collection of cruck-framed barns, dating from the sixteenth and early seventeenth centuries. Many more are to be found on the Pennine foothills to the north of the city.

Population

Towards the end of his life, Earl Gilbert decided to endow a hospital or almshouse for the aged poor of Sheffield. In order to determine the scale of poverty in the town and the outlying parts of the parish, a census was taken on 2 January 1616 by 'twenty-four of the most sufficient inhabitants there'. They counted 2,207 people in the town. of whom 725 (i.e. about a third of the population) were 'not able to live without the charity of their neighbours. These are all begging poore.' This makes grim reading, but at that time most English towns had a similar level of poverty. The situation improved during the second half of the seventeenth century, but the spectre of poverty was very real in Elizabethan and early Stuart times. The 1616 survey of Sheffield went on to record:

> 100 householders which relieve others. These (though the best sorte) are but poor artificers: among them is not one which can keepe a teame on his own land, and not above tenn who have grounds of their own that will keepe a cow.

> 160 householders, not able to relieve others. These are such (though they beg not) as are not able to abide the storme of one fortnight's sickness, but would be thereby driven to beggary.

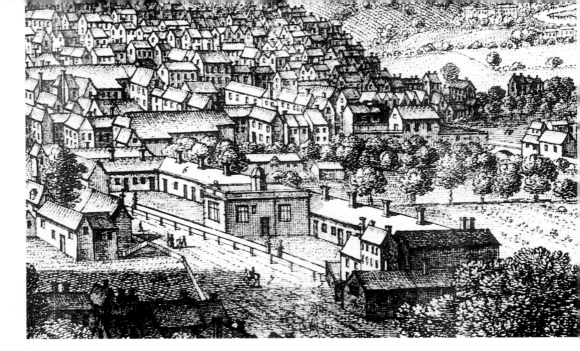

1,222 children and servants of the said householders: the greatest part of which are such as live of small wages, and are constrained to worke sore, to provide them necessaries.

Earl Gilbert's hospital was not started until half a century after his death, firstly because of a dispute over the will, then because of the Civil War. It was completed in 1673 on part of the former Castle Orchards, where the modern roundabout leads traffic to the Parkway, and was demolished in 1827 when the present Shrewsbury Hospital was opened in a healthier situation up the hill on Shrewsbury Road.

The 1616 census of 2,207 people in the central township of Sheffield is the first firm evidence that we have for the size of the local population. The figure is tiny by modern standards, but it should be judged rather by comparisons with contemporary towns. London dwarfed the rest with some 200,000 people, but the leading provincial cities had fewer than 20,000 inhabitants, and most market towns were smaller than Sheffield. The number of baptisms and burials recorded in the parish register between 1561 and 1640 show that Sheffield's population was growing at this time. During those eighty years the register recorded 1,866 more baptisms than burials. Similar growth is evident from a study of the registers of the surrounding rural parishes. Up to the

below Carbrook Hall, a remarkable survivor in the lower Don valley, dates from the early seventeenth century.
PHOTOGRAPH: CARNEGIE

A HISTORY OF SHEFFIELD

left Detail of Samuel and Nathaniel Buck, *East Prospect of Sheffield* (1745). The original Shrewsbury Hospital (6), built with an endowment by Earl Gilbert, is shown in the foreground. Lady's Bridge (9, centre right) marks the northern limit of the town. The fashionable hamlet of Bridgehouses, on the other side of the River Don, is top right.

SHEFFIELD LIBRARIES, ARCHIVES AND INFORMATION: LOCAL STUDIES

Civil War, the population of the Sheffield district was growing at the same rate as in the rest of England and suffered the same setbacks, notably in 1591–93 and 1597 when an unusual number of deaths were recorded in many parts of the country. Sheffield suffered from all the usual hazards to health that produced high rates of infant and child mortality and lowered the average expectation of life in Tudor and Stuart England, but it was less prone than most contemporary towns to the periodic epidemics that decimated the population. No virulent outbreaks of plague are recorded in the register.

Sheffield's population growth was the result both of natural increase and of immigration from the surrounding rural parishes. Settlers rarely came from further afield. For a brief period between 24 November 1653 and 5 December 1660 the marriage registers of Sheffield parish record the place of residence for both partners of the 459 weddings. No fewer than 372 grooms (81 per cent) and 356 brides (77.5 per cent) were said to be living either in the town or within the rural parts of Sheffield parish. No bridegroom came from further north than Leeds or further south than Nottingham and all but ten of them lived within 10 miles of the centre of Sheffield. Only ten brides came from beyond 10 miles and even these lived within a 20-mile radius of the town. The same geographical pattern of movement is evident from the apprenticeship and freemen books of the Cutlers' Company. Between 1625 and 1649 (the first twenty-five years of the Company's existence) 395 boys were apprenticed into the Hallamshire cutlery trades. The fathers of 22.3 per cent of these lads lived in Sheffield township, 20.1 per cent came from the rural parts of Sheffield parish, another 41.3 per cent resided within 21 miles of the town centre, and only 16.2 per cent lived 21 miles or more away. As the sons of existing freemen did not need to be formally apprenticed to their fathers and were not therefore included in these records, the number of locally born cutlers was even greater than these figures suggest.

The local origins of the men in the cutlery trades can also be judged by their surnames. The overwhelming majority of the freemen of the Cutlers' Company were members of long-established families, many of whom had been making

The Cutlers' Hall. The third Cutlers' Hall on this Church Street site was erected in 1832 and extended in 1865–67. The classical frontage hides a complex arrangement of rooms stretching back almost as far as Fargate. The Cutlers' Feast in the large Banqueting Hall remains the major social event in Sheffield.

PHOTOGRAPH: CARNEGIE

knives, scissors or other wares with a cutting edge since the Middle Ages. The 182 men whose names were recorded in a list of cutlers in 1614, ten years before the incorporation of the Company, included 12 Creswicks, 8 Carrs, 7 Websters, 6 Wilkinsons, 5 Parkins, 5 Pearsons and 5 Staniforths. The Creswicks provided six Masters Cutler between 1630 and 1667.

The Sheffield parish register of baptisms, marriages and burials begins on 27 March 1560. During the next 80 years 1,151 different surnames were recorded. Many of these names appear only briefly, but some crop up time and time again. The ten most common ones include Staniforth and Creswick, surnames that were coined in Hallamshire; the others are names of multiple origin that can be found elsewhere – Fox, Greaves, Hall, Hobson, Lee, Pearson, Smith and Taylor. The bearers of such names in Sheffield were, nevertheless, probably descended from men who had lived in Hallamshire when surnames were formed a couple of centuries or so earlier. Many of the common surnames in Elizabethan Sheffield were derived from local place-names: Bamford (or Bamforth), Birley, Barnsley, Beighton, Brewell (from Braithwell), Bullas (from Bullhouse), Crookes, Hoyland and Oxspring, as were the less common Dungworth, Housley and Osgathorpe. A few other surnames of this type had come from a little further north in the West Riding or from Derbyshire: Bilcliffe, Broadhead, Darwent, Firth, Greenwood, Heathcote, Hinch(c)liffe, Newsam, Wigfall, etc. These are the easiest to identify, but surnames derived from personal names, nicknames, topographical features and occupations were also common. They included such well-known Sheffield names as Bright, Carr, Cutts, Ellis, Hancock, Jeffcock, Jessop, Morton, Parkin, Rawson, Spooner, Stones, Trickett, Trippett, and Webster, amongst numerous others. As we have seen, some distinctive names, such as Hattersley, Scargill and Shemeld had been recorded close to Sheffield in the poll tax returns of 1379.

The Elizabethan parish register also contains a few surnames that stand out as being those of long-distance migrants. Today, nearly two out of three Mappins who subscribe to the national telephone system are listed in the Sheffield district. The Mappin Art Gallery and the firm of Mappin & Webb ensure the continued fame of this name, which was first recorded in 1593, when Derricke Mappin married Elizabeth Dunn at the parish church. His name suggests a Low Countries origin, but we have no idea how or why he came to live in Sheffield. He was not one of the immigrants of French descent who had been brought from the Weald by George, the sixth Earl of Shrewsbury, to establish charcoal blast furnaces and forges on his estates. This group included the Vintins, Perigoes, Husseys and Gelleys, a few of whose descendants still live in Sheffield. Some of the local Tylers, Jordans, Bartholomews and Gillams may also have arrived at this time, but we cannot be certain for other bearers of these names had settled in Hallamshire in previous eras.

These immigrants must have stood out amongst the rest of the local population, for most families had been settled in the neighbourhood for several generations. The continuity of local surnames is particularly marked in the cutlery trades. Other lines of continuity in these trades can be followed through the records of the apprenticeship system. Most local families had at least one member working in the metal trades and many had several. A shared interest in the manufacture of cutlery and links forged through marriage and apprenticeship gave the people of Hallamshire a real sense of common identity. By the sixteenth century, the place and the people had acquired a character whose distinctiveness was recognised throughout England.

Farming and industry

By the time of Harrison's survey of 1637 the old open-fields of Sheffield township had just about withered away. Only six small strips remained. From the survey it is clear that the 'Towne Field' had once stretched over the hill north-west of West Bar Green and north of Broad Lane. Not until the early eighteenth century were houses and workshops built on the slopes that became known as White Croft, Pea Croft and Lambert Croft. This townfield stretched as far as Crookesmoor in the west, to Shalesmoor in the east, and up to the closes of the farmers of Upperthorpe in the north. References to the townfield appear briefly in other records. Thus, in 1569 the Town Trustees paid for the repair of the townfield gate and in 1578 four people appeared before the manor court for not maintaining their hedges 'in the Townefilde of Sheffeld'. By this time the townfield was used for hay, not for cereals and was probably no longer farmed in common.

A few strips in what had once been the townfield of Sharrow survived into the eighteenth century, as did the strips of the open-fields of Crookes and Heeley and those on the flat land of the Lower Don Valley. At the time of Harrison's survey, Attercliffe was still farmed on a three-field system (Park, Crossgate and Dean Fields) and Darnall had a separate three-field system (Near, Middle and Park Fields) beyond the tiny brook that separated the two villages. In the western parts of Sheffield parish the farming system was very different, for there the inhabitants lived in isolated farms or small hamlets, most of which were arranged around small greens. Old names such as Bents Green and Nether Green are now applied to Sheffield suburbs.

Most farmers were copyhold tenants of the lord of Hallamshire, in other words they held their land by a copy of an agreement that had been written on the manorial court rolls. They could pass their farms on to their children at an agreed annual rent and an initial payment to the lord known as an entry fine, by the customary procedure of the manor court. Although the Church Burgesses had let their land to tenants on 21-year leases since 1555, it was not until Ladyday 1651 that the estate policy of the manor of Sheffield allowed the conversion of copyhold tenures to holdings by 21-year leases. A verdict of a manorial jury in 1650 concluded that copyholders had the right to fell and use any wood that grew on their own lands, to dig and sell any coal, slate or stone that lay under their lands, and to get stone, turf, clods, earth and clay from the commons. Throughout Hallamshire the typical farmer was a smallholder whose livelihood depended on his common rights on the surrounding moors and commons and often upon a second occupation, making knives or nails, weaving cloth or taking on any job

that came up. In 1545–46 a high proportion of the taxpayers in Hallamshire were
assessed on small amounts of land. In 1637 Harrison found that most farms were
smallholdings with less than ten acres and that more grass was grown than cereals. Just over half the area covered by his survey consisted of agricultural land.
The best soils covered the coal measure sandstones in the lower areas. The acid
soils above the 1,000 feet level were heather moors fit only for sheep and the
digging of peat for winter fuel. Energetic farmers had carved out numerous
'intakes' from the edge of the moors. The lord was happy to allow such piece-
meal enclosure, for the commons and wastes were extensive and he received extra
revenue from the rents that were paid.

When John Leland visited Sheffield about 1540, he wrote: 'Hallamshire hath
plenti of woodde, and yet ther is burnid much se cole'. Seacoal was the name for
what we simply call coal, in order to distinguish it from charcoal and white coal.
The name came from the Northumberland and Durham coalfield, which was
exploited far more intensively than the coalfield of Yorkshire, Derbyshire and
Nottinghamshire, for it had the inestimable advantage of cheap transport by sea.
Hallamshire was landlocked by comparison, so before the age of the canals and
the railways its coal could be sold competitively only in a regional market. The
chief local colliery was in the Earl of Shrewsbury's park, near Park Hill. George,
the sixth earl, was keen to increase his revenues by exploiting the coal and ironstone that outcropped on his land. As we have seen, he brought Frenchmen from
the Weald to erect charcoal blast furnaces in and around Sheffield. The Upper
and Nether Hammers at Attercliffe Forge were recorded by name in 1581 and
furnaces at Wadsley and Kimberworth were in operation by 1587. Some local
gentry families, seeing the success of these ventures, soon built furnaces and
forges on their own estates. Gilbert, the seventh earl, was content to lease his
ironworks to the Copleys, an ancient gentry family from Wadworth, near
Doncaster. During the first half of the seventeenth century Lionel Copley became
the leading ironmaster in south Yorkshire, with a business that included ironstone
mines, charcoal woods, furnaces and forges, and an outlet for sales via the river
port of Bawtry. In Derbyshire and Nottinghamshire, the iron trade was
dominated by George Sitwell of Renishaw Hall.

By this time Hallamshire had triumphed over its provincial rivals in the manufacture of cutlery. The London cutlers still dominated the market, particularly
for high-class cutlery. They complained from time to time that Hallamshire
cutlers were stamping their wares with the mark of the London dagger, but they
were not yet seriously troubled by the competition of a small town that was far
away and whose craftsmen concentrated most of their efforts on the cheap end
of the market. While the Earls of Shrewsbury were lords of Hallamshire the local
cutlery trades were regulated through the manor court, which issued marks and
insisted on common working practices, including a seven-year apprenticeship.
During the sixteenth century successive Earls of Shrewsbury had taken an active
interest in the cutlery trades. The sponsorship of such powerful figures was
certainly a benefit at the time. The lord's steward, for example, saw that Spanish
iron was imported though Bawtry, for the local ironstone could not provide the

sharp cutting edge that was required for knives and tools. This Spanish iron came from the Bilbao region and was brought most of the way by the relatively cheap method of water transport; during the seventeenth century, if not before, high-quality bars or iron and cementation steel were imported down the Rhine or via the Baltic and North Seas. Hallamshire was able to absorb the costs of importing its materials from abroad, for it had developed a long tradition of craft skills, often in the same families, and it possessed natural advantages in its superior grinding facilities that were provided by the quickly falling rivers and in the quality of its local grindstones, which were manufactured from the soft coal measure sandstones. In 1637 Harrison claimed that some 400–500 master workmen used the lord's wheels on a regular basis, renting grinding space for a few hours at a time. His figure may have been exaggerated, but by 1660 at least 49 sites on the Rivers Don, Sheaf, Porter, Loxley and Rivelin, with a few others on the Blackburn Brook and the Moss Beck, had been dammed for the grinding of cutlery, the milling of corn, the forging of iron, the smelting of lead, and other industrial purposes. Two out of every three of these wheels were geared to the grinding of cutlery and edge tools.

Manorial control of the cutlery trades came to an end with the death of Earl Gilbert in 1616. Two years before his death, the earl had allowed a jury of sixteen cutlers to take over responsibility for the issuing of marks and for 'receipts and disbursements'. They started by entering the marks of 182 cutlers who at that time were working in Hallamshire. The names have a strong local flavour. Two months after the first entry in the book seventeen north Derbyshire cutlers were admitted to the ranks. When an Act of Parliament was obtained in 1624 incorporating the Company of Cutlers, jurisdiction extended throughout Hallamshire and six miles beyond. The new Company was empowered to enrol apprentices, admit freemen, make orders and act on behalf of the membership. The preamble to the Act claimed that the major part of the local work-force was employed in the cutlery trades and that goods were made for a wide market, not only in 'most parts of this kingdom' but also in 'foreign countries'. Hemmed in as it was by the Pennines to the west, Hallamshire was nevertheless connected with all parts of England by a network of carriers' and packhorse routes. Local packmen were selling cutlery in Herefordshire and Worcestershire and exporting them through Chester by Elizabethan times, and a weekly carrying service to London had probably long been in existence by 1637, when John Taylor's *Carriers' Cosmographie* reported that 'The Carriers from Sheffield, in Yorkshire, doth lodge at the Castle in Woodstreet, they are to bee found on Thursdaies and Fridayes.' Much of the produce of Hallamshire was not carried laboriously overland, however, but was taken to Bawtry wharf, and then down the rivers Idle, Trent and Humber to the east coast and London.

Favourable literary references show that by the Elizabethan period Sheffield knives had a national reputation. When Peter Bales published his *Writing Schoolmaster* in 1590, he advised readers who were about to choose a penknife that 'a right Sheffield knife is best'. Table knives were still pointed and carried in a sheath, for the fashion for forks was considered an Italian effeminancy. Forks

Three Elizabethan knives. These are some of the knives which have been recovered in recent years from the mud banks of the River Thames. They can be identified as Sheffield knives by the marks that have been punched into the blades. The knife on the top has a bone handle with carved patterns, the one in the centre has an ivory handle, and the one at the bottom has bands of ivory, wood and bone, separated by brass washers. The knives are still pointed in the medieval manner. They were carried in a sheath attached to a man's belt. These were the sort of knives that were sold in Coventry in 1577, namely 'iiij [4] payre of sheafiel knyves, iij [3] in sheath … vj [6] dossen of hallomshire penn ware

AUTHOR, BY COURTESY OF SIMON MOOR

A HISTORY OF SHEFFIELD

did not become fashionable until Charles II used them at his court, and their use was not widespread before the end of the seventeenth century. The term 'cutler' covered a variety of skills, but some of the first members of the Company were described as scissorsmiths or as makers of shears and sickles. Other trades, such as the making of files or scythes were not admitted into the Company until later in the century.

In the margin:

*'a right Sheffield
knife is best.'*

PETER BALES, 1590

In recent years a group of enthusiasts known as the Thames Mudlarks have dug into the muddy foreshore of the river when the tide goes out. Among their finds, trapped in air-tight conditions that prevent corrosion, are considerable quantities of knives, some of which can be identified from their marks as having been made in Hallamshire. A representative sample of these are now on display in the Cutlers' Hall. They include simple, pointed knives with wooden handles such as Chaucer wrote about and some Elizabethan knives of better quality, hafted in bone, horn and other materials. They are eloquent testimony to the improved standards of production in the sixteenth century when the Talbots were taking a paternal interest in the fortunes of their tenants and when the grinding facilities offered by the local rivers were beginning to give the cutlers of Hallamshire a decided advantage over their provincial rivals.

Local government

As long as the Earls of Shrewsbury were lords of Hallamshire, the manorial court remained an effective body. The court baron met every three weeks to record transfers of land, and the court leet saw to petty law and order, each year electing a constable and other officers. The manor provided the Town Gaol, which was located underneath the Town Hall, and the Debtors' Gaol, which stood on the north side of King Street until its demolition in 1818.

The range of activities of the manorial court can be illustrated by the 'paynes' or by-laws that were agreed by the jury of the court leet in 1609:

Item a payne laid that no person or persons shall at any tyme hereafter wash any clothes, calfe heads, calfe meates, or swyne meates, or other things, within three yarde of the towne head well, new hall well, Burtland well or any other common well in and about the same towne for corruptinge the said wells in payne of and for every time 3*s*. 4*d* ...

the farmer or keeper of the backhowse oven shall bake mens breade well in the backhouse oven for a penny a mett and not to take or demand any more for the bakinge thereof ...

all the householders within the towne of Sheffeild shall bake ther Rye bread and wheate bread at the common backhouse oven and not in any little oven ...

all those persons which have any groundes lyinge in the towne feildes ... make and set good sufficient steeles [i.e. stiles] in the olde accustomed places that men may come and go thold waye ...

no mans sonnes, servants, or apprentices shall at any tyme hereafter play at certen games called the football, the trippe, the hornobilandes [a game played with sticks and a hard ball made of horn, with goals] or bads [played with sticks] nor any of them in the church yard or any other place of the town streetes ...

no manner of person or persons shall at any tyme after nyne of the clock until three of the clock in the morninge use walkinge or talkinge in the towne street whereby it shalbe anoyeance to those that be honest men and householders in the said towne ...

all those howsholders dwelling in the Church layne between Widow Jacksons house and George Fox his house before Penticost next shall remoove take and carry all such myre, smythie sleck, and filth, being in the towne streate against the houses ...

no howsholder within the towne of Sheffeild shall leave any dung hills before the dores either in streets or laynes but scower and carry them away.

The jurors also agreed that greenwood should not be cut down, nor hedges broken, that earth or mortar in Blind Lane and Balm Green should not be dug, and that hedges should be trimmed so as to allow loaded wains to get through. They insisted that ditches should be scoured, gates repaired and swine ringed. They proceeded to fine people who had broken such regulations or had been involved in 'a fray with blood' and to appoint offices who would put their by-laws into effect.

Sheffield was still a small seigneurial borough. All the major decisions affecting its affairs were taken by the lord or his officers, but the townsmen did have a certain amount of independence and were able to spend the rents of the lands that had been entrusted to them by the charter of 1297 on local services that would otherwise have had to be financed by the rates. During the reign of Edward VI part of the income from the Town Lands was confiscated by the Crown, but in 1554 Francis, the fifth Earl of Shrewsbury, was able to use his influence at Court to persuade Queen Mary to restore them and to create two new institutions to manage them. The major share of the property was given to a self-perpetuating body recruited from the parish gentry and the most prominent townsmen, who were styled the 'Twelve Capital Burgesses and Commonality of the Town and Parish of Sheffield', or the Church Burgesses in short. The first charge on their income was the maintenance of the parish church and the salaries of the three assistant ministers. (In the nineteenth century this arrangement had the unforeseen benefit of avoiding unseemly disputes with Nonconformists over the levying of parish rates for the upkeep of the established church, such as occurred in many other English towns.) The remainder of the revenue was spent on the town's business and the multifarious purposes of local government by another body, consisting entirely of townsmen, who in time became known as the Town Trustees. They too were (and are) self-perpetuating. Unlike their neighbouring townsmen in Doncaster (1461) or Chesterfield (1598), the Town Trustees never sought a charter of incorporation, under which the town would have been ruled by a mayor, aldermen and burgesses. Even after the death of Earl Gilbert in 1616 the townsmen did not take advantage of the continued absence of their lord to seek increased powers. Sheffield did not become a municipal borough until 1843.

The records of the Town Trust indicate the range of activities which they supported. For example, in 1572 they paid Thomas Creswick to make a pillory, and five years later they met the cost of repairing both the pillory and stocks. These stood close to the Town Hall, near the gates to the churchyard, facing down High Street. In 1580 they paid John Reades to make a cuck stool, which was used for ducking women who were notorious scolds. The manor also contributed to its upkeep; thus, in 1654 the constable's accounts include a payment 'for mending the Stocks, for bringing the Cuckstoole up to Barker poole.'

The Town Trustees also supported the overseers of the poor, who under the Acts of 1597–1601 were responsible for collecting local rates to pay for people whom they regarded as the deserving poor. The trustees' accounts include a payment of twelve pence in 1572 'to poore Oates wife, wydowe, being verye sycke and almost famyshed for lacke of food to her selfe and her children'. In 1580 they paid Edward Hellifield eight pence to remove a rogue from the town, and in 1590 they gave eight pence 'to Poole wiffe when she went to London' and twelve pence 'to William Woodhouse a poore boye that went up to London'. They assisted the constable too in various ways. In 1590, for instance, they paid him six shillings 'for the Carryeing of Henry Morton as a prisoner to Yorke', in 1592 they allowed eight pence 'for the conveying of a mayde forth of the Towne that came from London in tyme of the plag', and in 1595 they gave Hugh Roberts two shillings 'to pay the Watchmen with when the Gipsees were in the towne'. From time to time, the Town Trust also paid 'for mending of the Butt in the Wycker' (1572), 'a bowe string to the townshipe bow' (1573), walling the pinfold (1577), ringing the church bells on Queen Elizabeth's accession day (1585), and providing coats, badges and instruments for the waits, the town's musicians.

Religion

It is not surprising that Sheffielders became as staunchly Protestant as their lords, the Earls of Shrewsbury. Long before the Civil War, Sheffield had become a

Puritan stronghold. In 1635 the Archbishop of York was informed that the Vicar and all three of his assistants were fervent Puritans and that they were supported by many influential members of their congregation. The Revd Thomas Toller was Vicar from 1598 to 1635 and then (after the Archbishop had forced his resignation) assistant minister until his death in 1644. The Revd John Bright, who exchanged places with Toller in 1635, was the younger brother of Stephen Bright of Carbrook Hall and the uncle of Colonel John Bright, two of the leading Puritans, the wealthiest and most influential men in the parish. The Revd James Fisher, Vicar from 1648 until his ejection in 1662, ensured that Sheffield remained Puritan throughout the Civil War and the Commonwealth period.

A HISTORY OF SHEFFIELD

Carbrook Hall. *Sheffield...SWM*

The influence of the Puritans permeated the town. The Church Burgesses and the Town Trustees were overwhelmingly of that persuasion. So were the successive masters of the Free Grammar School at the western end of Campo Lane. The Church Burgesses' accounts record payments to a schoolmaster from 1564 onwards, then in 1603 the school was provided with a substantial endowment by Thomas Smith of Crowland, a Lincolnshire gentleman who had been born and bred in Sheffield. Like other contemporary grammar schools, the masters taught classics, some mathematics and the church catechism. The schoolhouse was rebuilt in 1648, partly with material from the dismantled castle.

The Puritans also restored the medieval chapels at Ecclesall and Attercliffe, which had been neglected since the Reformation. In 1622 Vicar Toller and the inhabitants of Ecclesall began to restore their chapel. Seven years later, work started on a new chapel at Hill Top, Attercliffe. The principal subscribers were William Spencer of Attercliffe Hall and Stephen Bright of Carbrook Hall. Stanley Gower, assistant minister and first curate at Attercliffe, afterwards achieved fame as a preacher before the House of Commons and a member of the Assembly of Divines at Westminster. The chapel at Ecclesall has been replaced by a later building, but the one at Attercliffe survives in part, much restored and reduced in size.

The Civil War

On 11 October 1642 Sir John Gell of Hopton, Derbyshire led his parliamentary army into Sheffield and took control of the town and castle. Stephen Bright had died at the beginning of the war, so it was his son, John Bright, who took the lead in rallying Sheffielders to the parliamentary cause. He soon rose to the rank of colonel under Sir Thomas Fairfax, the parliamentary commander in the North. He lost control of Sheffield, however, when in April 1643 royalist troops under the command of the Earl of Newcastle (William Cavendish of Welbeck and Bolsover) marched from Wakefield to Rotherham and Sheffield without encoun-

tering any resistance. Sir William Savile was placed in charge of a garrison in Sheffield Castle, the local ironworks were requisitioned to cast cannon, and the Puritan ministers were ejected from the parish church and the chapels. When Savile left, Major Thomas Beaumont, from Whitley, near Huddersfield, took command of a troop of horse and two hundred foot soldiers. The Royalists remained in control until the aftermath of their heavy defeat at Marston Moor in July 1644. During the following month a parliamentary force under Major-General Crawford moved into South Yorkshire. Sheffield castle was said to be 'strongly fortifyed with a broad and deep trench of eighteen foot deep, and water in it, a strong brest-work pallizadoed, a wall round of two yards thick, eight pieces of iron-ordnance, and two mortar pieces.' Crawford stationed a

left Some foundations of Sheffield Castle remain under the Castle Markets. Various excavations have been undertaken in the 1920s and recently, but we still have no precise idea of the size or layout of the town's most imposing and important medieval building.
PHOTOGRAPH: CARNEGIE

battery sixty yards away and submitted the castle to 24 hours of continuous bombardment. When heavier artillery arrived, the castle wall was breached. On 11 August 1644 the royalists surrendered. The lords of Hallamshire kept well away from Sheffield during the Civil War and eventually left for the Continent. It cost the Earl of Arundel and Surrey £6,000 to buy back his Sheffield estates at the end of the fighting. He never recovered his castle, for Parliament ordered that all the castles which had been fortified by the royalists should be demolished. In 1649–50 Sheffield Castle was razed to the ground. Pontefract and Tickhill castles were also made ruinous. In South Yorkshire only Conisbrough Castle was saved, for it was already insecure and had not been used during the Civil War.

Stone and other materials from the castle were sold to local people, or was pilfered. The lead was taken to be sold at Bawtry. The castle site was soon levelled as far as the steep slopes that descended to the rivers. It was used at first as an orchard, then as a bowling green, but gradually most of it was covered with buildings. The great ditch to the south, which had been 30 feet wide, 18 feet deep and full of water, was drained and filled with debris. The ditch to the east became the steep and narrow Castle Fold Lane. Today, only a few foundations remain under the present Castle Markets.

right Rural Sheffiel from Oughtibridge view (1737). Thes low-lying meadow by the River Do were known Colson Crofts o Fairbank's map o 1771. In the earl nineteenth centur they were covere by industri development an terraced house
SHEFFIELD GALLERIES A
MUSEUMS TRU

A HISTORY OF SHEFFIELD

CHAPTER 3 | # 'A town of considerable note for its manufactures'

NO OTHER TOWN in seventeenth-century England had such a specialised work-force as did Sheffield. Three out of every five men worked in the cutlery trades. But Sheffield was not alone in already having an industrialised economy. By the late seventeenth century Birmingham, Manchester, Leeds and some other places which had been mere market towns in the Middle Ages were known throughout the land for the goods that they produced. By the early eighteenth century their populations were growing at a surprising rate. By 1780 they had become markedly different from the elegant provincial towns that we think of as being typical of Georgian England. They and their surrounding districts had begun to assume the industrial characteristics of a new age. As the Revd Edward Goodwin wrote in the *Gentleman's Magazine* in 1764, Sheffield had become 'A town of considerable note for its manufactures'. Four years earlier, Horace Walpole had written to a friend that Sheffield was 'one of the foulest towns in England', meaning one of the dirtiest. He qualified this by observing that Sheffield was set 'in the most charming situation'.

The Dukes of Norfolk

Upon the payment of a large fine in 1648, Thomas Howard had recovered the Sheffield estates that had been taken from him during the Civil War. In 1660, when Charles II was restored to the throne, Thomas's grandson and namesake was created the fifth Duke of Norfolk, a title which the family had lost when the fourth Duke was executed in 1572. Although most of the dukes rarely visited Sheffield during the next two or three centuries, as lords of

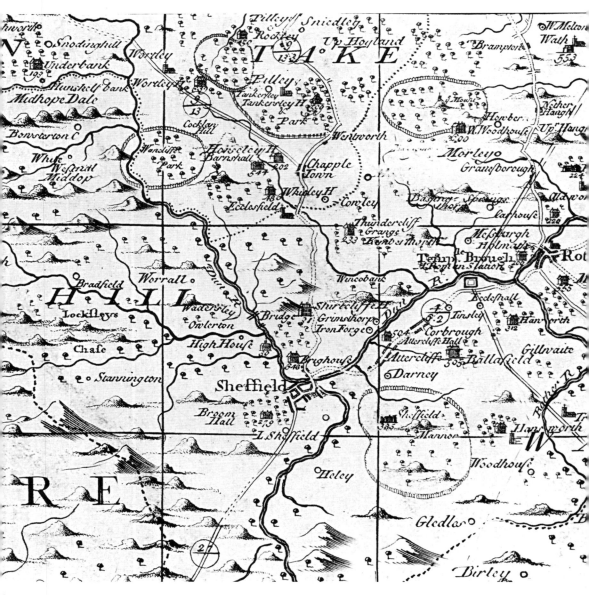

Detail of John Warburton's *Map of Yorkshire* (1718–20). This is the earliest large-scale map of Yorkshire. Warburton was accompanied on his tour of the county by the young Samuel Buck, who sketched towns and the houses of the nobility and gentry, in the hope of commissions for drawings. They failed to find enough subscribers to make the project worthwhile, but a few maps survive. The line of the Roman road through Templeborough is conjectural, but the map is useful in showing other roads before they were turnpiked. The mileage is recorded in both customary and statutory miles. The amount of land still enclosed within deer parks is striking. Sheffield Park had been converted to other uses by this time and the Manor Lodge largely dismantled.

the manor they remained enormously influential in local affairs. They did not take the close paternal interest that the Earls of Shrewsbury had, but they were keen to exploit the economic potential of Hallamshire, their most valuable estate.

Successive Dukes preferred to live first at Worksop and then at Arundel Castle, far away in Sussex. Henry, the seventh Duke, stayed at the Manor Lodge from time to time during the closing years of the seventeenth century, but he was exceptional. The Castle had been demolished and the Manor Lodge was by then old-fashioned in its design and facilities. It nevertheless still comprised a considerable group of buildings. In 1672 the lord's steward was taxed on 36 hearths there and his neighbour at the lodge paid for a further 21 hearths. Within a few years, however, it became apparent that large sums of money would have to be spent on repairs and improvements if the lodge were to remain a major residence. The eighth Duke decided that, as Worksop was so near and as Sheffield Park had already been turned over to farming and mining, the lodge would have to be dismantled. Demolition work began in 1708 and was concluded within two or three years, except for a few buildings which were converted to other purposes, such as John Fox's pottery. Fresh accommodation had to be provided for the Duke's steward, so a new house, known as the Lord's House, was built in Fargate in 1711. Five bays wide and two storeys high, with a triangular pediment and a hipped roof, it was the most elegant house in Sheffield at that time. A small, discreet Roman Catholic chapel was built to the rear, along Norfolk Row, on the site now occupied by St Marie's, the Catholic Cathedral.

When John Harrison surveyed the park in 1637 the enclosing wall was eight miles round. By 1693 the park wall was only three miles in circumference, for the rest of the area had already been divided into farms. By then the route from Gleadless through the park to the Sheaf Bridge was becoming a general right of

Details of Gosling's map (1736, left) and Fairbank's map of 1795 showing the area east of the Sheaf Bridge.

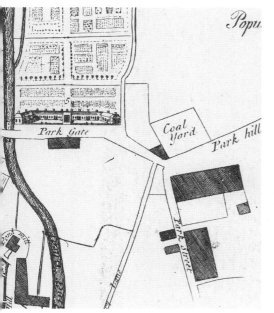

way for those who wished to travel to the town from the south-east and colliers had been allowed to settle on Park Hill near the Duke's mine. Ralph Gosling's map of 1736 marks a small settlement there; William Fairbank's map of the parish of Sheffield in 1795 shows a substantial suburb. The deer had gone, the Manor Lodge was in ruins, but the absentee lords still received a handsome income from their estate.

The deer had long been removed from Rivelin Chase and Shirecliffe Park also. It had become much more profitable to coppice the local woods for charcoal, white coal, pit props and the woodcraft trades. A map of Ecclesall Woods, drawn by John Gelley in 1725, shows the 21 sections into which the woods were divided so as to allow a regular cycle of coppicing. One of the sections was known as Dobbe Crofte Springe, a name that has been commemorated by Dobcroft Road. A tombstone in Ecclesall Woods marks the place where George Yardley, 'Woodcollier', was burnt to death in his cabin in 1786. All the local springwoods were carefully managed in this way. Even when coke became the fuel for smelting iron and lead in the second half of the eighteenth century, charcoal was still needed for the growing cementation steel industry.

The lords of Hallamshire also owned cutlers' grinding wheels and forges on the rivers and numerous farms and small holdings around the town which they let to tenants. In the 1730s the Duke of Norfolk converted the copyholds of over 1,000 acres of agricultural land in the Park, the Manor, Heeley, Little Sheffield, Upperthorpe, Neepsend, the Wicker, and Brightside into 21-year leases. The manorial court baron continued to register transfers of land held by the duke's tenants and, despite the absence of the lord, the manorial court leet met regularly throughout the later seventeenth and eighteenth centuries; indeed, the last court was held on 14 April 1909, though by then, it had few responsibilities. Records that survive from the Commonwealth period and the reign of Charles II show that in the third quarter of the seventeenth century the court was a flourishing institution and that its chief officer, the constable, exercised a wide range of responsibilities. A few examples from the constable's annual accounts from that period indicate his various roles:

Hadfield Wood
13-0-27
4

Stumpe Wood
21-2-13
10
and some 12

Dente Wood
8-2-4
3

Dobbe Croft Springe
8-2-4
5

Mirye Wood
7-2-16
8

Ffoxe hoyle bank
12-1-1
3

Luke Wood
14-2-16
6

Step ffoxe b
8-1-
7

Andrew Crooke the Ladyes Wood
37-1-13
10

Dale or Unwen Wood
16-1-27
16

Rowlinson or Crooke Wood
16-0-17
6

(indecipherable) Wood
14-1-2
1

John Bright Launde

Thomas Bright Wood
35-0-4
3

Dale or Unwen Wood
13-1-3
12

Dale or Urwen Wood
8-1-13
16

John Bright Wood
19-3-17
2

Ffoxe hill bank
45-1-22
2

John Bright Wood
20-1-9
6

Will Millward Wood
8-1-5
never cutte

Padfold (?) laund

John Bright Wood
20-1-9
6

Burrose Wood
19-0-32

Burrose Wood
12-2-8

Ecclesall Woods in the mid seventeenth century, showing how they were divided up into a number of coppice woods each worked by a different woodsman. The first set of figures gives the area of each parcel, while the final number gives the age of the underwood at the time the map was drawn.

SHEFFIELD ARCHIVES, WWM MP46, REDRAWN BY ADAM GREGORY, CARNEGIE

A HISTORY OF SHEFFIELD

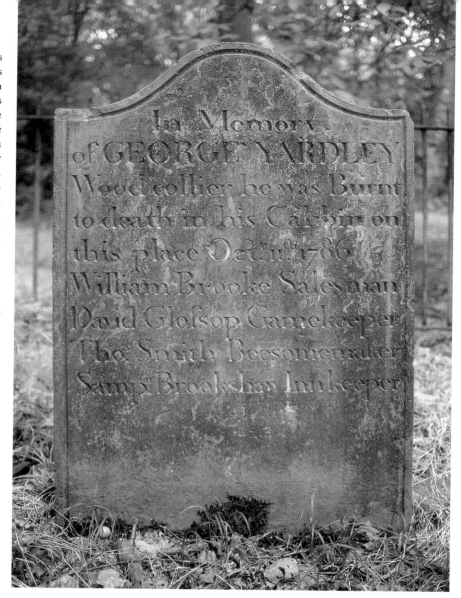

George Yardley's tombstone. This solitary memorial in Ecclesall Woods was erected by the friends of George Yardley, a 'woodcollier' or charcoal burner, who was burnt to death in his cabin on this spot in 1786. The names of the friends and their occupations are inscribed on the tombstone. The full text reads 'In Memory of GEORGE YARDLEY Woodcollier who was Burnt to death in his Cabbin on this place Oct. 11th 1786. William Brooke Salesman David Glossop Gamekeeper Tho. Smith Beesomemaker Samp^n Brookeshaw Innkeeper'

PHOTOGRAPH: CARNEGIE

1650: for quartering of Coll. Allureds men [i.e. parliamentary soldiers] at 2 or 3 severall times vizt. 111 men at one time for 2 dayes & 2 nights & 30 men at another time at 3*d.* per meale. £7 6*s.* 3*d.*

1654: for mending the Stocks, for bringing the Cuckstoole up to Barker poole ...

1660: to John Styring for writeing the pole booke, 10*s.* 0*d.* [i.e. collecting a poll tax] for our charge & horsehyre about paying in the polemoney, 10*s.* 6*d.*, paid to make up the pole booke, £1.

1661: spent & paid at the Coroners Quest where the boy was killed in the Colepitt, £1 2*s.* 0*d.* ...

1662: Given to poore Travellers, £2 13*s.* 4*d.*

Charges at Rotheram about Bruisters licenses, 1s. 6d. [i.e. brewsters: inn- and alehouse-keepers] ...

Spent amongst the Lords officers at the Rearing of the Maypole, 2s. 6d ...

For Ringing upon the 5th of November and on the King's birthday, 17s. 6d. ...

1663: to the Whaites [i.e. the town musicians] for goeing about the town on the faire even, 2s. od, to them & the watchmen in ale, 1s. 6d. ...

Charges about Mr Fisher [the ejected Vicar who had become a Fifth Monarchy Man and was involved in a plot against the government] seekeing & Carrying to Yorke, £1 17s. od.

1666: Charges in apprehending Steevenson & prosecuting him for Stealeing the Church Lead, 7s. od. ...

Charges of building a Centrie [i.e. sentry] house att Little Sheffield moore, £1 7s. od. [to watch for people coming from Eyam, which was stricken with the plague] ...

Charges about keeping people from Fullwood Spaw in the tyme that the sickness was at Eam, 6d. ...

1669: Charges of the Jury being Summoned to appear before the Clerk of Markett about altering measures, 14s. 9d. [The Dukes of Norfolk retained the right to levy market tolls until 1899.]

The medieval custom whereby the lord's tenants who held their property by a certain kind of tenure were expected to parade on Assembly Green, on the north bank of the River Don opposite the castle, each Easter Tuesday, continued long after 1660, when military tenures were abolished. The 'Sembly Quest' [short for Assembly Inquest] was recorded in 1383, but the tradition was probably already two or three centuries old by then. Harrison's survey of 1637 noted that 139 horsemen took part, but by the end of the seventeenth century only 60–80 men attended the parade. This ancient custom was hurriedly abolished after the Jacobite rising of 1715, when the Duke of Norfolk decided that it was unwise for the most prominent Catholic in England to parade a private army. Another link with Sheffield's medieval past was broken by this prudent decision.

The town

Our first maps and prints of the town date from the 1730s and 1740s. As we have seen, they have much to tell us about Sheffield's ancient past, as well as being prime sources of information on the lay out and appearance of the town on the eve of rapid expansion. The earliest surviving map was drawn in 1736 by Ralph Gosling, the master at the Writing School in Campo Lane. The following year, Thomas Oughtibridge, of Hatfield beyond Doncaster, sketched a view of the town from Pye Bank, and in 1745 Samuel and Nathaniel Buck drew a much more

William Fairbank's *Map of Sheffield* (1771). William Fairbank was the second of four generations of surveyors, a Quaker family who lived at Hartshead. The Fairbank collection at Sheffield Archives is the finest set of surveyors' maps, field books and papers in the country. The map shows the town still bordered by the Don and the Sheaf. The central street pattern is still largely intact, but Alsop Fields in the south was shortly to be developed for housing and industry. The western limits of the town were Moorhead, Barkers Pool and Townhead. In the north-west the town was spreading beyond its old limits, toward Shalesmoor.

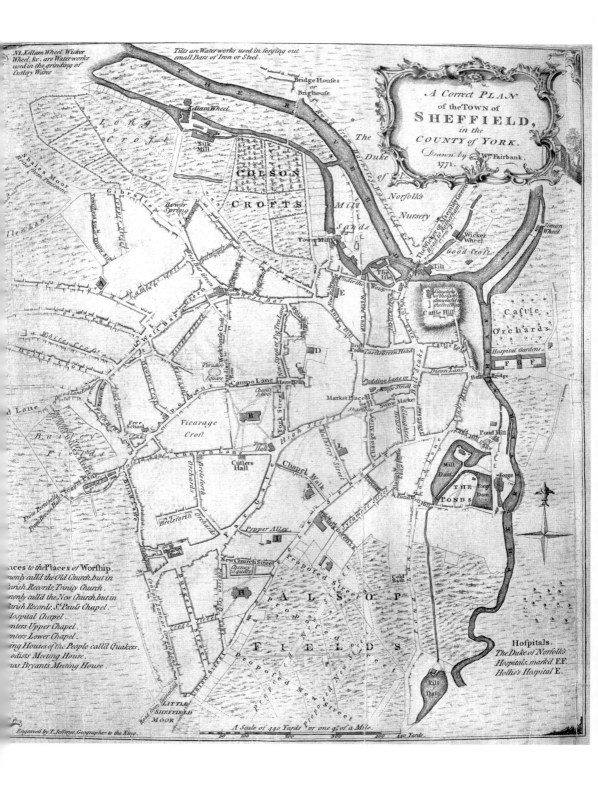

Carr
Darlands
Souther Hall
Elm Green
Bradfield H.
Nether Bank
J. Sparrow
Brush H.
Winco Bank
Souther Green
Bell H.
Paper M.
Wadsley B.
Wards End
Reason H.
Norwood H
Page H.
Camp
Bright Side
Crabtree
Grims thorp
Owlerton
Shirtcliff Hall
Hill House
Forge
Bridge
Pitts Moor
Turnpike
Forge
Attercliff Chap.
Broad Mead
Lane Head
White House
Walkley
SHEFFIELD
Over thorp
Atterclif Br.
Nunnery
Crook
Darna
Park Hill
Portobello
Broom Hall
Sheffield Manor
W
A
P
Little Sheffield
Sharrow Moor
Charrow Head
Green
Cherrytree Hill
Heatey
Woodth
Mechan
Edge
Newfield
High Stile
Edge End
Meres Brook
Field
Hammer Farm
Buton Hill
Holt
Mill Ho
Herding
Charlo

sophisticated view from Park Hill, which they called *East Prospect of Sheffield* ... We have to wait until 1771 for a better map than Gosling's. In that year, William Fairbank, the Quaker surveyor of Hartshead, published a map of the town and Thomas Jefferys made an accurate representation of the wider district as part of his map of Yorkshire, which he drew on the scale of one inch to one mile.

The maps show the continued importance of the Market Place at the heart of Sheffield. The former space to the north of King Street, stretching down to the Irish Cross and Castle Green Head, had been filled in long before Gosling's time. The area to the south of King Street was partly filled, in a higgledy-piggledy way, by the stalls of butchers and other traders. In the 1730s 34 butchers' shops were rented from the lord on 21-year leases. Gosling marked the butchers' shambles behind the market cross, which fronted onto the street which is still called Market Place. The present Haymarket was at that time named Beast Market, though it had already acquired its alternative description of Bull Stake, the name given to it on Fairbank's map of 1771. Here bulls were baited by savage dogs before they were slaughtered on market days. Fairbank also marked the Swine Market to the south of the shambles and noted the site of the slaughter houses alongside a gennel that led from the Market Place in the direction of the Ponds tanneries. The two maps show that the sale of livestock and the slaughtering, dressing, and sale of meat and hides were concentrated within a small area at the very the centre of the town.

The importance of the market was obvious to visitors. When Ralph Thoresby, the Leeds antiquary, came to Sheffield in 1681, he described the place as 'a large market town, most noted for knives, scissors, and iron-work' and in 1691 Sheffield's 'large corn market' was said to serve not only the town but also parts of Derbyshire, Nottinghamshire and the West Riding of Yorkshire. Two generations later, in 1764, the Revd Edward Goodwin wrote that Sheffield had a plentiful market on Tuesdays for butter, corn, cattle and fish, according to season, and a very good shambles. By then, the demands of the rapidly growing

population had intensified the pressure on the limited space of the Market Place until it could no longer cope. On market days extra stalls had to be placed all the way along High Street and near Townhead Cross, while the pot market was moved to Hicks Stile Field (soon to become Paradise Square). In 1784, when an Act of Parliament was at last obtained to re-arrange the market facilities, 108 shops and stalls belonging to butchers, tanners, shoemakers, fishmongers, pelt-mongers, hosiers, hatters, staymakers and a bookseller were said to occupy the old market place, and 76 stalls were spread out along the adjacent streets. Customers wandering up the High Street were offered a choice of earthenware, second-hand shoes, gingerbread, and cheese and bacon. Butter and eggs could be bought from the baskets of farmers' wives standing around the market cross, fruit and vegetables could be picked from carts which were squeezed into any available space, and further choices could be made from the shops of the dyers, coopers, tallow chandlers, fruiterers, hardwaremen, hatters, gardeners, curriers, breeches-makers and flax-dressers, and from hawkers in the streets or at the inns. The annual fairs were even more hectic, attracting, it was claimed, 28 cheese-mongers, 60 clothiers and linen-drapers, and sellers of gingerbread, toys and hardware 'too numerous to mention'.

When the lord and the townsmen agreed in 1784 that an improved Market Place was an absolute necessity, they stressed in their petition to Parliament the inadequacy of the available space, the congestion on market days, the 'very

A waggon trundles down the narrow High Street towards the Market Place. The Market Hall that was built in 1784 on the site of the old Shambles is shown on the right.

improper situation' of the slaughter houses and their offensive sights and smells. After improvements had been made, the *Sheffield Register* observed on 4 August 1787 that the markets, which:

> used to be held in a confused, irregular manner, in the streets, and which travellers have frequently complained of as dangerous and disagreeable, are now confined to particular places. The newly erected market place which is neatly elegant in appearance and commodious in the construction contains the butchers, hucksters, part of the gardeners, etc, the rest with the dealers in earthenware, fruiterers and others stand in Paradise Square – a large convenient place in the centre of the town. By these agreeable regulations the streets have a better appearance, and carriages pass free from interruption, without endangering the foot passengers.

A rental for the New Market, on 25 March 1790, recorded 215 shops and stalls, a third of which, including those of 25 shoemakers and 10 breechesmakers, traded in goods other than food.

Under the terms of the Act of 1784, the old shops, stalls, shambles and market cross were removed, the streets were widened and property frontages were straightened. A new market hall and a shambles were built, livestock were removed from the central streets to a more spacious site in the Wicker, and slaughter-houses were erected along a new street called Castlegate that was laid out on the southern bank of the River Don. From then on, corn was sold in front of the market hall, the Beast Market became the Hay Market, and the Swine Market became the Fruit Market. Sheffield had (somewhat belatedly) adjusted its market facilities in a similar manner to towns all over England which were having to cope with the impact of population and economic growth on their historic centres.

A detail of Fairbank's 1771 plan of Sheffield showing the newly laid out Paradise Square, the workhouse, the churchyard, the town hall and schools. Fairbank marked only the buildings that fronted the streets, but by this time most of the old open spaces had been filled with houses and workshops.

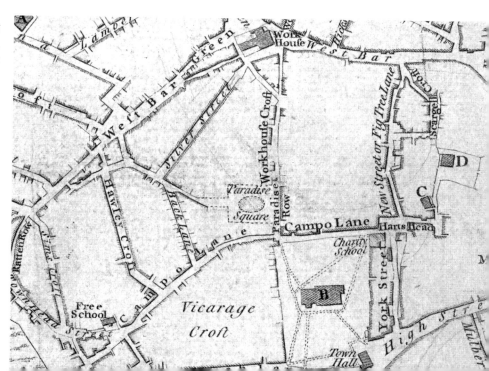

The town depicted on Gosling's and Fairbank's maps and the prints of Oughtibridge and the Bucks was surrounded by pasture and arable land, and contained numerous orchards and gardens within its borders. Some of the central streets bore picturesque names like Orchard Street, Mulberry Street and Fig Tree Lane. Cowhouses were a common sight at the edges of the town, and pig sties were located at the rear of houses in the central streets. Dr William Buchan of Hartshead wrote in the late 1760s: 'There is hardly a journeyman cutler who does not possess a piece of ground which he cultivates as a garden'. Gosling's map shows that in 1736 space was still readily available for housing development near the centre of the town, particularly at Hartshead, on Church Burgess land known as Wade's Orchard, and at Hick's Stile Field, the steeply sloping meadow where the pot market was held on Tuesdays. In the year that Gosling drew his map, Joseph Broadbent, a cutlery merchant and prominent Quaker of Hartshead, built five houses at the top of this meadow and named them Paradise Row; in 1771 his eldest son, Thomas, built the houses which form the other three sides of Paradise Square, Sheffield's only piece of attractive Georgian development.

During the eighteenth century, the streets in the centre of the town were gradually filled with housing. By the 1720s new streets such as Hawley Croft were being lined with houses, cottages and smithies down the steep slope to the north of Campo Lane and on the flatter land by West Bar Green. The first expansion beyond the old limits occurred on the north side of Broad Lane, where Hollis Croft, White Croft, Pea Croft, Lambert Croft and Scotland Street followed the curving boundaries of the old strips of the former open-fields. Scotland Street was perhaps a nickname for the furthest point north in Sheffield; it was not there

Paradise Square. Sheffield's only Georgian square. Built by the Broadbents on the steeply sloping site of the former Hick's Stile Field, this residential quarter has been converted into offices. Large public gatherings were held here in the eighteenth and nineteenth centuries, some religious, others political.
PHOTOGRAPH: CARNEGIE

St Paul's and Cheney Square, c. 1855, by Godfrey Sykes
SHEFFIELD GALLERIES AND MUSEUMS TRUST

  A HISTORY OF SHEFFIELD

in Gosling's time and was referred to simply as 'Scotland' in a rate book of 1755–56. Other Sheffield nicknames included Little London, on the road south beyond Heeley, and the Isle of Wight for the low-lying district near Millsands, which was normally just called The Isle. Pudding Lane and Paternoster Row were named after London streets. A few of the other minor place-names that were coined in the eighteenth century commemorated battles in distant countries. Gibraltar was captured by the British in 1704 and Portobello was the scene of a British victory over the Spaniards near Panama in 1739. At Port Mahon, in Minorca, in 1756 the French defeated a British force under Admiral Bing, who was tried upon his return to England and executed. A Sheffield mob burned his effigy.

When the Earl of Oxford and his party visited Sheffield in 1725, his chaplain wrote:

> There has been a great part of the town, which was made up chiefly of wooden houses, rebuilt within these few years, and now makes no mean figure in brick particularly towards the north side of it, where there [are] abundance of new erections upon new foundations by which the town has lately been consider-ably enlarged.

Space for houses and workshops was also available at the southern edge of the town. Here, Upper Chapel had been built in Pepper Alley (named after a Mr Pepper) in 1700 and St Paul's Church had been erected by Cheyney Square (named after a Dr Cheyney) in the 1720s. The land that lay between St Paul's

St Paul's Church. Edward Blore's view of 1819 shows the Baroque church that was Sheffield's most stylish eighteenth-century building. Erected as a chapel-of-ease in the 1720s, it was demolished just before the Second World War. The site is now the Peace Gardens.

Church and Coal Pit Lane (now Cambridge Street) at the south-western edge of the town belonged to the Church Burgesses. No streets or houses were marked here on Gosling's map, but in 1737 the Church Burgesses started to grant 800-year building leases, and open spaces such as this one, Sims Croft and Brailsforth Orchards (now Orchard Square) began to be filled with buildings. A 1756 rate book mentioned the new Burgess Street in the south-west, and fifteen years later Fairbank's map marked the new Cross Street (now Cross Burgess Street). By then, the old lane that had once marked the boundary of the lord's park had been re-fashioned as Union Street. As the date is too late for the name to refer to the Act of Union with Scotland (1707), the street was probably just a link road in the same sense as Cross Street. It ran into Norfolk Street, the new road that followed the old park boundary along the back of the High Street gardens, the former burgage plots of the medieval town. Norfolk Street was first named in local records in 1747. It soon became one of the most important streets in Sheffield. In 1764 the Revd Edward Goodwin thought that the best houses in the town stood in the High Street and Norfolk Street, near St Paul's Church, and in Paradise Row.

When the Duke of Norfolk's deer park was converted into farms, the space between Norfolk and Union Streets to the west and the River Sheaf to the east became known as Alsop Farm or Alsop Fields after the tenant. Gosling's map marked buildings extending along Pond Lane, but otherwise Alsop Fields remained intact. In 1771, however, Fairbank showed buildings on the eastern side of Norfolk Street and development along the new Sycamore Street, Bowling Green Lane and Petticoat Lane. The rest of Alsop Fields was staked out in a grid pattern of 'Proposed New Streets'. Another map by William Fairbank, surveyed

An engraving of the first Cutlers' Hall, from J. S. Fletcher's *A Picturesque History of Yorkshire* (c.1900). Built in 1638, it was replaced by a New Hall on the present site in 1725.

in 1797, shows that the proposed scheme had by then been put into effect. The new streets (some of which survive as narrow and straight lanes on sloping land near the Central Library and the railway station) took their names from the lord of the manor. Charles Howard was Duke of Norfolk and Earl of Surrey and Arundel, his main residence was in Sussex, and his agent was Vincent Eyre, so there were plenty of names to choose from. The new streets were quickly lined with houses, factories and workshops. The Alsop Fields scheme had no monumental public buildings and did not segregate residences from industrial buildings.

These new developments were modest in aspiration and achievement when compared with the best work in contemporary towns. Sheffield was slow to respond to the movement which has been described as an eighteenth-century urban renaissance. The town did not have rich merchants who could afford to build fine houses, like those in Leeds or Nottingham, nor a wealthy corporation which could redesign the layout of the town and commission grand public buildings. The baroque architecture of St Paul's Church added a little dignity, but the Cutlers' Hall of 1725, the Nonconformist meeting-houses, the charity school and the workhouse were all plain and functional.

Writing about the Sheffield of his childhood in the 1760s, Samuel Roberts observed that, 'The town was then in a very rude state in every respect, it being only partially flagged, with many stones loose.' The notorious open sewer at the top of Castle Green, known as Truelove's Gutter after an old Sheffield family, had been cleared by the Town Trust in 1694, and a few oil lamps had been installed in the main streets during the winter of 1734–35, but these and similar minor improvements were little to boast about. Sheffield was not a social centre which attracted the gentry from the surrounding countryside, as Doncaster did, for it was commonly perceived as a dirty manufacturing place. It did, however, follow the example of other towns in the provision of social events,

albeit rather belatedly and comparatively modestly. Horse races were held on Crookesmoor from 1711 until the enclosure of the commons in the 1780s. Assemblies (chiefly for dancing and card playing) were held in the Boys' Charity School from at least 1735, and in 1762 special Assembly Rooms were built in Norfolk Street. Facilities for cultural events did not improve until well into the second half of the eighteenth century. Sheffield did not have its own newspaper until 1754 (and that did not last very long), and although travelling players had often performed in the yard of the Angel Inn, the town did not have a theatre until 1763. The first musical festival was held in 1769, and the subscription library was founded in 1771.

Sheffield retained the appearance of an old market town, soiled by its industry. An anonymous visitor in 1768 thought that: 'The town of Sheffield is very large and populous, but exceedingly dirty and ill paved. What makes it more disagreeable is the excessive smoke from the great multitude of forges which this town is crowded with.' Those inhabitants who were not employed in the cutlery industry earned their livings chiefly in the food, clothing and footwear, building, and retail trades. A number of modest inns and (by 1687) a coffee house surrounded the Market Place and stretched along the High Street. A government enquiry in 1686 reported that Sheffield had 119 guest beds and 270 stables, that is more than Rotherham and Barnsley, but about the same as Chesterfield and considerably fewer than Leeds, Wakefield and Doncaster. It also had an

Hartshead. The house known as No 1 Hartshead is the earliest surviving brick house in Sheffield. It was built for Nicholas Broadbent, scissorsmith and trader, in 1728. The Broadbents were prominent Quakers whose meeting house stood nearby.

astonishing number of alehouses. A list of those licensed at the quarter sessions in 1679 suggests that Sheffield had either an inn or an alehouse to every six or seven households. The inns were modest in scale and style when compared to the grand coaching inns of the main thoroughfares of Georgian England. The alehouses were converted parlours and kitchens.

At the time of the hearth tax returns of 1672 the central township of Sheffield had one or two poor quarters and the best houses were grouped together in High Street, but generally speaking the rich and the poor were not housed in separate residential areas. Although the town had hardly any notable buildings, at that time no fewer than 205 houses offered reasonable comfort with at least three hearths to heat the rooms. The east prospect of the town depicted by the Bucks two or three generations later in 1745 points to a similar conclusion: most Sheffielders were not rich, but neither were they poor. Nevertheless, the most unfortunate of the inhabitants of the central township fared no better than the poorest cottagers in the countryside. Surveys of 66 dwellings in Sheffield in 1611 and 1616 included descriptions of twelve cottages which consisted of only a single bay of housing with perhaps a lean-to at the back. For example, Nicholas Shooter had just '1 small Cottage 1 bay thatcht' in the Water Lane–Castle Green district, which was the poorest part of the town.

By the time that the 1616 survey of the Church Burgesses' properties was updated in 1672, many of the old thatched roofs had been replaced with stone slates. The smallness of some of the cottages and the presence of smithies and barns is illustrated by the following extracts:

Phillipp Stainroid: 1 house 3 bays and 3 outshutts thatcht 2 Smythies under one roofe and a barn of 2 bayes slated ...

Cottages on Balm Green by William Botham, 1802. These were built on a former piece of common land, near the present City Hall, without gardens or well-defined property boundaries. They appear to date from the first half of the eighteenth century. No stone-built cottages from this period survive in Sheffield.

Willm. Norris: A house butting on west barr ... and two Smythies joyneing together with a backsyde ...

James Harrison: A house slated ... of 2 bayes ... alsoe a parlour of a bay slated and a Kitchin and 2 Smythies thatcht ...

William Walker: a house 2 bayes slated in water lane ... with a chamber over it a kitchin and a Smythie each a bay slated ...

Francis Stainford: a house 2 bayes and 2 outshutts slated in water lane a smythie and a kitchin 2 bays slated ...

Alex Hydes: a house in Castle Green 2 bayes slated ... an old barn of a bay an outshutt thatcht ...

Thomas Hoyle (Sam. Sanderson): 1 house 3 bayes slated att the Bullstake a kitchin 1 bay slated a stable and a barn 2 baies with a Cowhouse 1 bay all slated ...

Thomas Creswicke: a house of 2 bayes slated butting W[est] on the High Street with a Kitchin and Smythie of 2 bayes slated, with a Court and backsyde in the which is a barne of two baies slated ...

George Oxspring: A Thatcht house of 3 baies butting west on the street ... alsoe a new dwelling house slated of a bay and an halfe A stable 1 bay and an outshutt thatcht a barn 2 baies slated.

During the seventeenth century the old wooden buildings were gradually replaced by new cottages with stone walls and stone slate roofs. These sturdier structures did not necessarily offer more space, however. For example, a cottage in Castle Green that was leased from the Church Burgesses in 1713 consisted of no more than a living room (or 'house'), a chamber and a cellar, and a cottage in Snig Hill in 1731 consisted simply of a 'house', a chamber and a garret.

These seventeenth- and eighteenth-century cottages have all been demolished, and we need not mourn their passing, but a few were shown on the Bucks's east prospect of 1745, and a watercolour of 1802 by William Botham depicts a row of three ancient, stone-built cottages on Balm Green, which were one-and-a-half or two storeys high, but with only a single room on the ground floor. The central township of Sheffield was gradually filled with domestic and industrial buildings as the eighteenth century progressed. In 1774 James Wheat claimed in his *Observations on the Present State of the Poor in Sheffield* that:

> Their Houses, if such they can be called, are miserable cabins, small, low, close, dark and dirty, where unpolluted Air seldom enters – here a father, a mother, and their children often reside in one room, and often sleep in one Bed, or if they happen to be possessed of two, they are generally of such wretched quality as to be fit only to generate filth, vermin and disease.

Of course, only a small minority of families lived in such appalling conditions. The standard of living for most Sheffielders was far better than that.

As we have seen, the Earl of Oxford's chaplain commented in 1725 that the

A HISTORY OF SHEFFIELD

Sheffield parish church, as rebuilt in the late eighteenth century, from an engraving by J. Rogers after a drawing by N. Whittock.

old wooden houses of the town were being replaced by new brick buildings. The Manor Lodge had been adorned by a pair of brick towers in the 1570s, when brick was used only on prestigious buildings such as castles, country houses and colleges, but the first building in Sheffield to use brick throughout was Upper Chapel, which was erected in 1700. In 1848 the chapel was refronted in stone, but the original brickwork can still be seen at the sides and to the rear of the building, almost to roof height. Brickmakers are first recorded in the Sheffield parish register about the same time. The town had a plentiful supply of brick-making earths and soon it was considered both economical and fashionable to build with

this material. By 1764 the Revd Edward Goodwin could report that, 'The buildings are in general of brick'. In the nineteenth century Sheffield continued to follow the example of Leeds and Wakefield in preferring brick rather than local sandstone, which was the choice of Huddersfield, Bradford and Halifax and other, smaller towns on the edges of the Pennines.

The earliest surviving brick house in Sheffield is that now known as No. 1 Hartshead, which was built three storeys high and five bays wide in 1728 by Nicholas Broadbent. Brick was also used for the houses that were erected by other members of his family in Paradise Square. The fashionable houses in the new suburb of Bridgehouses, to the north of the River Don, were probably built in a similar manner, but none has survived. Other prominent surviving examples from the second half of the eighteenth century include the brick house at the end of Surrey Street, which was built for the Leader family (manufacturers of Old Sheffield Plate), and Mount Pleasant, which Francis Hurt erected in 1786 in what was then a rural part of the parish. Both these buildings are now used for educational purposes.

Population

Daniel Defoe's account of Sheffield, which he included in *A Tour through the Whole Island of Great Britain* (1724–26), was based on a visit of about 1710–12. Defoe regarded Sheffield as 'populous and large', for he was judging it by contemporary standards and not by later ones. In 1736 the population of the central township was counted in a special census that was taken to support the case for completing the new St Paul's Church. Ralph Gosling's map noted 9,695 people, but omitted a further 246 Roman Catholics and 180 Quakers, whose presence raised the total number to 10,121. The people who lived in the central urban township in 1736 formed a much larger community than did the 2,207 people who were counted in the same district in 1616. The urban population had increased four and a half times in the space of 120 years, and most of this rise had taken place after 1700. As a further 4,410 parishioners lived in the rural townships, the total population of Sheffield parish in 1736 was 14,531. This figure is directly comparable with that of the 135,310 inhabitants of the new borough who were recorded in the census return of 1851. The population had started to rise significantly by 1736, but the greatest advances were yet to come.

Upon his visit to Sheffield in 1725, the Earl of Oxford's chaplain commented on 'the health of the place, which few towns so populous enjoy with such constancy as they do'. He observed the beneficial effects of the regular cleansing of the streets by water released from Barker's Pool, when the inhabitants took 'the opportunity of sweeping into it all their uncleanly encumbrances'. (The water flowed down Fargate, High Street, Market Place, Water Lane, and into the Don.) Sheffield stood on a ridge, well above the river valleys, and thus benefited from both the wind and natural drainage. The fires of the smithies that helped to keep people warm in winter may have helped to keep illness at bay, but Sheffielders commonly claimed that it was the smoke which kept them healthy! The town suffered occasional serious outbreaks of infectious diseases, but these sudden

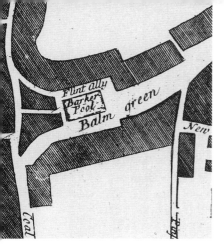

epidemics did not appear as regularly as in most other places. Many children died in the summer of 1715 from a mysterious infection, and the course of other epidemics can be traced in the parish registers during 1723, 1726 and 1728–29. The cause of death was rarely noted, but the different patterns of mortality suggest a variety of diseases. In the parish of Sheffield the spring of 1723 and the winter of 1728–29 were the worst seasons on record for high numbers of deaths.

A detail of Ralph Gosling's map of Sheffield showing the area around Barker's Pool and Balm Green.
SHEFFIELD LIBRARIES, ARCHIVES AND INFORMATION: LOCAL STUDIES

In the early eighteenth century, Sheffield's population growth was checked but not reversed by such deadly viruses. The town began to grow in an astonishing way. Young immigrants from the surrounding countryside helped to swell the number of the town's inhabitants, yet these rural parishes grew at the same time. Marriage registers and apprentice books demonstrate that immigrants came from the same places as their predecessors in the seventeenth century, and the Attercliffe township poor law records show that even the poor did not travel very far. Few immigrants came to Hallamshire from beyond the West Riding or Derbyshire. Most of them headed for the town, but others built cottages on the edges of the commons and wastes, in such places as Grenoside or Gleadless. Immigration alone cannot explain the growth of eighteenth-century Sheffield, however. Population levels rose throughout Hallamshire and by the middle years of the century the whole of England was experiencing the beginnings of spectacular,

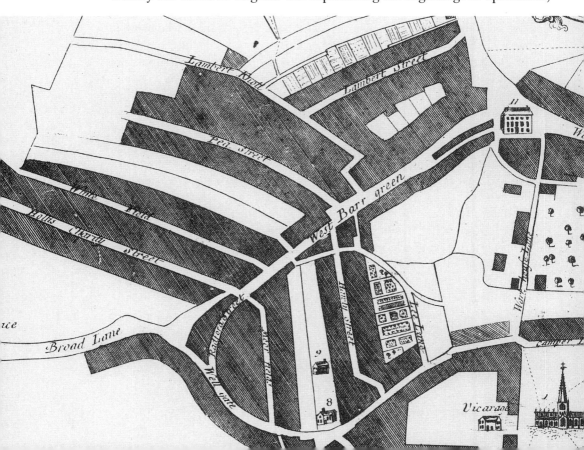

unprecedented growth. It is now accepted by historical demographers that earlier marriages and therefore more births account for about two-thirds of this rise in national population levels and that lower death rates explain the rest. Young couples were able to marry at an earlier age than their parents because of the increased opportunities to find employment.

The limited range of local poor-law records that have survived suggest that early eighteenth-century Sheffield was not as poverty stricken as it had been a hundred years previously. The local economy was now strong enough to support a much larger population at a higher standard of living than it had been able to in the latter years of the Earls of Shrewsbury. The paupers in the workhouse formed only a very small proportion of the inhabitants of the parish and the amount of money spent on them and the rest of 'the deserving poor' was modest.

A workhouse had been built on West Bar Green, at the north-western edge of the town, in 1628. This was a timber-framed structure, used only for the accommodation and employment of poor children. It sufficed for a century or so, until Sheffield became one of the first towns to build a new workhouse after the passing of the Workhouse Test Act (1723). Overseers of the poor were empowered to refuse relief to anyone who was not prepared to live in the workhouse and work at the tasks that were given them. The new brick building, three storeys high and five bays wide, was built on the same site as the old wooden structure that it replaced. It was marked prominently on Gosling's map, amongst the new houses and workshops that were going up all around. It was enlarged in 1759 and was used as a workhouse until its demolition in the early nineteenth century.

Throughout Hallamshire, both in the town and the countryside, the persistence of the same family names over the generations strikes anyone who browses through the parish registers. The stability of a core group of families in contrast to the comings and goings of others. reinforced the sense of common identity that the inhabitants of Hallamshire already possessed through a shared involvement in the cutlery trades. Many of these surnames were local in origin. When a hearth tax was levied on the central township of Sheffield in 1672 the 494 householders had 264 different surnames between them. The most common were Creswick (12), Webster (10), Staniforth (8), Hancock (8), Barlow/Barley (7), Ellis (7), Rogers (7), Turner (7), Bright (6), Fox (6), Pearson (6), Roberts (6), Scargill (6), Stacy (6), Bullas (5), Clayton (5), Steven (5), Stones (5), Shore (5), Taylor (5), and Twigg (5). Each of these names had long been familiar in the area. Minor place-names within Hallamshire had given rise to the very common surnames Creswick and Staniforth and to other names such as Burley (1), Crookes (4), Hawley (3), Howsley (2), and Shirtcliff (3). Distinctive surnames such as Scargill (6), and Shemeld (3), had also been recorded locally in the fourteenth century. Most of those Sheffielders who were taxed on their smithies as well as their domestic hearths sprang from ancient Hallamshire families such as these.

Some surnames, however, betray their origins elsewhere in the West Riding of Yorkshire or in neighbouring counties. The Dewsburys, Dodsworths, Hellifields, Lockwoods, Oxleys, Rockleys, Sorsbys, Swindens, Stainlands, Waterhouses, Wigfields and Wadsworths came from further north in the West Riding. The

Two late seventeenth-century Sheffield knives, found in the mud banks of the River Thames. The style of the knife on the top is not much different from that of knives made a hundred years earlier. It was made about 1660 and has a bone handle. The one below has a curving ivory handle and a blade that ends in a small point. Its mark can be identified from the records of the Cutlers' Company as that granted to Joseph Carr, who was made a freeman of the company in 1675.

AUTHOR, BY COURTESY OF SIMON MOORE

A HISTORY OF SHEFFIELD

Broadbents, Cleggs and Kirkhams had crossed the Pennines from Lancashire, the Bradburys, Brammalls, Cuttforthaighs, Hides and Poyntons came from Cheshire, the Brailsforths from south Derbyshire, and the Binghams from Nottinghamshire. No doubt some householders with common surnames had also migrated from these places. The drift was from the north and the west and few people had travelled very far. Many had entered Hallamshire as apprentices in the cutlery trades and had stayed to become 'little mesters'.

Cutlery

We have seen that by the middle of the seventeenth century Sheffield had a more specialised occupational structure than any other town in England. Three out of every five of its men worked at one branch or other of the cutlery trades. In his

Two eighteenth-century Sheffield pocket knives, recovered from the mud banks of the River Thames. The making of 'spring knives' was a Sheffield speciality from at least Elizabethan times. The bone handle of the knife on the right is hardly spoilt, but little remains of the tortoise-shell that was used for hafting the knife on the left. The blades are still sharp and the knives snap shut, despite their long burial in the Thames mud.

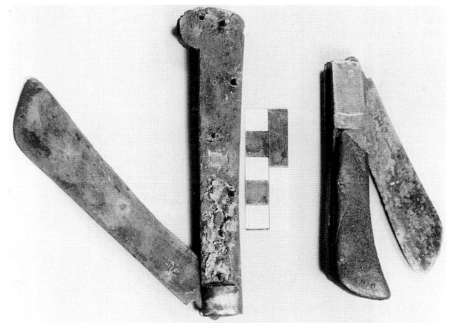

Forging hand files. Henry Martin is shown using a distinctly shaped filemaker's hammer, *c.* 1902 (the date of the Almanac on the wall), to forge a saw file at Thomas Turton's Suffolk Works. By this time the hand-cutting of files had largely gone in Sheffield, though it survived in the inter-war period in outlying villages, notably Ecclesfield.

A grinder at his wheel: a model at Kelham Island Industrial Museum.

PHOTOGRAPH CARNEGIE: COURTESY OF SHEFFIELD INDUSTRIAL MUSEUMS TRUST

left

Reconstructed blade forger's smithy which once stood at the top of St Philip's Road, showing the hearth, bellows, and stithy and stock' the anvil and stone base) where the cutler worked.

SHEFFIELD INDUSTRIAL MUSEUMS TRUST

Worthies of England (1662), Thomas Fuller wrote that most of the common knives of English country people were made in Yorkshire and that Sheffield, 'a remarkable market', was 'the staple town for this commodity ... One may justly wonder how a knife may be sold for one penny'. Despite their under-recording of the exempted poor, the hearth tax returns of 1672 list about 600 metalworkers' smithies in Hallamshire and adjacent parts of South Yorkshire and north Derbyshire. The central township of Sheffield contained 224 of these smithies. Beyond the Market Place and the High Street, nearly every house had a work-shop attached to it or one standing at the rear. Some workshops contained more than one smithy hearth, but normally a single hearth sufficed. In all, Sheffield had a smithy to every 2.2 houses. No wonder the town had acquired a reputation for being a smoky, industrial place. Even more cutlers worked in Sheffield than these figures suggest, for the most skilled workers did not do their own forging in a smithy but bought blades from others and spent their time assembling and finishing goods in a work chamber. Inventories of personal estate that survive in probate records suggest that one in every four cutlers had work chambers, but no smithies.

Over 200 inventories of personal possessions were attached to wills made by Sheffield cutlers in the forty years between 1690 and 1739. Together, they provide a clear picture of the standard of living and the nature of the workshops (or 'smithies') of the typical 'little mester' who was making table knives, pen- and pocket knives and scissors for a mass market. Having served an apprenticeship, some men simply continued to work as labourers, or 'journeymen', but most began their own small businesses in humble buildings in their backyards. Smithies were built of stone or brick, sometimes as 'lean-tos' at the rear of a house, some-times as out-buildings. The cutler heated his rods of iron and steel in a coal-fired hearth which he blasted from time to time with a pair of bellows. He worked at

Saw makers. This photograph, taken c. 1902, shows the skills of craftsmen at the Suffolk Works. John Henry Simpson, on the left, is setting the teeth of a saw, while the man who is standing is sharpening teeth with a file. Saw-making was established as a specialist trade in Sheffield during the second half of the eighteenth century. By 1900 most saws were set by machine.

an anvil which was set on a stone base known as a 'stithy and stock'. When a blade was forged into shape, it was cooled and hardened in a 'coultrough'. The inventories also noted workboards, vices and hammers.

The next step was to grind the steel part of the blade to a cutting edge. Until well into the eighteenth century grinding was not a specialist occupation, except in the scythe trade, which involved much heavier work. Most forgers took their own blades to the grinding wheels in the river valleys, where they rented space and ground their own wares. By 1748 sufficient men worked full-time as grinders to form a mutual-help organisation, the Grinders' Sick Club, and in 1770 Arthur Young noted that the dangerous nature of the job meant that the grinders were the best-paid craftsmen in town. Minute particles from the grindstones were inhaled and lungs were thus worn away. Terrible accidents sometimes occurred when a revolving grinding wheel fractured or spun off its frame. Grinding became a notorious trade in the nineteenth-century steam-powered factories, when 'grinders' asthma' caused many premature deaths from damaged lungs. The occupation was less hazardous in earlier times when grinding was a part-time job in a more open setting.

Hand grinding of
Carver blades at
Suffolk Works
(Thomas Turner &
Co.), 1902.

The remaining tasks were the polishing of the blades and the fitting of handles, or 'hafting' as it was known. The best-quality table knives of the second half of the seventeenth century were different in design from the pointed knives of earlier times, though they were still normally seven or eight inches long. Now that forks were becoming accepted at the table, knives no longer needed to be pointed. Their blades were made slightly wider and were curved, with a broad tip and a sturdier handle. Most knives long continued to have sharp points in the old manner, however, for the majority of the population were slow to adopt the use of the fork. Handles had anciently been made from wood, bone, horn, brass, ivory and tortoiseshell, and some craftsmen had long been skilled in the use of silver, agate and gold. These men did not forge or grind their own blades, but spent their working time in their chambers on the well-paid jobs of assembling and finishing.

A cutler who had obtained his freedom of the Cutlers' Company and who had set up as a 'little mester' was able to arrange his working time to his own convenience, providing that he met his targets by the end of the week. He therefore celebrated 'Saint Monday' as a holiday and worked hard and long each Thursday and Friday. When trade flourished he earned high wages. In 1770 Arthur Young was told that 'Upon the whole, the manufacturers of Sheffield make immense earnings ... in general they get from 9s. to 20s. a week.'

The probate inventory of Joseph Brammall, filesmith, 1698. Among the equipment in the smithy (listed at the top of the right-hand column) were 'three paire of bellows & their furniture', twelve 'stythyes & their Stocks', 24 hammers of various sizes, grinding stones, weighing scales and troughs. In a 'closet over the house' was 'A vice and a workboard' valued at 18s. The files, 'in severall Rooms' totalled some 600 dozen and were valued at £123 11s. 8d. Nearly £118 was owed by 21 named individuals, many from London, although Brammall himself owed some £240. Credit was essential to the running of a successful business. Despite the large scale of his metal-working operation, two cows, a horse, sheep and geese were also to be found in the barn and cowhouse.

The proportion of the work-force that was occupied in the cutlery trades
remained constant as the population grew in the eighteenth century. The typical
unit of production long remained the 'little mester' and his apprentice, with perhaps a journeyman or two, but as the century advanced the number of
journeymen who worked for others undoubtedly increased. The rural cutlers of
Hallamshire were more traditional than the townsmen in their arrangements. In
1672 the number of smithies per house (51 to 123) in the township of Attercliffe-
cum-Darnall was almost as high as in central Sheffield. One in every three houses
there had a smithy attached to it. North of the River Don in Brightside bierlow
22 of the 100 householders possessed a total of 30 smithies. In the western parts
of Sheffield parish, however, the proportion of the work-force that was involved
in the manufacture of cutlery was similar to that in the surrounding countryside,
for only 37 smithies were recorded amongst the 286 houses there.

The sub-division of labour in the manufacture of knives, which became
marked during the later seventeenth and early eighteenth centuries, was matched
by the emergence of specialist trades that concentrated on the making of particular products. The first of these new trades was that of filemaking. Cutlers had
long made their own files, but in the 1650s the Sheffield marriage register recorded
the first specialist filesmiths. The trade quickly attracted others, for the demand
for files continued to grow. In 1682 the Cutlers' Company agreed to accept 21
filesmiths into membership. One of these men was Joseph Brammall, whose
inventory upon his death in 1698 recorded no fewer than 600 dozen files, and
debts owed to him by London merchants. No doubt some of his wares were sold
in America, together with other Hallamshire wares. Sheffield led the way in the
in the manufacture of files, though Birmingham soon followed. By the early eighteenth century the filemakers were outnumbered only by the makers of knives
and scissors. The making of files by hand started as an urban trade, but ended
nearly three hundred years later as a depressed rural craft, long after machines
had taken over in the town. Nowadays, new technology has largely removed the
need for files; and in the 1990s the last Sheffield file manufacturers closed their
businesses.

The new craft of button making was particularly attractive to poor immigrants
for the trade lay outside the jurisdiction of the Cutlers' Company and was therefore unregulated. The first Sheffield buttons were made either of horn, metal or
alcomy (a base alloy that resembled gold). No button makers were named in the
marriage register in the 1650s, but at the end of the seventeenth century the baptism and burial register recorded sixteen. The trade was adopted in Birmingham
and the Black Country about the same time. Most buttons were made quickly and
cheaply, unlike the silver buttons that were the height of fashion. The quality end
of the business was highly profitable, so when Thomas Boulsover discovered how
to plate copper with silver in 1743 he set up a successful business as a button
maker. His buttons were stamped from a die on a fused metal sheet, then cut out,
polished and burnished until they were hardly distinguishable from genuine silver
buttons. His business prospered. The manufacture of small metal boxes for
keeping tobacco, snuff, money, or bits and pieces had also been started by

craftsmen in the late seventeenth century. This trade too was revolutionised by the discovery of Old Sheffield Plate.

Other new crafts were pursued on a more modest scale. One was the making of awls, i.e. small, pointed tools with wooden handles that were used by shoe-makers for piercing holes in leather. The first mention of awlblade makers in Sheffield occurs during the middle years of the seventeenth century; fourteen awl-bladesmiths joined the Cutlers' Company in 1676 at the height of the battle over the payment of hearth tax. The first local reference to a razor maker occurs in 1681, though cutlers had previously made razors as a side-line. Few other crafts-men turned to this trade on a full-time basis until well into the eighteenth century. As we have seen, forks were becoming accepted as an eating utensil during the reign of Charles II, but the first reference to a Sheffield forkmaker is as late as 1700. The old trade of sheather continued for another generation until men finally stopped carrying a knife in a sheath attached to a belt around their waist. Gales and Martin's *Sheffield Directory* of 1787 lists other new tradesmen, including the eleven manufacturers of 'Lancets and Phlemes', a fleam being a lancet for bleed-ing horses. Meanwhile, one old trade had long since disappeared. The Twigges of Attercliffe had made arrowheads until 1660, but from then onwards we hear no more of this medieval craft.

The cutlers who made high-quality knives lived and worked in central Sheffield, whereas 'common wares' were made throughout Hallamshire. Scissorsmiths were found in the townships of Sheffield and Attercliffe-cum-Darnall, and certain other metal trades were confined to particular rural parishes on the fringes. The nailmakers lived in the central and northern parts of Ecclesfield parish and in other hamlets and scattered farmsteads near the slitting mills at Wortley, Masborough and Renishaw. Scythe making was the distinctive occupation of the men of the parish of Norton, and the manufacture of sickles was concentrated in the Moss valley, in Eckington parish. These two parishes had captured a large part of the agricultural edge-tool industry by the seventeenth century. Norton men sold their scythes in the market towns of northern England and lowland Scotland, while the scythe makers of Belbroughton and neighbour-ing parishes to the south-west of Birmingham sold their products in the south of England. When William Blythe of Norton Lees died in 1632, he had a stock of 2,000 scythes ready for sale. His son and namesake had a similar number in 1666. Thirty-five Norton scythemakers were admitted into the Cutlers' Company in 1681. They shared only eight family names.

A few axe makers were mentioned occasionally in the rural parishes around Sheffield during the seventeenth and early eighteenth centuries, and the local forges made saws and other wood-working tools, as well as frying pans and other utensils, but the great days of the expansion of the tool industry were yet to come. For instance, no saw makers were recorded in the Sheffield parish register before Robert Marples in 1747, but by 1787 ten saw manufacturers had set up business in the newer parts of the town.

Sheffield was still overwhelmingly dependent on its cutlery industry. The Cutlers' Company had become established as the leading institution in town. The

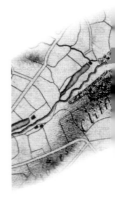

right A tilt hammer preserved at Abbeydale Industrial Hamlet. The German method of using water-powered tilt hammers to reduce bar iron to smaller dimensions was used increasingly in Sheffield from the 1730s onwards. On a visit here in 1769 Arthur Young observed 'the tilting mill, which is a blacksmith's immense hammer in constant motion on an anvil, worked by water-wheels, and by the same power the bellows of a forge adjoining kept regularly blown. The force of this mechanism is prodigious; so great that you cannot lay your hand upon gate at three perches distance, without feeling a strong trembling motion which is communi-cated to all the earth around

PHOTOGRAPH: CARNEG

A HISTORY OF SHEFFIELD

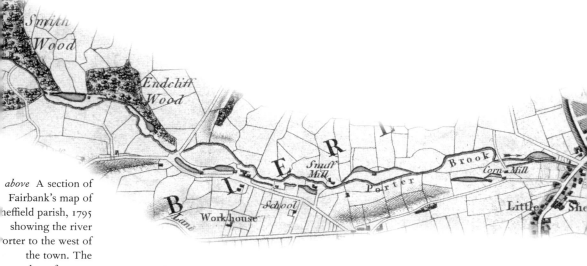

Company had built a hall in 1638 and had replaced it with a new one on the same site in 1725–26. They had shown their worth during the reign of Charles II when they succeeded in their battle to prevent the hearth tax being levied on smithies as well as houses. The Cutlers' Feast had become a major event to which the local aristocracy and gentry were invited. A tight control was kept on the admittance of freemen via the apprenticeship system. The Company had at first tried to restrict growth, thinking that this policy would preserve their members' livelihood, but by the early 1720s they had changed their attitude and had become enthusiastic advocates of expansion. They began to challenge the role of London merchants by selling their goods through other outlets and they championed the scheme to make the River Don navigable. Previously, a Sheffield trader such as Thomas Hollis could get rich only by setting up business in London, but now the Shores, Broadbents, Parkins and Roebucks had become merchants based in Sheffield.

The expansion of the cutlery trades is evident from the greatly increased number of water-powered grinding sites. Sheffield's five rivers powered 49 works by 1660, and at least another 41 by 1740. Even before Benjamin Huntsman invented crucible steel or Thomas Boulsover began to make Old Sheffield Plate, 90 of the 115 places where water mills were ever constructed in the river valleys were already in existence. Two out of every three of these sites were used for grinding cutlery and edge tools. This is only part of the story, however, for at many sites extra buildings and grinding wheels were added to the existing facilities. The growth in capacity during the later seventeenth century and the first half of the eighteenth century was enormous. Water power was crucial in Sheffield's development. No other place in Britain had such a concentration of sites. The demand for more space for grinders was the strongest impetus, but by 1740 five forges and three new sites for tilt hammers were also in production. Many more were marked on William Fairbank's map of Sheffield parish in 1795.

Iron and steel

The masters who controlled the production of iron in South Yorkshire and north Derbyshire in the seventeenth and early eighteenth centuries were members of gentry families, led by the Spencers of Cannon Hall and the Sitwells of Renishaw Hall. Among the possessions of the Spencers and their partners were the charcoal blast furnace at Rockley and the Top Forge at Wortley, which survive as major monuments of industrial archaeology. The management of the ironworks at Attercliffe was entrusted to John Fell (1666–1724), whose younger brother Thomas was in Jamaica in 1699 selling Attercliffe products. John's son and namesake (1696–1762) succeeded his father and built New Hall, Attercliffe, 'a handsome brick house with spacious gardens', whose name is preserved by Newhall Road. By the middle years of the eighteenth century coke was replacing charcoal as the fuel that was used in the local iron industry. Samuel and Aaron Walker, who had begun to experiment in an 'Air Furnace' in an 'old nailor's smithy' at Grenoside in 1741, moved to Masborough five years later in order to be near the navigable river and eventually became the leading ironmasters in the north of England. Meanwhile, the second John Fell's adopted son, Richard Swallow, adapted Attercliffe Forge to coke smelting and thus preserved its position as a leading producer of iron ware.

For much of the eighteenth century the manufacture of iron goods was on a larger scale than the production of steel. It was not yet clear that steel would play so important a part in the history of Sheffield. We have seen that from the sixteenth century onwards Hallamshire cutlers had imported their raw materials from the Continent of Europe. Iron bars from Oregrund in Sweden eventually became the most highly prized. In South Yorkshire, imported bar iron was first

left Detail of Thomas Oughtibridge's *View of Sheffield* (1737). The pair of bottle-shaped kilns (5) at the edge of the town are Samuel Shore's cementation steel furnaces. They are the only ones shown in the view, but it is known that Thomas Parkin owned another steel-works out of sight in Balm Green (by the present City Hall). Shore's furnaces are commemorated by the street name Steelhouse Lane. Sheffield had a long history as a cutlery centre before it acquired a reputation for making steel.

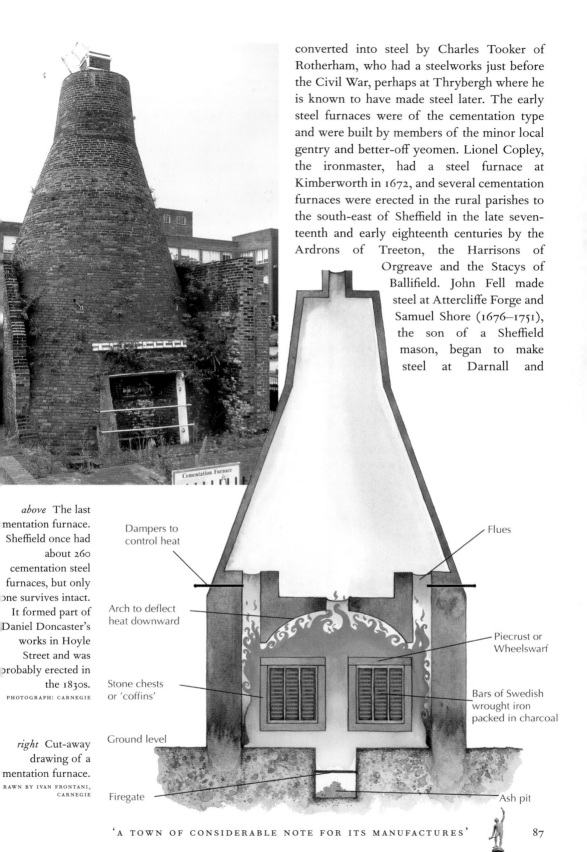

converted into steel by Charles Tooker of Rotherham, who had a steelworks just before the Civil War, perhaps at Thrybergh where he is known to have made steel later. The early steel furnaces were of the cementation type and were built by members of the minor local gentry and better-off yeomen. Lionel Copley, the ironmaster, had a steel furnace at Kimberworth in 1672, and several cementation furnaces were erected in the rural parishes to the south-east of Sheffield in the late seventeenth and early eighteenth centuries by the Ardrons of Treeton, the Harrisons of Orgreave and the Stacys of Ballifield. John Fell made steel at Attercliffe Forge and Samuel Shore (1676–1751), the son of a Sheffield mason, began to make steel at Darnall and

above The last cementation furnace. Sheffield once had about 260 cementation steel furnaces, but only one survives intact. It formed part of Daniel Doncaster's works in Hoyle Street and was probably erected in the 1830s.
PHOTOGRAPH: CARNEGIE

right Cut-away drawing of a cementation furnace.
DRAWN BY IVAN FRONTANI, CARNEGIE

Dampers to control heat

Flues

Arch to deflect heat downward

Piecrust or Wheelswarf

Stone chests or 'coffins'

Bars of Swedish wrought iron packed in charcoal

Ground level

Firegate

Ash pit

Woodhouse and then in the town itself. Thomas Oughtibridge's view of Sheffield in 1737 shows a pair of bottle-shaped cementation furnaces that Shore had built at the edge of the town in what became known as Steelhouse Lane. Out of sight was a steel furnace which Thomas Parkin had built by 1716 in Balm Green and possibly another of Shore's at Castle Hill. These were the only steelworks that had been erected in Sheffield by the time that Benjamin Huntsman began his experiments a few years later.

Only one cementation furnace survives in a virtually complete state in Sheffield. This is the one that was built in the 1830s by the firm of Daniel Doncaster in Hoyle Street and which was last heated (for the purpose of making a film) in 1951. (It can be seen near the bottom of the hill by which Supertrams descend from the University of Sheffield to Shalesmoor.) Cementation furnaces were built of brick around two sandstone chests shaped like coffins, which were placed above a coal fire and below a cone-shaped chimney. Wrought-iron bars about three inches wide, a half or three-quarters of an inch thick, and as long as could be fitted in, were placed in the chests and separated from each other by layers of charcoal. The chests were then sealed, often with 'swarf' from grinding wheels, so that gases were excluded while the coal fuel was brought to a bright red heat (1050–1100°C) and kept at that temperature for up to a week. The furnace and its contents were then allowed to cool over the following week, by

Clock made in Sheffield by Benjamin Huntsman, now on display at the Kelham Island Industrial Museum.
PHOTOGRAPH: CARNEGIE

Benjamin Huntsman's house. Huntsman moved from Handsworth to Attercliffe Green in 1751. He later moved a short distance across the road to establish a new steelworks at what became known as Huntsman's Row. His house, which is now the Britannia Inn, has the date 1772 in large figures in its gable end. They are reputedly made of Huntsman's cast steel.
PHOTOGRAPH: L. NUTTALL

A HISTORY OF SHEFFIELD

which time carbon had spread from the charcoal to the bars of iron. The finished product was known as 'blister steel' because of the huge blisters on its surface.

By 1740 enough cementation steel was probably being made in and near Hallamshire to meet local demand. The principal purchasers of steel were the cutlers and tool makers. The south Yorkshire steel industry took root and flourished because the expanding Hallamshire cutlery industry, which was already centuries old, provided such a ready market for its products. In time, the Sheffield steel industry was to outgrow the cutlery industry in both volume and value, but in the seventeenth and eighteenth centuries the 'light trades' still reigned supreme.

But although blister steel could be forged into excellent knife blades, its imperfections and lack of consistency made it unsuitable for the manufacture of rolls, dies, wire, and fine work. Benjamin Huntsman, a Doncaster clockmaker, born in Epworth in 1704 of Quaker parents, had a particular problem with springs and pendulums and resolved to make steel of better quality. His invention of 'cast steel', which he poured from heated clay crucibles into moulds, is traditionally dated to 1742, but it was perfected over many years of trial and error. It was the most important discovery ever made in Sheffield and in time it transformed the whole character of the place.

Huntsman moved from Doncaster to Handsworth in 1742 so as to be at the heart of the local steel-making region. His new home and workplace were demolished about 1933, but they are recorded in an old photograph and a watercolour painting. Here he began to experiment by remelting the cut-off ends of bars of blister steel in small pots, or 'crucibles', which were similar to those that goldsmiths and glassmakers used. He encountered much difficulty in finding or making crucibles that could stand the heat of the coke fire, which was raised to more than 1525°C for between three and five hours in order to reduce the steel to a molten state and to burn off all impurities. Crucibles also needed to be strong enough to take the weight of the steel and to resist any corroding effect in the process, and they had to be sufficiently robust to be man-handled with a giant pair of tongs when the liquid contents were teemed into the ingot moulds. It is very likely that Huntsman was familiar with the crucibles made from Bolsterstone clay that were in use at the nearby Catcliffe glass furnace (which still stands alongside the Parkway as it nears the M1), but he is known to have imported some of his crucibles from Holland. Huntsman's experiments were also timely in that it had just become accepted in the iron- and brass-making industries that coke fuel could not only reach higher temperatures than charcoal, but could stay incandescent for a longer period. Coke could also resist the weight of a crucible much better than charcoal. In South Yorkshire excellent coke could be made from coal mined from the Barnsley seam. Another advantage was that ganister clay from south-west Yorkshire was an ideal refractory material with which to line the furnace and its chimney so that the walls would not crumble in the heat. The materials were at hand, but Huntsman was faced with so many technical and design problems that it took years for him to get everything right.

Abbeydale Industrial Hamlet contains the best-preserved example of a crucible furnace. On descending to the cellar space, the visitor can see how a strong

  A HISTORY OF SHEFFIELD

above Ganister – a highly siliceous sedimentary rock found beneath coal seams – was mined locally and ground to a powder by a ganister mill such as this. It was then used as a refractory material for lining steel furnaces.

left The very large, brick chimney stack identifies the function of this building at Abbeydale Industrial Hamlet as a crucible furnace. Commonly depicted on nineteenth-century views of Sheffield industry, they are now a rare sight.

PHOTOGRAPHS: CARNEGIE

left Crucible furnace, Abbeydale Industrial Hamlet. Clay crucibles are stacked on the top shelf, with a few re-used ones below. The holes in which they were placed have been opened at the bottom. Tools for handling the heated crucibles and a besom made of birch twigs stand by for duty.

PHOTOGRAPH: CARNEGIE

through-draught created and maintained sufficient heat to melt the cementation steel in the various crucible holes and what strength and skill were required to lift a crucible and pour the molten steel into a mould. Crucible furnaces are immediately recognisable from the outside by their square block of chimneys, so different in appearance from the bottle-shaped cementation furnaces, but few survive in the town whose fortunes were transformed by Huntsman's invention. For over a hundred years, until Bessemer's converter brought about another revolution in production, the crucible method was the only way of casting an ingot of steel. The Sheffield–Rotherham region was not a major centre of steel production before Huntsman's discovery, but during the following century it became the major steel-producing centre in the world.

By 1751 Huntsman's experiments were successful and his business was expanding. He decided to give up clock making and become a full-time steel maker at a much larger holding on the east side of Attercliffe Green. During the same year, the River Don Navigation had opened just down the road at Tinsley. The short move from Handsworth to Attercliffe was a decisive one, long remembered by his firm which always headed its stationery 'Established 1751'.

Benjamin Huntsman stayed at Attercliffe Green for at least twelve years but

Crucible steel making at Cammell's in the 1930s. Almost 200 years after Huntsman's invention, high-quality crucible steel remained an essential component of the steel industry

SHEFFIELD INDUSTRIAL MUSEUMS TRUST

by 1770 he had moved a short distance to premises on the other side of the road, a little further south in the Darnall direction, on a site known later as Huntsman's Row. He reputedly fixed the date '1772' in large figures of his own steel in the gable end of a building next to Huntsman's Row, presumed to be his residence and now the Britannia Inn. The firm that he founded remained here until 1899, when they opened a new works in Coleridge Road, nearer Sheffield. All traces of his works at Attercliffe have been obliterated.

Huntsman kept his invention secret and no real competitors emerged before the mid-1760s. He was satisfied with a relatively small business that brought him a reasonable income. His modest memorial in the churchyard at Hill Top reads: 'Benjamin Huntsman of Attercliffe, steel refiner. Died June 20, 1776, aged 72 years.' In time, however, the invention of crucible steel came to be seen not only as the major cause of Sheffield and Rotherham's pre-eminence as a steel manu-facturing district, but as the chief reason for the continued success of the Hallamshire cutlery industry.

Old Sheffield Plate

While Huntsman was experimenting with crucible steel, another local man was laying the foundations of a new Sheffield industry. In 1743 Thomas Boulsover, a Norfolk Street cutler, discovered that when silver and copper were fused together they could be hammered and worked as one metal, so as to have the external appearance of silver. He immediately recognised the commercial possibilities of his discovery, for plated silver was so much cheaper than solid silver. He developed a method by which a thin rectangular sheet of silver was attached firmly to a much thicker ingot of copper of similar size. The two materials were heated until they fused. The combined ingot was then allowed to cool and was afterwards cleansed with fine sand and water before it was rolled out into a plated sheet ready for stamping or crafting. Boulsover had to roll, hammer, stamp and solder his products by hand and was therefore limited to making small artefacts such as buttons and knife handles. Huntsman's steel was not yet available for rolls, dies and stamps. The rolling process was critical and Boulsover's successors soon began to use polished crucible-steel rolls. It was also heavy work, performed either by horses or by water wheels. In the early 1760s Tudor & Co. had a horse-mill off Norfolk Street (now Tudor Square) and John Hoyland & Co. and Joseph Hancock built plate-rolling mills at Cooper Wheel on the River Sheaf and at Old Park on the River Don.

Thomas Boulsover (1705–88) rapidly made a fortune from his new trade. Plated wares that were sold at half the price of silver were sold readily to a public that was increasingly interested in fashionable dress and display. In 1749 Boulsover leased land in Beeley Wood to build his own grinding wheel, which in partnership with Joseph Broadbent, the Quaker merchant of Hartshead, he later converted into Nova Scotia Tilts. In 1752 he obtained a loan from Strelley Pegge of Beauchief Hall, esquire, with which to purchase Whiteley Wood Hall and an estate of some 100 acres. He diversified further within the next few years by building a forge on the River Porter near his new residence so that he could forge and roll steel to make into saws and fenders. Meanwhile, others (in Birmingham as well as in Sheffield) were profiting from his invention and were producing a much wider range of household goods, starting with candlesticks, saucepans and coffee pots. The same firms soon turned their hands to making solid silver artefacts as well. Recognition of the achievements of Sheffield and Birmingham craftsmen and acknowledgement of the rapid growth of this trade came in 1773 when both towns were permitted to open Assay Offices.

From about 1750 Joseph Hancock (c.1711–91) developed a business that was soon larger than Boulsover's. Starting with snuff boxes, he is credited with widening the trade from the production of 'accessories' such as buttons, buckles and knife handles to the larger and more valuable hollow ware artefacts of the types that are on display at Weston Park Museum. He, rather than Boulsover, became known as 'the Father of the Old Sheffield Plate Trade'. Prominent among the other businesses that sprang up in the 1760s were those of John Hoyland & Co. and the partnership of Tudor, Sherburn & Leader, which was established in 1762. Partnerships were necessary because of the high initial outlay. Sherburn, for instance, provided most of the £3,000 that backed his business with Henry Tudor, a London chaser, and Thomas Leader, a London snuff-box and watch-and-instrument case maker. Likewise, Roberts, Cadman & Co. invested £2,800 when their partnership was established in 1786. Partnerships were also necessary because of the combinations of different craft skills that were required: platers, silversmiths, die-cutters, chasers, piercers, etc, as well as travellers and book keepers. The range of skills and the scale of production in the plating trade were very different from those in the contemporary cutlery industry. The silver platers needed more equipment and greater working space. They could not operate in the small smithies and chambers of the cutlers.

An Old Sheffield Plate basket, made by John Hoyland in 1768.

An Old Sheffield Plate coffee pot with a hinged lid and a wooden handle. This elegant pot, with chased decoration, was made by Matthew Fenton, *c.* 1765 in his factory in Mulberry Street. It is now on display in Weston Park Museum.

SHEFFIELD GALLERIES AND MUSEUMS TRUST

An Old Sheffield Plate candlestick in the form of a 'caryatid', a carved female figure, made by J. Rowbotham of Sheffield in the mid-eighteenth century.

SHEFFIELD GALLERIES AND MUSEUMS TRUST

Two accounts of the early days of the Old Sheffield Plate industry were written by Charles Dixon (1776–1852), candlestick maker, and Samuel Roberts II (1763–1848), who ranks with Matthew Boulton of Birmingham as the leading craftsman in the trade. Dixon observed that:

> When the trade was first begun workmen were obtained from the silversmiths' shops in London as foremen or managers, and a great number of copper braziers were employed to raise and hammer the parts of some of the articles. All the parts of the candlesticks were made from the dies under the stamp hammer, and put together to form the pedestal or shaft, and were invariably hard soldered (or silver soldered), which was a considerable expense, besides the quantity of labour they took more time to execute the work.

Many skilled cutlers were also employed:

> At one time good workmen were considered very valuable and there have been instances of men owing their masters £100 at a time.

In a letter to a newspaper in 1843, Samuel Roberts remembered that:

> As the trade was completely new in Sheffield – where no similar goods, of any metal, had been made, workmen at all qualified to manufacture them had to be sought from London, York, Newcastle, Birmingham, etc. Those who chose to come were, of course, generally indifferent characters – many of them very bad ones; therefore during the first forty years the journeymen platers were, as a body, the most unsteady, depraved, and idle of all other workmen. They were not only depraved themselves, but the source of depravity in others. They were, in fact, in many respects a pest to the town. The masters could neither do without them, nor obtain better. They were therefore forced to give them high wages, and to wink at all their irregularities. From this cause the masters were continually enticing the workmen from each other's houses, giving them a kind of security. There were in consequence continual disputes between masters and workmen, and between masters and masters about them.

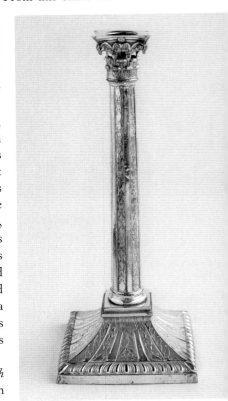

An Old Sheffield Plate candlestick made by Thomas Law, *c.* 1760, now on display at Weston Park Museum. Law made silver ware as well as plated goods and was Master Cutler in 1753. The decoration on his candlestick is die-stamped.
SHEFFIELD GALLERIES AND MUSEUMS TRUST

The high wages on offer for skilled work eventually attracted workmen of a higher quality.

At the cheap end of the market for household utensils, particularly teapots and spoons, Britannia metal became an acceptable replacement for pewter. In or about 1769 James Vickers, a Methodist living in Garden Street, invented what he was content to call white metal. In Gales and Martin's *Sheffield Directory* of 1787 Vickers was named as the sole maker of 'measures, teapots, castor frames, salts, spoons, etc.' in white metal, but a dozen or so firms were listed as 'makers of White Metal and metal-framed knives.' Ten years later, another directory named both James Vickers and Richard Constantine as 'White Metal manufacturers', and Froggat, Couldwell & Lean as 'Manufacturers of Britannia Metal Goods, & Silver Platers and factors, Eyre Street'. This is the first reference to the 'Britannia' name, which was presumably coined for marketing purposes.

In 1770 Arthur Young published *A Tour through the North of England*. He had travelled to Sheffield from Rotherham and had found the road 'execrably bad, very stony, and excessively full of holes'. He went on to note that:

> Sheffield contains about 30,000 inhabitants, the chief of which are employed in the manufacture of hard-ware: The great branches are the plating-work, the cutlery, the lead works, and the silk mill ... In the plated work some hundreds

of hands are employed; the men's pay extends from 9*s*. a week to £60 a year: In works of curiosity, it must be supposed that dexterous hands are paid very great wages. Girls earn 4*s*. 6*d*. and 5*s*. a week; some even to 9*s*. No men are employed that earn less than 9*s*. The day's work, including the hours of cessation, is thirteen … Upon the whole, the manufacturers of Sheffield make immense earnings … in general they get from 9*s*. to 20*s*. a week; and the women and children are all employed in various branches, and earn very good wages.

Other industries

Young also visited the silk mill that had been erected about 1760 at the northern edge of the town, near the present Kelham Island Industrial Museum. He wrote:

A detail of Fairbank's 1771 map of Sheffield showing the silk mill and Kelham Wheel. See page 55 for a view of Colson Crofts in 1737.

Here is likewise a silk mill, a copy from the famous one at Derby, which employs 152 hands, chiefly women and children; the women earn 5 or 6*s*. a week by the pound; girls at first are paid but 1*s*., or 1*s*. 2*d*. a week, but rise gradually higher, till they arrive at the same wages as the women … All the motions of this complicated system are set to work by one water-wheel, which communicates motion to others, and they to many different ones, until many thousand wheels and powers are set to work from the original simple one.

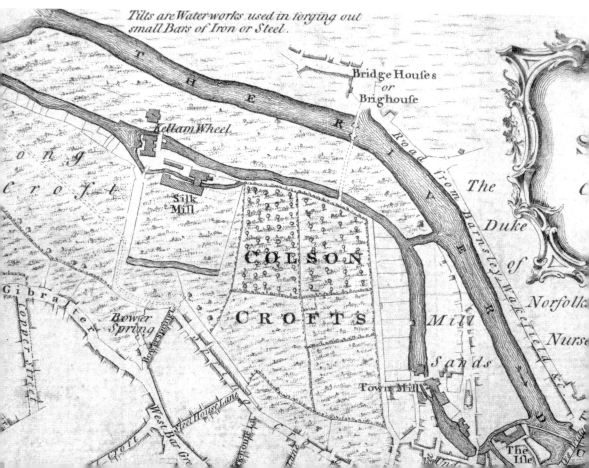

They use Bengal, China, Turkey, Piedmont, and America raw silk ... This mill works up 150 lb of raw silk a week all the year round, or 7800 per annum. The erection, of the whole building, with all the mechanism it contains, cost about £7,000.

The silk mill had been built by William Bower on the model of the famous Derby Silk Mill of *c.*1720, which also became the prototype of the later cotton mills built by Richard Arkwright at Cromford. The silk industry spread to Macclesfield, Leek and other places in the north midlands, so it is not surprising to find that a business was started in Sheffield. If it now seems an unusual venture that failed in the long run, for a time it was the largest works in the town. But it did not prosper, and the *Sheffield Public Advertiser* of 15 January 1774 advertised the

Sale of lease – Wm Bower, bankrupt – at Sheffield. The large and extensive Building, with one of the compleatest set of Silk Mills in this Kingdom, a good Dwelling-house, Offices, Gardens, etc. The Silk Mills are in very good Repair, are still employed, and as a great number of Women and Children have been made useful at a vast Expense, it must make this Purchase very desirable, the Premises having cost within a few Years, at least £7,000. Likewise the whole of that curious Machinery known by the Name of the KELHAM WHEELS for grinding and glazing the Cutlery; this consists of two Ends and one Chamber, containing Thirty nine Troughs, lett to different Tenants at £195 per Annum; they are generally underlett, and at a very small Expense may be much improved.

As we shall see, the works was converted into a cotton mill and eventually into a workhouse. The site is commemorated by the name of Cotton Mill Street.

Another unusual industrial building at the southern edge of the town was the lead mill, a name now well known to Sheffield's youngsters as a popular venue for music and dancing. The mill was said to be 'newly erected' in 1759 on the site of a grinding wheel which had been leased to a scissorsmith. Water from both the Sheaf and the Porter was used to power a large wheel, which by the 1850s had been replaced by steam power. A report of 1865 mentions lead refining, the production of both white and red lead, and the grinding of paint. It must have been an unhealthy place in which to work.

Several other family businesses operated on a smaller scale over the generations. The Rawsons, Aldams, Shemelds, Hooles, Sandersons and others owned or leased tanneries in the Ponds and in rural parts of Sheffield parish, such as Walkley, Upperthorpe, Crookes, Wardsend, Raisen Hall and Grimesthorpe. Hides were obtained locally and from Smithfield Market as back carriage for traders who sold Hallamshire wares in London. Running water, lime, and oak bark were readily available. The tanners produced an essential supply of leather for shoes, garments, harness, horse collars, saddles, straps, bags and bottles, together with bellows, grinders' beltings and sheaths for local cutlers. Sheffield also had its millers, butchers, grocers, drapers and all the other trades that were normally associated with a market town.

A guide stoop o 1734 on the hil north of Sheffielc The West Ridin JPs ordered th erection of guid stoops at junction in 1733. Thi unusual six-side example stands a Dyson Co1 between Peniston and Stocksbridge One side show here marks the wa to Sheffield an Rotherham, th other to Barnsle Pontefract an Doncaste Travellers needed face the inscriptio then take the turnin on the right. Larg numbers of guid stoops can be foun in south-we Yorkshire and nort Derbyshire (wher they date fro 1709). They a contemporary wit many of th surviving packhors bridges and wer part of an attempt t improve travellin conditions ju before the era o turnpike road
SHEILA EDWAR

A HISTORY OF SHEFFIELD

Communications

At the beginning of the eighteenth century, Sheffield was on neither a major thoroughfare nor a navigable river. Bawtry wharf lay twenty difficult miles away to the east. The highways that approached the town from the north or the south had to negotiate steep hills and deep valleys, while to the west lay the formidable obstacle of the Pennines. Few English towns were as landlocked as Sheffield. Yet salesmen travelling with loaded packhorses or wains and carts managed to sell Hallamshire wares in far away places. Travel was often tedious but it was not impossible. The moors to the west of Sheffield provide plenty of visual evidence of old tracks heading to and from the town. Many of the guide stoops that the Derbyshire JPs ordered to be erected in 1709 bear an inscription pointing the way to Sheffield on one of their four sides. For example, a stoop near Longshaw Lodge marks the way to 'Shafild', 'Chasterfild', 'Tidswel', and 'Hatharsich and so to Chapil in Lee Frith'. In the summer months travellers could cross the moors without too much difficulty.

It remained far cheaper to send bulky goods by water, wherever that was possible. The advantage of having a navigable river that came right up to the town

eaf Quay, at the terminus of the Sheffield Canal. The former office building of the Sheaf Works that William reaves founded in the 1820s to make cutlery, steel and edge-tools alongside the new canal was converted into a Tom obbleigh pub in 1989.

OTOGRAPH: CARNEGIE

became increasingly obvious when similar schemes were put into effect elsewhere. The Aire and Calder Navigation was begun in 1699 to link Leeds and Wakefield with the sea. The Cutlers' Company had not shown much enthusiasm when the idea of making the Don navigable had first been promoted in 1698 and again in 1704, but by the 1720s they had been converted to an expansionist outlook and had become enthusiastic champions of the navigation scheme. A bill was presented to Parliament in 1721, but its progress was thwarted by the Duke of Norfolk, who feared that the water supply to Attercliffe Forge and four other of his dams in the Lower Don Valley would be affected. Five years passed before a compromise plan was agreed, whereby the navigation would go no further west than Tinsley. Two Acts in 1726–27 gave Doncaster corporation control of the river below their town and the Cutlers' Company the more difficult task of making the Don navigable up to Tinsley Wharf and of maintaining the road from Tinsley to Sheffield. By 1740 the river had been made navigable as far as Rotherham, and in 1751 the scheme was completed. It proved highly successful and of major assistance in encouraging the growth of the local economy. Crucible steel, Old Sheffield Plate, and the Don Navigation were three dramatic developments in the middle years of the eighteenth century, which together signalled the beginnings of a great change in the fortunes of the town.

Once the navigation project was finished, local landowners and business men started to think about forming turnpike trusts to improve the roads. Sheffielders had again been slow to respond to a new idea that been taken up quickly in some other parts of the country. Early turnpike roads set out not to replace old highways but to maintain and improve them through the collection of tolls. The lack of adequate technology and of experienced road builders meant that the surveyors employed by the trusts had to be content with old methods of repair applied more thoroughly and regularly than before. Their main achievement was to provide routes that were firm and wide enough to take wheeled traffic. Short detours, especially up the steepest hills, were made, but it was not until the early years of the nineteenth century that entirely new routes were created by local turnpike trusts.

The first turnpike road in south Yorkshire was that which came over Woodhead to the Don navigation at Doncaster and Rotherham, an ancient highway from Cheshire that was improved in 1741. Another fifteen years passed before an Act was obtained to turnpike one of the roads leading out of Sheffield. This was the highway that ran down The Moor and along London Road to the county boundary at Heeley Bridge and on towards Chesterfield and Derby, where it joined the road from Manchester to London. William Fairbank's map of the parish of Sheffield in 1795 and Peter Burdett's map of Derbyshire of 1763 show how the road climbed from Heeley up Derbyshire Lane (not the present street of this name) to Little Norton and along the edge of Norton Park. It left Norton via Dyche Lane and Coal Aston before dropping down Green Lane into Dronfield. Beyond Unstone, it followed what is now merely a narrow lane to Old Whittington and continued that way into Chesterfield. An anonymous traveller along this road in 1768 described it as 'very bad, exceedingly hilly and

100   A HISTORY OF SHEFFIELD

Old Toll Bar, Pitsmoor. M.25.248.

Toll Bar House, Pitsmoor. The original turnpike road followed the line of Pitsmoor Road (right), but in 1836 a new route was created down Burngreave Road (left) and the toll bar was erected at the junction.

disagreeable in every respect. The rock beaten small is the only material here, as in many other places, they have to repair them with.' In 1795 the present Chesterfield Road was created from Heeley Bridge through Woodseats and Meadowhead to Dronfield and across Whittington Moor to Chesterfield, a much more direct route than the 1756 turnpike road which had stuck to the line of the previous highway.

Having improved their road to the south, Sheffielders turned their attention to the north and in 1758 joined forces with the landowners and businessmen of Leeds and Wakefield to obtain powers to turnpike the road through Barnsley. This road left Sheffield by Lady's Bridge, Nursery Street and the steep slope of Pye Bank. In 1829 James Mills surveyed the route and concluded that only a small portion of it was suitable for rapid travelling. He advocated 'the substitution of a good road for the incorrigibly bad one, for it is notorious that the Inns of Sheffield prefer sending their posting by way of Doncaster to avoid the hills on the present Road.' Another observer reckoned that the whole route from Derby through Sheffield to Leeds was one of the worst roads in England. In 1836 some of these criticisms were met by the provision of a new route up a gentler incline from the Wicker through Burngreave to Pitsmoor, where an old toll house still stands at the junction with the previous turnpike road; the original toll house stood a little further down the earlier road. From Pitsmoor, the turnpike followed the line of the present road, down to Fir Vale, over Sheffield Lane Top, and along Ecclesfield Common. There, however, it turned right along Nether Lane to Chapeltown, rather than attempt the steep hill up Coit Lane (the modern road past Ecclesfield School). The route continued via Hoyland Common, Birdwell, Worsbrough village and Mount Vernon into Barnsley and then north over Old Mill Bridge. Critics of the tolls levied by the Sheffield–Leeds trust were told that they 'must own the vast amendment it is, from the uncommon badness of the Road' before it was turnpiked.

Detail of Peter Burdett's *Map of Derbyshire* (1763–67), the earliest large-scale map of the county. Drawn on the scale of one inch to one mile, Burdett's map is an invaluable source of information about the local landscape. It marks the early turnpike roads and the local lanes, the commons and wastes before parliamentary enclosure, the coppice woods and the villages and hamlets that lay to the south-west of Sheffield. The thick line in the centre of the map divides the hundreds or wapentakes of High Peak and Scarsdale and continues northwards as the county boundary.

The road to Manchester was the next to be improved. In 1749 Manchester men had turnpiked their road to Buxton, via Sparrowpit Gate. Nine years later, the old highways from Sheffield to both Buxton and the junction at Sparrowpit Gate were brought to the same standard. The road climbed out of Sheffield via Sharrow Lane and Psalter Lane (the medieval route whereby salt was brought the other way from Cheshire). Having reached Banner Cross, the road turned sharply right to Bents Green and proceeded directly to Ringinglow. The three-storeyed, octagonal 'Round House' at Ringinglow was built as a toll house in 1795, or shortly afterwards. Here, the road split into two. One branch went straight ahead towards Callow Bank, Hathersage, Hope and Castleton, then up Winnats Pass and across the moors to Sparrowpit Gate. The other branch turned left and headed across Houndkirk Moor to Fox House and through the Longshaw estate to Grindleford Bridge, where it started the steep ascent of the Sir William hill, continuing in a direct line along the ridge to Tideswell and so on to Buxton. This route still gives a vivid impression of the nature of the early turnpike roads, which stuck rigidly to the line of the ancient highways.

The road out of Sheffield along the lower Don valley via Attercliffe was the next to receive attention. In 1758 the Don Navigation Company improved the road from Lady's Bridge as far as Tinsley Wharf, and two years later an Act was obtained to turnpike the continuation of this road via Whiston, Wickersley and Tickhill to Bawtry. In 1764 the road that headed in a south-easterly direction from Attercliffe through Darnall and Handsworth was turnpiked as far as Worksop. The road from Tinsley to Doncaster was turnpiked in the same year. These are major roads which are still busy with traffic.

In 1777 an Act was obtained to turnpike the road from Sheffield to Halifax. This left the town at West Bar Green, crossed Shalesmoor, and headed for Wadsley Bridge. Here, it turned right up the hill, then left via Fox Hill to the older part of Grenoside, before heading across Wharncliffe Chase towards Penistone and Huddersfield. The present Halifax Road through the lower part of Grenoside to the Crown Inn was made fifty years later.

A few more routes were turnpiked in the following years. In 1778 the road from Sheaf Bridge up Duke Street and through the former deer park to Gleadless was turnpiked as far as Gander Lane, Eckington, where it joined the road to Mansfield. Three years later, the Hathersage–Greenhill Moor road via Fox House, Owler Bar, Holmesfield and Bradway met the Sheffield–Chesterfield turnpike in Norton parish, and the Totley–Stoney Middleton road linked with the route from Chesterfield to Chapel en le Frith. Their completion brought a temporary end to twenty-five years of improvements. As we shall see, it was not until the early years of the nineteenth century that turnpike trusts in the Sheffield area constructed entirely new roads along routes that had never been attempted before. Together, these old and new highways formed the basis of the modern road system until the coming of the motorways.

Politics and religion

Despite the continued absence of the manorial lord, the old machinery of the seigneurial borough survived into the nineteenth century. Sheffield was not even a quarter session town until 1699 and the nearest JPs were at Broom Hall and Thrybergh. A variety of institutions with overlapping jurisdictions governed the town and parish. Suited to an earlier age, none had sufficient powers to deal with the problems of rapid expansion. The Town Trust was reformed in 1681, but the other institutions – manorial courts, the civil parish, the Church Burgesses, and the Cutlers' Company – continued much as before. After the Restoration, the leading families – the Brights of Carbrook and the Spencers of Attercliffe – withdrew from the district. Who then ran the town? To a large measure, it was the attorneys.

In English towns in the second half of the seventeenth century the number of professional men rose significantly. In Sheffield, as in other places, the most successful group were the attorneys, or solicitors as they would now be called. They acquired enough wealth to be regarded as urban gentry from the fees that they charged for court cases, the drawing up of property deeds and settlements, the drafting and executing of wills, the arrangement of credit in the form of mortgages, bills, bonds and other securities, and from their salaries as manorial stewards and clerks to the other local institutions. They registered deeds at Wakefield, took wills to be proved at York and Lichfield, attended the quarter sessions, and travelled to the ecclesiastical courts at York and the courts of Chancery and Exchequer at London.

A legal profession was firmly established in the town during the 1660s and 1670s. At first, the most prominent names were those of Chappell, Simpson and Lee. Thomas Chappell (1639–93) was descended through three generations of Roberts from John Chappell of Darnall, who died in 1576. He was succeeded in his Fargate office by his son, Thomas, and his grandson, Robert, who died in his early forties in 1736. George Lee (died 1687) was a member of a prolific Sheffield family, much involved in local affairs. Their members included lead merchants, dyers, doctors, cutlers, a clergyman, an ironmonger, a grocer and a barber. William Simpson was different in being an immigrant. The son of the Vicar of Blythe (Notts), he was an able man whose services were in demand well beyond Sheffield,. His position as one of the most prosperous men in High Street was recognised by the grant of a coat of arms. He was the first Town Trustee to hold the executive position of Town Collector and one of the nine men who were honoured in 1681 by the title of honorary freeman of the Cutlers' Company. Simpson was involved in numerous business partnerships and by 1687 had made sufficient money to buy Babworth Hall, near Retford, where his family continued to live until the end of the nineteenth century. His legal firm passed from Richard Bacon to Thomas Wright and then to Francis Sitwell, names that recur frequently in local records.

The most successful of all the Sheffield attorneys, however, was Joseph Banks (1665–1727), who came from north-west Yorkshire to work with Thomas Chappell. Banks lived in 'The New Great House, in the Prior Row, near the Church gates' and was well connected in local Dissenting circles. He inherited Shirecliffe Hall, through his wife's father, Rowland Hancock, a Nonconformist minister, and rode in one of the few private carriages in Sheffield. As agent to the Dukes of Norfolk, Leeds, and Newcastle, a partner in local industrial enterprises, and the leading attorney in town, he was able to acquire a fortune. He left Sheffield at the age of 37 to live at Scofton (Notts), and later at Revesby (Lincolnshire). The Banks family became prominent Lincolnshire gentry; his great-grandson was Sir Joseph Banks, the famous naturalist.

Sheffield had few other professionals in the late seventeenth and early eighteenth centuries and the middlemen who sold cutlery and other local wares were rarely described as merchants. Sheffield was not a social centre which attracted the neighbouring gentry, as Doncaster was able to, nor was it of political importance, having no MP or any administrative responsibilities beyond Hallamshire. Its leading inhabitants were not as wealthy as their counterparts in other towns, so, as we have seen, Sheffield lacked fine town houses and grand public buildings. On the other hand, it was relatively free of political tension, for it had no prizes to fight over. Most of the freeholders who went to the trouble of travelling to York for the county elections supported the Whigs. In religion, the

Sheffield parish church (1793). This view was taken shortly after the completion of extensive alterations to the medieval parish church, now the Cathedral. The fifteenth-century tower and spire were not touched and remain intact to this day, but the large Gothic windows had only just been inserted. In the centre distance is the new chapel-of-ease of St James, built by Vicar Wilkinson. Its former position is commemorated by street names.

old attachment to the Puritan cause turned many of the inhabitants towards Nonconformity.

The Puritan families that had dominated Sheffield until the restoration of King Charles II in 1660 became the influential Nonconformists of the latter years of the century. The same men long continued to serve as Church Burgesses and Town Trustees and to support ministers whose religious beliefs they shared. But the Church of England was no longer under their control. After 1662 its ministers had to conform to a series of parliamentary Acts; those who refused to conform were ejected from their livings. The Vicar of Sheffield and his assistant ministers were amongst those who were replaced by clergymen who accepted the doctrines of the Anglican church. The medieval church of St Peter, together with the chapels at Attercliffe and Ecclesall and the chapel at the Shrewsbury Hospital, were supposed to serve the whole of the enormous parish of Sheffield. By 1736 the population of this parish had reached 14,531. Clearly, the accommodation provided by these places of worship was inadequate. Many people chose instead to attend the services in the Nonconformist meeting-houses, and thousands more stayed away from any form of organised religion.

In his *Autobiography and Select Remains*, Samuel Roberts described the parish church that he attended in his childhood during the 1760s:

> The Church itself was then one of the most gloomy, irregularly pewed places of worship in the kingdom. It seemed as if, after the work of pewing had

begun, every person who chose had formed a pew for himself in his own way,
to his own size, height, and shape, There were several galleries, but all formed,
as it seemed, in the same way as the pews; some of them on pillars, and some
hung in chains. The Lord's closet was a gloomy structure. High under the
lofty centre arch, spanned from side to side, the massive Rood Loft; behind
which, filling up the apex of the arch, were the King's Arms, painted most
gloriously, and magnificently large. Under the clock, in a large glass case, yet
scarcely perceptible in the gloom, was the pendulum, blazoned with an enormous staring gilt sun, solemnly and mysteriously moving from side to side,
with a loud heart-piercing tick or tack at each vibration. Seen through the large
centre arch was the gloomy solemn chancel, with the altar table, and the
massive armour-clad marble effigies of the noble Talbots, and their ladies,
stretched side by side; one of them with two; all of them [the Talbots] guarded
by the enormous black oak eagle with its wide outstretched wings. All these
things seen in the dimmest gloom by the feeble aid of a few candles.

Plans of the nave and the galleries, drawn in William Fairbank's field books in
1798, confirm Roberts's description of a cluttered interior. Yet the church was
full only on the rare occasions that the Archbishop of York came for special

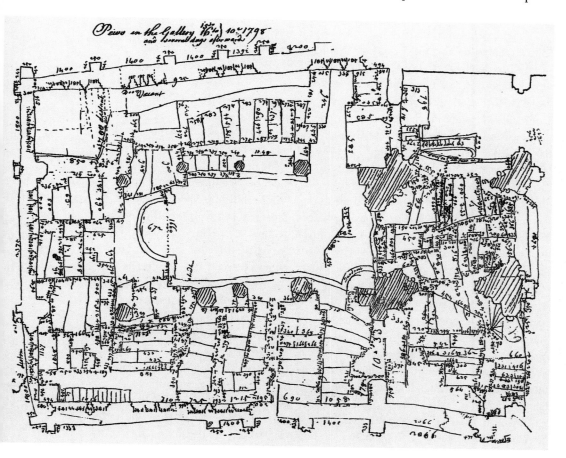

W. Keeling, *St Paul's Church* (1885). When St Paul's was built in the 1720s it stood at the south-western edge of the town. The row of houses to the left is contemporary. The dome on top of the tower was added in 1769, though it may have been part of the original design. St Paul's was Sheffield's most stylish eighteenth-century building.
BISHOPS' HOUSE MUSEUM

confirmation services. In 1743 Archbishop Herring was informed that 500 communicants had attended the Easter services, a seemingly large number, but one that formed only a small proportion of the total inhabitants of the parish.

The lack of adequate space at the parish church prompted the parishioners to raise a public subscription for a chapel-of-ease nearby. In 1718 Robert Downes, a Sheffield goldsmith, started the subscription with an offer of £1,000 and an annual stipend of £30 for a minister. Sufficient money was pledged for the first stone to be laid on 28 May 1720 on a piece of ground that had been purchased near Pincheon Croft Lane (the later Pinstone Street). St Paul's was designed in the Baroque style and was soon the most distinguished building in the town. Unfortunately, a protracted dispute over who should present the curate prevented the consecration of the church for another twenty years. Downes claimed that as the principal subscriber he should have the right to present his nephew, but the Vicar of Sheffield and the patron of the living, William Jessop of Broom Hall, insisted that the right was theirs. Political differences between the Tory Downes and the Whig Jessop poisoned the atmosphere. The Archbishop of York refused to arbitrate and the Archdeacon was powerless. The local census referred to earlier established the case for a new church to accommodate the growing population, and the Master Cutler offered to organise another subscription, but the dispute was not resolved until 1739, when Downes licensed the building as a meeting-house for Protestant Dissenters. A compromise was quickly agreed whereby the presentation was placed in the hands of the Vicar, on the understanding that he would appoint another of Downes's nephews in the first instance. The new church was consecrated in May 1740. It obtained baptism and burial rights three years later, and marriage rights in 1848, and remained a prominent Sheffield landmark for more than two centuries until its demolition just before the Second World War. The site is now occupied by the open space of the Peace Gardens.

During the late seventeenth and early eighteenth centuries the vitality of the Nonconformist meeting-houses in and around Sheffield provided a sharp contrast

Upper Chapel. In 1700 the Sheffield Dissenting congregation, which had previously met at New Hall, Snig Hill, opened their new meeting house at the top of Norfolk Street. It was the first brick building in town. In 1848 it was re-fronted in stone. It acquired its name Upper Chapel in 1715, when a group broke away to start the Nether Chapel lower down the street. Upper Chapel became Unitarian, Nether Chapel Congregational.
PHOTOGRAPH: L. NUTTALL

to the slothfulness of the Church of England. Many of the ministers who were ejected from their livings in 1662 for refusing to conform to the Anglican church stayed in the district as chaplains to the gentry families that stuck to their Puritan beliefs. Francis Jessop of Broom Hall used his influence as a Justice of the Peace to protect fellow Nonconformists from the penalties of the law. Regular prayer-meetings and services were held in 'conventicles' at the gentry halls at Shirecliffe, Carbrook and Attercliffe. From 1686 to 1689 the Revd Richard Franklin had taught future Nonconformist ministers and the sons of prominent Dissenters at an academy in Attercliffe Hall, the former seat of the Spencer family. The Attercliffe Academy was revived in 1691 by the Revd Timothy Jollie, the pastor of Sheffield Independent congregation from 1681 until his death in 1714. Under his leadership, it became one of the leading educational establishments of its day, attracting pupils from far and wide.

Most of the leading townsmen adhered to the Nonconformist cause. In 1676 a national return known as the Compton ecclesiastical census estimated that 10 per cent of the inhabitants of the parish of Sheffield were Dissenters (the alternative contemporary name for Nonconformists). The great majority of the other 90 per cent hardly ever attended any place of religious worship. Relationships between members of the various denominations at the time were generally good. When the 'Glorious Revolution' of 1688 ushered in a new era of official toleration, the Sheffield Dissenters met at New Hall, Snig Hill, until they completed their chapel in Pepper Alley in 1700. John Evans's list of Nonconformist

congregations in 1715 claimed that 1,163 people, that is about a sixth or a seventh of the town's population, attended services there, forming the largest Dissenting congregation in Yorkshire. The meeting-house acquired the name of Upper Chapel in 1715, upon the death of Timothy Jollie and a subsequent theological dispute which was focused on the choice of his successor. About 200 members stuck to their Calvinist beliefs and built Nether (i.e. lower) Chapel in the snicket that became known as Chapel Walk. The split attracted much attention as the first to take place in northern Nonconformity. The members of Upper Chapel gradually moved to a Unitarian position, but the worshippers at Nether Chapel remained Congregationalist. The modern United Reformed Church at the back of Marks & Spencers is the third chapel to be built on the site.

The Nonconformist cause declined during the course of the eighteenth century. In 1743 Archbishop Herring was informed that about 2,000 families lived in the parish of Sheffield, of whom 250 were Dissenters. A combined congregation of about 700 attended Upper and Nether Chapels every Sunday, 40 Dissenters met at Attercliffe, and another small group worshipped at Fulwood, in the chapel that was founded in 1729 under the terms of William Ronksley's will and which is now Unitarian.

The census of 1736 counted 180 Quakers in the town of Sheffield. The Friends had obtained their first local converts in the neighbouring countryside. George Fox had preached on Cinder Hill Green, near Handsworth, in 1653 and 1654 and on the second occasion had stayed at the home of Thomas Stacy of Ballifield. A regular meeting at Ballifield Hall was established and soon a meeting-house was built at Woodhouse. Thomas Stacy's brothers, Malin and Robert, and their families were the local leaders of groups of Quakers who emigrated in the 1670s and 1680s to West New Jersey. The continued attraction of America helps to explain why the number of Quakers in Yorkshire, Derbyshire and Nottinghamshire declined in the early eighteenth century. George Fox's initial appeal had been to the poor, but wealthier people like some of the South Yorkshire ironmasters soon became Friends. In Sheffield, the Broadbents of Hartshead were the most prominent Quakers. Others included the Aldams, tanners of Walkley, and the Fairbanks, Sheffield's four generations of surveyors. In 1705 the Sheffield Friends built a meeting-house just down the lane from the Broadbents's house; its memory is preserved in the name Meeting House Lane.

At the time of the 1736 census 246 Roman Catholics attended the chapel to the rear of the Lord's House in Fargate. As the lord of the manor was the leading lay Catholic in England, the congregation were able to meet regularly even though such meetings were illegal. Little is known of this congregation because of the need for secrecy, but in 1767 they numbered 319 and were served by two priests, whose stipends were paid by the Duke of Norfolk. Their presence did not lead to any violent local controversy. As we shall see, the Methodists had a much harder time.

Sheffielders who did not want to worship at the parish church therefore had plenty of choice amongst the other denominations. In the seventeenth century, in particular, church services and theological discussion occupied much of the

D.Martin, *Sheffield from Broomhall Spring* (1791). Across the fields from a viewpoint west of the town can be seen the spire of the parish church (left) and the tower of St Paul's (right). Within a couple of generations the fields would be covered with houses in a series of planned developments.

SHEFFIELD INDUSTRIAL MUSEUMS TRUST

time of the wealthier inhabitants of Hallamshire and that of many of the less well-off. Most people, however, were neither members of a church nor a chapel; they stayed away from the services altogether.

Sheffield was an 'open' society. It was not ruled by a self-perpetuating oligarchy of families like contemporary Nottingham. Both the pious and the materially successful were well regarded. Immigrants could make their way in Hallamshire and even become Master Cutler. Although the town of Sheffield had no resident magistrate and responsibility for law and order was not clearly defined, the place was not considered unruly and did not have a criminal subculture. Few Sheffielders were tried at York for capital offences. Antiquated as they were, the institutions of local government managed to preserve law and order, relieve the poor, and maintain essential services.

By the end of the eighteenth century, however, Sheffield had acquired a reputation as a radical place, much given to the expression of demands for political reform, and the lack of a local barracks was causing the authorities much concern. The change came about with the huge growth of the population. For most of the century Sheffielders had rarely got excited over politics. In 1715, at the time of the Jacobite rebellion, '800 Footmen arm'd with Firelocks and Scythes prepared to meet the rebels'. Thirty years later, when Bonnie Prince Charlie's Highlanders were marching south through Manchester to Derby someone wrote in the parish register: 'The Rebells expected and great alarm in the town'. But on both occasions fears were not turned into reality. The first time that a mob was used for political purposes was in 1723 when opponents of the Don Navigation Bill were intimidated. The first mob violence was directed at the Methodists, whose meeting-house was destroyed in a riot on 25 May 1743. The authorities were to rue their turning of a blind eye to this outrage. The first Methodist preachers had come to Sheffield in 1738. By 1741 a meeting-house had been built in Cheney Square, near St Paul's Church. The new building that was erected after the riot of 1743 was in turn demolished by rioters, when Charles Wesley attempted to preach. He wrote:

> In the afternoon I came to the flock in Sheffield, who are as sheep among wolves; the ministers having so stirred up the people, that they are ready to tear the Methodists in pieces. At six o'clock I went to the Society-house next door to our brother Bennet's. Hell from beneath was moved to oppose us. As soon as I was in the desk, with David Taylor, the Hords began to lift up their voices. An officer, in the army, contradicted and blasphemed. I took no notice of him, but sang on. The stones threw thick, striking the desk and the people. I gave out, that I should preach in the street and look them in the face.

Wesley led his congregation to safety while the mob demolished the chapel:

> We returned to our brother Bennet's, and gave ourselves up to prayer. The rioters followed, and exceeded in outrage all I have seen before. Those at Moorfields, Cardiff, and Walsall, were lambs to these.

The Methodists were eventually left in peace, but their progress was slow. In 1773 the Sheffield circuit, which covered north Derbyshire and most of South Yorkshire, had only 910 members. The great days of expansion were yet to come.

The next time that a mob got out of hand was in 1756, when, shortly after the burning of Admiral Bing's effigy (referred to earlier) several hundred people attacked Nettleship's granaries at the Pond Mill and threatened to pull down the houses of the factors in a spontaneous protest against high corn prices, which had risen in a week from 17 shillings to a guinea. The riot was reported in the *Derby Mercury* of 10 September 1756: 'The Gentlemen of the Town assembled to consider how to put an end to the Disturbance, when the Bellman was ordered to cry that wheat should be sold at fifteen shillings the load.' This action having no effect, the Riot Act was read, and the constable and his helpers tried ineffectively to control the crowd until they were chased off the streets. As the mob took control, one dealer sold his wheat at 10 shillings a load. On the Wednesday night the rioters 'assembled about 12 o'clock and forced into the Pond Mill and destroyed all the corn and flour they could meet with, and publically declared they would destroy all the mills, and afterwards pull down the Houses of the Factors'. The disturbances continued till Friday. They were the first real sign that the authorities might not be able to control popular protest.

CHAPTER 4

From town to borough

BETWEEN 1736 AND 1801 the population of Sheffield tripled. We have seen that in 1736 the central township had 10,121 inhabitants and that the whole of the parish (including the town) contained 14,531. By the time of the first official census in 1801 the population of the central township had risen to 31,314 and that of the parish to 45,755. Fifty years later, the inhabitants of the new borough of Sheffield (which covered the same area as the old parish) numbered 135,310. The pace of growth was astonishing. The British population was rising at an unprecedented rate, and the rise was particularly marked in the industrial districts such as Hallamshire. Long before the great steelworks were built in the east end of the parish, Sheffield had been transformed into a burgeoning industrial town, one of the wonders of the age, and one beset by unprecedented problems.

The town

The town had been improved in minor ways by various schemes during the late eighteenth and early nineteenth centuries. The nature of these changes was captured in some doggerel verses written by James Wills, which he published in 1827 under the title of *The Contrast, or the Improvements of Sheffield*. Some of his worst verses catalogued the changes to the Market Place in 1784:

> Near the silk draper's shop [now the Fruit Market], stood
> The Shambles, most dismal, were then made of wood,
> The sheds of the stalls almost closing, amain,
> Form'd an archway for customers, out of the rain;
> Down the centre, a channel, the filth to convey;
> And some lighted candles, almost at mid-day.
> But now, 'tis commodious, and forms a good square,
> With abundance of fruit and potatoes sold there ...
>
> Not fifty years since, at the Market-place head,
> Were the broad shallow tubs to sell oat-meal, for bread;
> And near them, the Slaughter-house stood in disgrace,
> Being a nuisance to all those who pass'd by the place ...

His descriptions of other parts of the town leave no doubts that improvements were needed:

The Barker's-pool noted for nuisance indeed,
Green over with venom, where insects did breed,
And forming a square, with large gates in the wall,
Where the Rev. Charles Wesley to sinners did call ...

Proceed then up Church-lane, that poor narrow place,
With wood buildings projecting; 'twas quite a disgrace,
The roofs nearly meeting, a dark dreary street,
Might justly be styled 'the robber's retreat',
Where shops were so darken'd for want of true light,
Appear'd quite at noontide, as though it were night:
But now, what improvement is made in Church-lane,
Fine shops for each tradesman, whereby he may gain.

In 1785 Vicar Wilkinson had allowed the removal of a 9 ft strip of the church-yard so that Church Lane could be widened; it was widened again in 1866–67 and 1891, and for the Supertram in 1994. In 1784 Wilkinson had also sold the old vicarage and most of the triangular piece of land known as Vicarage Croft, which lay immediately west of the parish church, for private building. The proceeds went towards the erection of a new chapel-of-ease dedicated to St James, which was opened in 1788. The chapel was fashionable for a time, but has long been demolished. St James's Street, St James's Row and Vicar Lane survive as street names.

The expansion of the town and the growth of some of the settlements in the rural parts of the parish can be observed by a comparison of a series of local maps and by noting the detail on a fine collection of views painted in oils or water colours. William Fairbank's new map of the town in 1797 marked the streets that

William Fairbank's *Map of Sheffield*, 1797. The map shows the first planned developments as the town expanded in the latter part of the eighteenth century. The grid patterns of the new streets make a sharp contrast to the winding roads and lanes of previous centuries. Alsop Fields is now divided into plots right down to the Porter Brook though many are not yet built upon. The wedge-shaped area to the south is the newly enclosed Little Sheffield Moor (now known simply as The Moor). The town has expanded to the west beyond its old border on Coal Pit Lane (Cambridge Street) where another regular pattern of streets has just been created

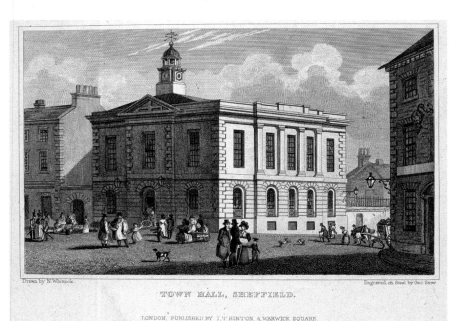

Drawn by N.Whittock.   Engraved on Steel by Geo. Stow.

TOWN HALL, SHEFFIELD.

LONDON, PUBLISHED BY I.T.HINTON, 4, WARWICK SQUARE.

The town hall, erected in Waingate in 1808, drawn by N.Whittock and engraved by George Stow.

  A HISTORY OF SHEFFIELD

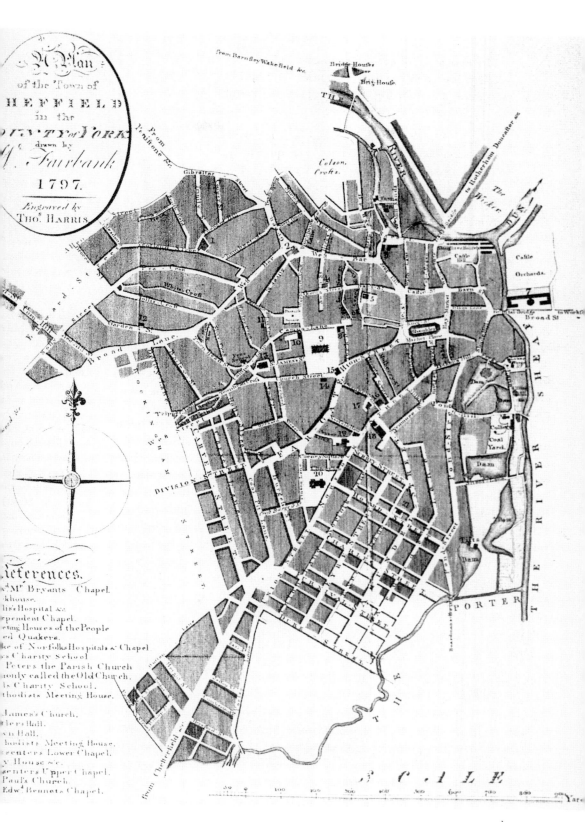

A Plan
of the Town of
SHEFFIELD
in the
COUNTY of YORK
drawn by
W. Fairbank
1797.

Engraved by
Tho.s Harris

References.

and Mr Bryants Chapel.
..khouse.
..lis's Hospital &c.
..pendent Chapel.
..eting Houses of the People
..ed Quakers.
..ke of Norfolks Hospitals & Chapel
..'s Charity School
.. Peters the Parish Church
..monly called the Old Church.
..ls Charity School.
..thodists Meeting House.

.. James's Church.
..lers Hall.
..n Hall.
..hodists Meeting House.
..centers Lower Chapel.
..y House &c.
..centers Upper Chapel.
..Pauls Church
..Edwd Bennets Chapel.

SCALE

50 0 100   200   300   400   500   600   700   800
                                                                    Yards

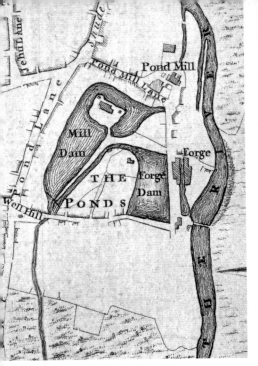
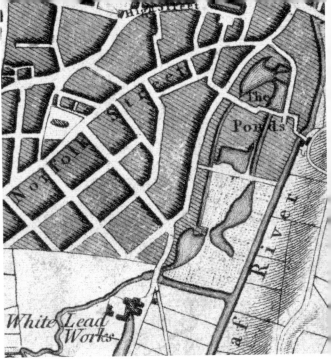

had been laid out since his earlier map of 1771. By 1797 the Alsop Fields scheme was well advanced; all the plots on the 'Proposed New Streets' of 1771, except those in the south-east, were now occupied by houses or industrial buildings. The builders had got as far south as Duke Street and had not yet developed Earl Street, apart from a small section coming off the Moor. The regularity of the grid pattern offered a sharp contrast with the narrow, winding streets of the older part of the town. This regularity was matched only by the new developments on the western edge of Sheffield, just across the township boundary. For the first time, the town had spread beyond its medieval limits into Ecclesall bierlow. Little Sheffield Moor ('The Moor' of today) had recently been enclosed and had been built upon throughout, the houses and workshops forming a strange, wedge-shaped extension to the town. South Street, the main road down the Moor towards Chesterfield, was the broadest thoroughfare in Sheffield. Short, parallel streets ran off this highway as far as the former borders of the common. On Fairbank's map of 1797 these old boundaries were marked by the new Button Lane, Young Street, and Porter Lane, and by the Porter Brook.

A grid pattern of new streets had been laid out north-west of Moorhead and west of Coal Pit Lane and Holly Street (the former Blind Lane), on land that belonged to Earl Fitzwilliam, of Wentworth Woodhouse, the lord of the manor of Ecclesall. The earl had inherited this property through his uncle, the second Marquis of Rockingham, the husband of Mary Bright of Ecclesall. Eventually, the two principal roads in this new part of the town were named Rockingham Street and Fitzwilliam Street; Bright Street was one of the short roads on the former moor. In 1797 Rockingham Street was still at the 'proposed' stage and Fitzwilliam Street was not yet planned. So far, the scheme had produced the parallel Carver Lane and Carver Street, crossed by Division Street. They extended

Details from Fairbank's maps of 1771 and 1795, showing the development of the area around the medieval ponds. The White Lead Works was said to be 'newly erected' in 1759, on the site of an old cutler's grinding wheel. Further downstream lay the Pond Tilt (a forge erected in 1732–33), the old corn mill, and the Pond Forge (developed from 1765 by John Kenyon of Middlewood Forge) Slaughter houses, tanneries and breweries were also sited in this insalubrious district

  A HISTORY OF SHEFFIELD

A section of John Leather's map of Sheffield (1823). Alsop Fields and The Moor had been built upon, but the western expansion into Ecclesall township (or bierlow) was only just beginning. However, land on both sides of the new turnpike road to Glossop and Manchester was designated 'Building Ground' and laid out in orderly streets.

as far north as West Street, which was at an early stage of development, for it was not yet linked with Townhead and Church Street, but stopped in the east at a T-junction with Holly Street. Fairbank's 1797 map also reveals that the town was spreading northwards and that some buildings had been erected on newly enclosed land in the Wicker and along Nursery Street towards Neepsend. Alongside the River Sheaf, the Ponds district was now covered with buildings and was destined to become a slum area.

A near-contemporary view of *Sheffield from Broomhall Spring* (1791, *see* p. 111) by David Martin shows that St Paul's Church was still near the southern edge of the town, surrounded by plain Georgian houses, some in rows but with others arranged haphazardly. Cows grazed the fields that had not been converted into building plots. As yet, neither Wilkinson Street nor Glossop Road connected the town with the rural settlements to the west.

By the time that John Leather published his map of Sheffield in 1823, the orchards, gardens and other spaces within the old boundaries of the town were completely filled with buildings. The Alsop Fields development had been finished as far as the Porter Brook, the township boundary in the south, beyond which lay the hamlet of Little Sheffield. Park Hill had become a large suburb to the east of the town, and in the north the Wicker had become a distinctive new district in the loop of the River Don. To the east of the Wicker, Savile Street had acquired its name, but as yet few buildings had been erected along it. The houses that extended along Nursery Street now almost joined those of the earlier suburb of Bridgehouses, which too was growing quickly and changing out of all recognition.

By the 1820s the town was also expanding in a north-westerly direction across the former Shalesmoor, but both the General Infirmary (1797) and the new St Philip's Church (1828) stood alone in the countryside. Leather's map marks 'Building Ground' between Shalesmoor and Port Mahon, to the west of Allen

In 1794 Captain David Robertson, based at Sheffield's first barracks in Wood Street, drew many local scenes in the countryside around Sheffield. Here at Heeley the River Sheaf was dammed to power a cutler's grinding wheel.

Shrewsbury Hospital. The original hospital was built in the 1660s under the terms of the will of Gilbert, the seven[th] Earl of Shrewsbury. It was a hospital in the old sense of the word, namely a group of almshouses, arranged around [a] chapel. In 1827 the old hospital, which stood just inside the former deer park, near the River Sheaf, was dismantle[d] because of flooding and pollution, and the present buildings were erected higher up the hill, in Shrewsbury Road, [in] a fashionable Gothic style and with a chapel as the centrepiec[e]

A HISTORY OF SHEFFIELD

The Cholera Monument, Norfolk Park. Erected in 1834–35 to M.E. Hadfield's design, it marks the burial ground that was reserved for those who died in the epidemic of 1832.

PHOTOGRAPH: CARNEGIE

Street, as a sign of things to come. A grander scheme was planned to the west of Rockingham Street, which was now largely built up. The stimulus for this scheme was the new turnpike road that crossed the Pennines over the Snake Pass to Glossop and Manchester. This road came out of town along Church Street, which had recently been linked to West Street by the curving line of the new Bow Street. (The curve is still there, but the whole length of the road is now called West Street.) The highway headed west towards Broomhill under the name of Glossop Road. Leather's map marks a planned development on either side of it; a middle-class suburb that would be free of the smoke of the town, for the prevailing wind was in the west. This new suburb stretched from an as-yet unnamed street (later, Broomspring Lane) in the south as far north as Broad Lane and

Robertson's drawings provide a unique record of the rural nature of the settlements alongside the River Don as it flowed through the northern part of the parish of Sheffield. Neepsend, Shirecliffe are shown (*above*), with Bacon Island to the right. The River Loxley (*below*) joins the Don, near the old barracks.

Two more drawings by Captain David Robertson in 1794, near the old barracks. The River Loxley is bridged at the bottom of Walkley Lane (*above*) and the River Don flows southwards into the town of Sheffield (*below*).

Brook Hill. Much of the land belonged to the Broom Hall estate, which had been owned by the Revd James Wilkinson, Vicar and Magistrate, whose name is commemorated in Wilkinson Street. In the 1830s and 1840s the Church Burgesses built the solid, three-storeyed, detached brick houses (that now serve as offices) on the south side of Glossop Road, and later erected a parallel row on the north side. Leather's map shows that further development was planned near Leavy Greave at the western end of Portobello Street, as far as Western Bank. Lanes had been laid out across this 'Building Ground', but as yet most sites were unoccupied. The new church of St George stood beyond the western limits of the

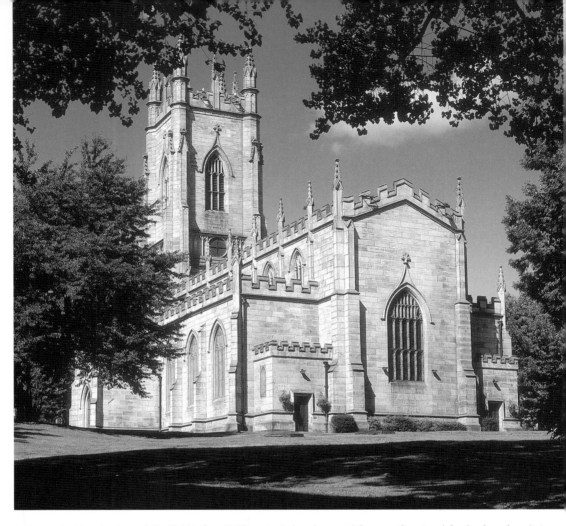

St George's Church. One of Sheffield's four 'Million Act' churches, paid for out of national funds, the others being St Philip's, St Mary's, and Christ Church, Attercliffe. Designed by the local firm of Woodhead & Hurst, and opened in 1825, it followed the fashionable revival of the Perpendicular Gothic style of the late Middle Ages. St George's was a prominent landmark in the new middle-class residential district to the west of the town centre. In 1994 it was converted into a lecture theatre and students' flats for the University of Sheffield.

PHOTOGRAPH: CARNEGIE

town, at the edge of the scheme. The whole of this district soon became a desirable suburb. Mark Firth lived at Broomspring House, at the top of Wilkinson Street, and Samuel Plimsoll lived for a time in Leavy Greave. The Glossop Road development was the first middle-class suburb in Sheffield that deliberately eschewed industrial premises. In Alsop Fields, Rockingham Street, and Portobello houses for both the middle and the working classes had been erected next to foundries and workshops. In Glossop Road and Wilkinson Street the houses were surrounded by gardens and kept well away from the smoke and noise of industry; they were far too expensive for the working classes.

The grid patterns of new streets to the south and west of the old town were vividly portrayed on a map published by J. Tayler in 1832. Tayler's map also shows

right Snake Pass, late summer, 2004. The turnpike road from Sheffield to Glossop and Manchester was a new route of 1818–21. Previously, Manchester was reached via Ringinglow, the Winnats Pass and Chapel-en-le-Frith or via Woodhead.

PHOTOGRAPH: CARNEGIE

  A HISTORY OF SHEFFIELD

how Park Hill had grown into a large suburb, equal in size to the Alsop Fields development, which was now complete. To the east stood the Hyde Park cricket ground, which had replaced an earlier ground in Darnall as the major centre of cricket in Sheffield. The Shrewsbury Hospital had recently been removed from its seventeenth-century site on the banks of the River Sheaf and had been rebuilt on the hillside. The new 'Cholera Burying Ground' had been laid out nearby and was soon to have its monument in the form of a slender spire. William Cowen's picture, *Sheffield from Shrewsbury Road* (1838)

depicts the late Georgian town across the Sheaf as a crowded mixture of houses and industrial buildings; the only public buildings of note were the churches.

By 1832 Little Sheffield was strung out along London Road as far as Highfield, and three parallel streets – Hermitage Street, New George Street and Sheldon Street – stretched towards the new St Mary's Church. By 1850 all the building plots in these streets were occupied by houses. South-west of the former Little Sheffield Moor a new grid of streets was laid out across a proposed 'Building Ground' as far as Broomspring Lane. These planned streets included the dog-legged Hanover Street, which was projected as far as Wilkinson Street. Its continuation as the present busy Upper Hanover Street had not then been contemplated. At the top of Wilkinson Street, the row of houses that curves into

North-East view of the Cricket Ground, at Darnall, N.r Sheffield.

North-east view of Darnall cricket ground, 1894. The ground was opened in 1822 for the newly formed Wednesday Cricket Club as a business venture of George Steer of the Cricket House Inn, Manor Hill. Within a few years it had become one of the finest cricket grounds in the country, with seats for 8,000 spectators and 'a noble brick pavilion'.
SHEFFIELD LIBRARIES, ARCHIVES AND INFORMATION: LOCAL STUDIES

Glossop Road, including the present Post Office, had just been built. Several larger houses, set well back in their gardens, offered attractive homes to the better-off by the junction of Glossop Road and Clarkehouse Road, but Broom Hill still appeared distant and rural. Some of the new buildings in the west had attracted humorous nicknames. 'Mount Pisgah', where Moses viewed the promised land, had been re-located at the western end of Crookesmoor, and Jericho, a common name for an out-of-the-way place, where houses were 'jerry-built', was identified in a Fairbank survey as '16 houses built by Samuel Turner in 1792 and called Jericho'.

North of the River Don, the Wicker and Bridgehouses nearly met to form one large working-class suburb, but Pitsmoor remained a separate village strung out along the turnpike road at the top of the hill. Blonk Street took its name from Benjamin Blonk's scissor works at the old Wicker grinding wheel. Meanwhile, industry and housing were creeping up the Don Valley, but St Philip's Church

A section of a map
of Sheffield by J.
Tayler (1832).

and the General Infirmary were still separated by fields from the Philadelphia Works, and the Barracks still occupied a site in the countryside. The low-lying Colson Crofts, depicted on the eighteenth-century maps of the town, had long since been built over, and by now rows of terraced cottages extended off Moorfields, along Dun Street, Dun Fields and Acorn Street, around a foundry, a brewery, and the Ebenezer Methodist Chapel, as far as the Globe Works in the north. These cottages, built of bricks with blue slate roofs, provided the standard

working-class accommodation that was available in Sheffield at that time. They consisted of single rooms on the ground floor and first floor, a cellar, and an attic room. In many northern industrial towns the cellar was used as living space, but this was not the practice in Sheffield. The ground-floor room served as a kitchen, dining room, living room, the place for bathing in a tin bath in front of the fire, and the space for drying wet clothes on a rainy day. The floor was paved with stone flags, an oven and a boiler were fixed at either side of the fire, and worn grindstones were placed in front of the fire for cooking. The husband and wife slept in the chamber with their younger children, while their older ones, or a lodger, slept in the attic. Cottages such as these were surrounded on three sides by neighbouring buildings, for they stood 'back-to-back', one fronting the street and the other facing into an unpaved yard or court, which contained the water pump and the privies. The typical builders of such cottages were speculators of

William Ibbitt, *South-east View of the Town of Sheffield*, 1854. A view of the new borough from Park Hill, looking across the gloomy Ponds district to the market area and the spires of St Peter's, St Marie's, and St Paul's. The western limits of the town are marked by St George's and St Philip's. Industry has spread along the Don Valley but the hills are not yet covered with housing. On the right, a train pulls out of the Victoria station on the newly completed railway line from Manchester. Greaves's Sheaf Works and the Duke of Norfolk's Park colliery are sited close to the canal basin. Sheffield was beginning to acquire an industrial East End.

modest means who had insufficient resources to erect more than a few buildings; they are commemorated by many a street name. A local building regulation of 1864 forbade the building of any more back-to-backs. Thousands of such buildings had been erected by then, but only an odd one or two examples have survived modern clearance schemes.

A map of Sheffield drawn by J. Rapkin in 1850 shows that by then the new streets on the edges of the old town were fully fronted by houses, but in the middle-class districts to the west many building plots were still available. The Broom Hall estate, which was to become Sheffield's finest Victorian suburb, was at an early stage of development. H. P. Parker's *View of Sheffield from the South East* (1843), taken from Sky Edge, offers a splendid panorama in the year that Sheffield was incorporated as a borough. The churches stand prominently on the ridge of the old town and at the limits of the expanding settlement. Tall chimneys belch forth smoke, and the town looks compact and congested, yet is everywhere surrounded by fields and distant moors. William Ibbitt's *North West View of Sheffield from Parkwood Spring* (c.1850) confirms the evidence of the maps in showing St Philip's Church and the General Infirmary in a rural setting by the

A section of a map of Sheffield drawn by J. Rapkin in 1850. Note that for convenience of reproduction the map has been rotated and north is now at the left.

'The town is very ugly and gloomy; it is scarcely possible to say that there is a single good street, or an imposing or interesting public building.

SAMUEL SIDNEY, 1851

Back of numbers 18 and 20, Court number 2, Furnace Hill, 1930.

  A HISTORY OF SHEFFIELD

River Don and St George's Church on the hill, marking the western limits of the town. His more famous *South-East View of Sheffield* (1854) echoes Parker in providing a powerful sense of the growing industrial borough. Greaves's Sheaf Works dominates the canal basin in the east, a foretaste of the even larger works that would soon be erected.

The entry for 'Sheffield' in Samuel Lewis, *A Topographical Dictionary of England* (1835), speaks of the

numerous streets, which, with the exception of one or two of the principal, are narrow and inconvenient: the houses, chiefly of brick, have obtained from the works a sombre appearance, and are intermingled with many of very ancient character; the chief portion is within the angle formed by the rivers, but there are considerable ranges of building on the opposite banks.

Samuel Sidney's *Rides on Railways* (1851) did not consider Sheffield to be a tourist attraction:

The town is very ugly and gloomy; it is scarcely possible to say that there is a single good street, or an imposing or interesting public building, – shops, warehouses and factories, and mean houses run zig-zagging up and down the slopes of the tongues of land, or peninsulas, that extend into the rivers or rather streamlets, of the Porter, the Rivling, the Loxley, the Sheaf, and the Don.

Sidney conceded, however, that, 'Almost all the merchants and manufacturers reside in the suburbs, in villas built of white stone on terraces commanding a lovely prospect.' Sheffield's golden frame enclosed the grimy town.

Public health

In 1795 John Aikin, a Manchester man, concluded that Sheffield was certainly a healthy place when compared with Manchester and Liverpool. It was true that the infant mortality rate was scandalously high, and that deadly illnesses such as scarlet fever remained scourges throughout the nineteenth century, but Sheffield's exposure to the cleansing effect of wind and rain, its lack of cellar dwellings, and its natural drainage except in the river valleys ensured that its inhabitants did not suffer as much as did those who lived in other industrial districts. The town's major health disaster occurred in 1832 when Asiatic cholera struck in July and by November had killed 402 people, including the Master Cutler. Inadequate sanitation allowed the disease to spread. When cholera came again in 1849, Sheffield was prepared. In that year, only 1 per cent of cases proved fatal, whereas 32.5 per cent of cases had succumbed in 1832.

The old town of Sheffield had depended on natural springs and public wells for its water supply, but these sources proved inadequate once the population started to rise dramatically. From the 1690s onwards various schemes for supplementing the natural supply were considered. In 1713–14 the Duke of Norfolk and the Town Trust gave permission to John Goodwin, a Bawtry wharfinger, and Robert Littlewood, a Thrybergh millwright, to bring water from springs near the White House, Upperthorpe, by pipes in the highways, to a piece of waste ground near Townhead Cross. Thomas Oughtibridge included the new Waterworks in his view of the town in 1737. In that year Joshua Matthewman joined Goodwin and Littlewood in building a reservoir at White House. In 1782, upon the enclosure of the commons, his son, Joseph Matthewman, began to build reservoirs at Crookesmoor.'The New Dam' was marked on a Fairbank survey of 1787. By 1832 a series of six large dams and four smaller ones had been constructed; the last two were in use until after the Second World War. The dams were shown on Leather's and Tayler's maps and were a dramatic landscape feature of T. C. Holland's *Sheffield from the Reservoirs. Crookesmoor*, painted in 1826. The water was piped from Crookesmoor to a dam that was sited just to the north of the present Sheffield University Supertram stop, from where it was piped via a stone cistern in Division Street to all parts of the town.

Between 1830 and 1848 the newly incorporated Sheffield Waterworks Company built a storage reservoir at Redmires to impound the flood waters of the Wyming Brook. Water flowed by gravitation along a conduit to the Hadfield service reservoir at Crookes and thence down into the Crookesmoor dams. The Middle Redmires reservoir was completed by 1836. A report of 1843 concluded that an 'ample' supply of water was provided three times a week through pipes in the principal streets of the town. Householders stored water in tanks or cisterns, which were often sited underground. The Lower Redmires reservoir was finished in 1849, the Upper not till 1854. As we shall see, in the second half of the nineteenth century many more schemes were necessary to meet the increasing demands of both domestic and industrial users.

'The steep declivity, the smooth and uniform surface and washing by the rain, and the absence of dirty debris from the manufactures of the town, give [Sheffield] an air of cleanliness which is very agreeable.

JAMES SMITH, 1840S

'The town of
Sheffield lies in
the heart of
finely swelling
hills that rise all
round it,
adorned with
well-cultivated
fields, beautiful
plantations, and
enclosures, with
a vast number of
elegant seats of
gentleman ...'

REVD WILLIAM
MACRITCHIE, 1795

Sheffield may have been healthier than most industrial towns, but it made an unfavourable impression on visitors. In 1801 Lady Caroline Stuart-Wortley wrote, 'I never was in so stinking, dirty and savage a place.' She had arrived in the only carriage in town, and so had attracted much unwelcome attention. Nor was she alone in her impressions. The various handbooks and gazetteers that were published in the nineteenth century all commented on the unpleasant smoke. It was only a minor consolation that another woman, Mrs Hughes of Uffington, thought that Sheffield was 'one degree better than the abominable town of Birmingham.'

In 1841 the Revd J. C. Symons wrote that Sheffield was

one of the dirtiest and most smoky towns I ever saw. There are a quantity of small forges without high chimneys. The town is also very hilly, and the smoke ascends to the streets, instead of leaving them ... One cannot be long in the town without experiencing the necessary inhalation of soot ... There are, however, a number of persons who think the smoke healthy.

A contemporary 'Report on the condition of the Town of Sheffield', by James Smith, which was published as part of the *Royal Commission on health of towns*, estimated that Sheffield's population of 85,076 was accommodated in 25,000 houses, most of which were 'better ventilated and better cleansed by rain than the streets of most towns' because of their elevated situation. Smith observed that:

The newer parts are laid out with more regularity ... The streets are regularly swept and cleansed under the authorities, and the refuse is carried off by the scavengers and deposited in a dung-yard in the lower part of the town, where it is made up for sale ... The steep declivity, the smooth and uniform surface and washing by the rain, and the absence of dirty debris from the manufactures of the town, give it an air of cleanliness which is very agreeable ... still there are many portions where the working classes reside confined, ill-ventilated, ill-drained, and filthy. In general, however, the dungsteads and privies are more tidily kept than in most of the towns visited.

Here, as elsewhere, the greatest amount of sickness prevails in undrained, ill-ventilated, and filthy localities. There is a flat and ill-drained portion of the town, on the south side of the river, where much fever prevails. The streets in this part of the town are frequently covered with water several feet deep during floods, and many low dwellings are inundated.

There are some cottages lately built for working classes, which are of a very good construction. These houses are built back-to-back; but so well are they arranged that they have a good ventilation ... The sewage water is discharged into the river, polluting the stream ... There are no public gardens or open space of any extent for the people to walk and enjoy themselves in, but the country is open and hilly.

A report by J. C. Hall, *On the prevention and treatment of the Sheffield grinders' disease* (1857) noted that:

SHEFFIELD, FROM THE RESERVOIRS CROOKS MO

To His Grace The Duke of Norfolk &c &c &c

By Permission This Plate is most respectfully dedicated by His Grace's obliged and Obedient

T.C.Hofland, *Sheffield from Crookesmoor* (1826). The reservoirs at Crookesmoor provided most of Sheffield's drinkir water. The view down the valley shows the General Infirmary and the new St Philip's Church in a rural setting. St George's Church occupies a lofty position on the right of the picture and the spire of the parish church can be seen in the middle distance.

> In Sheffield, the artisans generally have a house for themselves, and those who live in the suburbs frequently a garden. In times of good trade, at least, it is unusual to find two families under the same roof, and there is hardly an instance of an inhabited cellar in the town ... There is probably less of the confined alley and narrow cul-de-sac in Sheffield than in many other manufacturing towns, and ... a good deal has been done of late years to improve the sewers and surface drains of the town.

He concluded that much more improvement was nevertheless required.

In 1848, the second edition of James Haywood and William Lee, *A Report on the Sanatory Condition of the Borough of Sheffield* commented on the worst parts of the town that they could find:

> Taking the district included between the two rivers Sheaf and Porter, commencing at Pond-mill and Shoreham-street, and including Suffolk-road,

Fornham-street, Pond-street, Shemeld-croft and the adjoining populous districts to the Gas House, we pass through the oldest and worst constructed part of the town; the courts on each side of Pond-street, contain poor miserable dwellings, with low rooms imperfectly lighted and ventilated, and subject to all the nuisances arising from filthy surface drainage and exhalations from the various stagnant ponds. The amount of filth derived from the main sewers and manufactories, and deposited in these places is inconceivable, and the stench given off in summer, when the river is low, is most offensive ...

Of Lee-croft, Hawley-croft, School-croft, and Sims-croft, we may remark generally that the houses are irregularly built, though of a respectable construction. Many, however, are dirty, as also are the yards in this locality. The mass of buildings in Sims-croft, particularly those at the lower end, are of a meaner character than the former, and are inhabited principally by Irish ... the district bounded by Beet-street, Upper and Lower Allen-street, Gibraltar-street, Westbar-green, Tenter-street, and Broad-lane ... [is] more densely populated in relation to its extent than any district previously mentioned ... The houses, especially those erected in the yards (which are of a very confined character), are ill constructed, badly lighted and ventilated; being built back to

The Master Cutler's Tombstone, Norfolk Park. John Blake, the Master Cutler in the year that cholera first struck many of Britain's largest towns, was one of the 402 Sheffielders who died from the epidemic between July and November 1832. His tombstone lies a few yards away from the memorial that was erected to the victims.

PHOTOGRAPH: CARNEGIE

back, and generally of three storeys high, which of itself is an impediment to the free access of light and air; and from the accumulations of filth and bad drainage in the lower part of the district the atmosphere is loaded with miasma to a degree which is highly pernicious ... the particles of soot floating about in the atmosphere [are] so numerous that people [are] prevented from having recourse to the most common method of ventilation by opening windows and doors; in many places the evil is so extensive that the inhabitants find the greatest difficulty in maintaining personal or domestic cleanliness ... We are aware that a strong feeling prevails amongst the manufacturers, most of whom are opposed to any interference on this subject.

The men who served on royal commissions and other enquiries were deliberately looking for the worst examples in order to press the case for reform. Their descriptions of life in the slums depict an appalling state of affairs, but these should not mislead us into thinking that the entire working-class population of Sheffield lived in such miserable conditions. The majority of the Sheffield working-class regarded themselves as 'respectable' members of society who were not to be classified with the shifty and the drunken, nor with the unfortunate. The most wretched were the poor Irish immigrants who came fleeing famine in search of work as casual labourers. Their numbers were much smaller than the Irish immigrants in Merseyside and the Lancashire cotton towns, however, and considerably fewer than those who settled in Leeds.

Meanwhile, the provision of medical services was a matter for continued public debate. Sheffield's first modern hospital, the General Infirmary, was built by public subscription in 1797, in the midst of fields beyond the north-western border

The General Infirmary. Sheffield' first modern hospita (as distinct from the 'hospitals' or almshouses endowe by Gilbert Talbot and Thomas Hollis in the seventeenth century) was the General Infirmary, built by public subscription in gree fields to the north o the town and opene in 1797.
PHOTOGRAPH: L. NUTTALL

A HISTORY OF SHEFFIELD

Sheffield General Cemetery was designed by Samuel Worth for the Sheffield General Cemetery Company and opened in 1836. Like other early public cemeteries, it was landscaped in the French manner. It was originally used by Nonconformists, whose chapel was built in an Egypto-Greek style. The Anglican cemetery, which was laid out to the east by Robert Marnock in the late 1840s, was served by the Gothic-style chapel, seen here, designed by William Flockton and opened in 1850. The cemetery was bought by the city council in 1979 and most of it was bulldozed seven years later. Since the 1980s a group of volunteers has been active in restoring the cemetery, but much work remains to be done.
PHOTOGRAPH: CARNEGIE

of the town. A surgeon-apothecary, Hall Overend, ran a private medical school, which was continued by his son, Wilson Overend. In 1835 a mob, fuelled by rumours that the bodies in the dissecting room in Eyre Street were robbed from graves, in the manner of the notorious Burke and Hare gangs elsewhere a few years before, ransacked the building. Another medical school, which had been founded in 1829 in Surrey Street by Dr Arnold Knight and a group of medical men, is recognised as one of the forerunners of the University of Sheffield. By the early 1830s the General Infirmary could no longer deal adequately with all the medical needs of the growing town. In 1832 – the year that cholera struck – a Public Dispensary was opened, first in Tudor Place, and then shortly afterwards in West Street. It was later developed into the Royal Hospital and survived until 1978, just before the opening of the Royal Hallamshire Hospital.

The manner in which the town was governed did not facilitate reform. A new institution was added to the various bodies that had existed for centuries when, in 1818, Sheffield obtained an Improvement Act. The town was belatedly following the example of others, and in so doing chose the least democratic form of institution. Sheffield's 80 Improvement Commissioners were not elected, but were appointed by the Town Trustees, the Master Cutler and the two Wardens of the Cutlers' Company. They were given the power of 'cleansing, lighting, watching and otherwise improving the town of Sheffield', through the levying of local rates. Their jurisdiction was confined to a radius within three-quarters of a mile of the parish church, and their responsibilities did not include drainage or sewerage. Nevertheless, Samuel Lewis was able to report in 1835 that,

A HISTORY OF SHEFFIELD

'Considerable improvements have taken place, under the provisions of an act obtained in 1818, by which the town is partially paved, and lighted with gas by a company whose extensive works are situated at Shude Hill, near the bridge over the river Sheaf '.

An equal lack of enthusiasm was evident when the opportunity arose for the whole of Sheffield parish to be incorporated as a borough. Only the fear of being policed by a county force under the direction of rural magistrates, persuaded a majority to apply for a royal charter. This was granted on 24 August 1843. The first elections for the borough council were held on 1 November 1843, after which William Jeffcock was chosen as the first mayor. The new system did not herald a new age of reform, however. The town council did not appoint a health committee until December 1846.

Communications

Gales and Martin's *Sheffield Directory* of 1787 lists the coach services and carriers' routes that linked the town to all parts of Britain. Coaches set off from either the Angel Inn in the Market Place or the Tontine Inn in Haymarket. They were advertised to reach Birmingham, Carlisle, Doncaster, Edinburgh, Hull, Leeds, London and Manchester, and to link with other services to more distant places. Thus, the coach to Birmingham left the Angel at 3 o'clock in the morning, every day except Sunday, and went via Chesterfield, Derby, Burton-upon-Trent and Lichfield to the Swan Inn, Birmingham. A return service was available at the same hour. The Manchester coach used the Buxton turnpike road, three days a week, but the service ran only in summer. A 'Heavy Coach' from the Angel departed every evening for London, through Chesterfield, Mansfield, Nottingham, Leicester and Northampton, and the 'Mail Coach' set off at 5 o'clock in the morning along the same route. The daily 'Tontine Coach' went to London by way of Rotherham, Worksop, Newark, Grantham and Stamford. Sheffield's first stage coach service, operated by Samuel Glanville, landlord of the Angel, had started in 1760. Three years later, the London journey was reduced to three days and the frequency of the service was increased to three times a week. The London service was considerably improved in 1798 when a 'Post Coach', starting from the Royal Oak in Pond Street thrice a week, arrived at its destination in 31 hours; an extra hour was required on the return journey.

Meanwhile, the humble carrier's cart continued to take parcels and people to the neighbouring villages and market towns, usually on a weekly basis, and the sturdier waggons provided slow but reliable services to all parts of the land. For example, Swinden's Cart left the Bird-in-Hand, Church Lane, every Tuesday for Stoney Middleton and Tideswell, where goods could be forwarded to Buxton, and every Tuesday evening Royle's Waggon set off from the Travellers in West Bar along the turnpike road to Leeds, where goods could be forwarded to 'Newcastle, Carlisle, and all Parts of the North'. Three waggons crossed the Pennines to Manchester all the year round, by way of Chapel-en-le-Frith or over Woodhead. In the early years of the nineteenth century, coaches, waggons and

Hunter's Bar Toll House. The toll house was built in 1811 on the new Ecclesall Road, which provided an easier route out of town into Derbyshire than the ancient one via Psalter Lane. Brocco Bank is to the left. The Turnpike Trust was not profitable and was closed on 31 October 1884. Reuben Thompson's horse bus service is shown left as the last payer of tolls. After the photograph was taken, he passed through the toll bar, turned around, and re-entered Sheffield as the first to use the road without paying tolls! The stone posts now stand amidst the greenery of the traffic roundabout at the bottom of Brocco Bank.

carts, linked with water carriage, gradually provided a comprehensive network of services. Sheffield remained difficult to reach from all directions except the east, but its encircling hills were increasingly passable.

In the late eighteenth and early nineteenth centuries the local turnpike road system was completed. For the first time, new routes were created. In 1803 the Hathersage–Greenhill Moor turnpike trust (created in 1781) was authorised to construct a route that left London Road at Highfield to follow the Sheaf valley through Abbeydale and Totley, then up the hill to Owler Bar and down the other side to Baslow. Two years later, the Wadsley–Langsett turnpike road followed the Don and Little Don from Wadsley Bridge, through Deepcar and Stocksbridge to the Flouch Inn, where it joined the older turnpike road from Doncaster and Rotherham to Manchester via Woodhead. Between 1812 and 1819 a new western route left Hunter's Bar and climbed the hill to Banner Cross, where instead of veering right to Ringinglow it continued through Whirlow to Fox House. The old highway across Houndkirk Moor gradually decayed. Finally, in 1818 the most ambitious scheme of all was begun. This was the turnpike road to Glossop and Manchester over the Snake Pass (so-called because half way between Ashopton and Glossop the Duke of Devonshire built an inn, which was distinguished by the sign of the Cavendish snake). In 1821 this dramatic new road along the northern side of Kinderscout and over Bleaklow was opened.

right Virtually all that remains that is recognisably part of the Victoria Station of the Great Central Railway.

A HISTORY OF SHEFFIELD

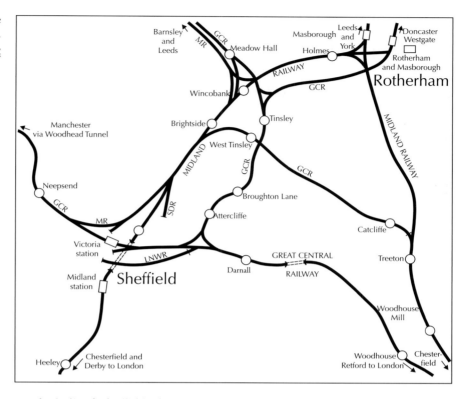

The railways of the Sheffield district.

DRAWN BY ADAM GREGORY, CARNEGIE

The bulk of Sheffield's heavy imports and exports came and went by the Don Navigation, which had reached its western limit at Tinsley Wharf in 1751. The

success of the navigation encouraged new attempts to bring the waterway all the way to Sheffield. A way round the opposition of those whose works were dependent on the water power provided by the River Don had to be found. Eventually, it was agreed that a new canal would have to be dug and a series of locks constructed at the western edge of Tinsley. In 1819 the Sheffield Canal was finished right up to the Canal Basin, near the confluence of the Don and the Sheaf. Within four years, Greaves's enormous Sheaf Works had been built alongside it. The canal was an important stimulus to the industrialisation of Sheffield's east end.

The railway was an even greater stimulus. At first, it seemed as if Sheffield was going to be side-lined by this revolution in transport, for the surrounding hills needed expensive tunnels and cuttings. George Stephenson's North Midland Railway, which was started in 1837 and opened in 1840, passed to the east of the town, via Chesterfield and Rotherham to Leeds. A five-mile line from Wicker station to Rotherham was opened on 31 October 1838, but this was small consolation. Sheffield was not connected directly with

Chesterfield until 1 February 1870, when the line via Dronfield and the Bradway tunnel (1 mile 267 yards) to the fine new Midland station was opened. The difficult route across the Pennines to Manchester was completed much earlier, however. The first train left from the temporary terminus at Bridgehouses on 14 July 1845, though Woodhead Tunnel was not opened until 22 December of that year. It took another six years to build the massive Wicker Arches, which carried the railway over the River Don for 660 yards to the Victoria station. This plain, functional building was opened on 15 September 1851.

The rural parts of the parish

The landscape of the rural districts of the parish of Sheffield was changed considerably by the process of parliamentary enclosure, by which the owners of the major part of the land could override the opposition of those who preferred to retain the common pastures and wastes in their ancient form for their traditional purposes. In the Sheffield district enclosure was concerned largely with the commons and moors, for the strips of the open fields had long ceased to be farmed in common and many had already been consolidated into larger blocks. Only Attercliffe, Darnall and Crookes still had fields where the long, thin pattern of strips was recognisable. The first township to obtain an Act of Parliament to enclose its commons and wastes was Ecclesall bierlow in 1779; the process of

A coloured version of E.Blore's *Sheffield from Attercliffe Road* (1819). The canal had finally reached Sheffield in the year that Blore took this view. 'Smoky Sheffield' was already a thriving industrial town. Soon it would expand in an easterly direction and the rural nature of the foreground of this drawing would be transformed. In 1819, however, Salmon Pastures was still a pleasant place by the river.

n by W.Westall A.R.A.   Engraved by Ed:

A HISTORY OF SHEFFIELD

Many of the local commons and wastes were converted into grouse-shooting moors after enclosure. In 1897 the Duke of Norfolk sold Stanage or Hallam Moors to William Wilson of Beauchief Hall. Ten years later Wilson employed a young mason, George Broomhead, to carve runnels and basins in large rocks so that grouse could drink there. Pleased by the success of the first six near Stanage Pole, Wilson ordered two further series in the next few years, making a total of 108 basins. All but five can still be found with diligent searching.

PHOTOGRAPH: AUTHOR

surveying, considering claims and awarding new allotments to the Marquis of Rockingham, lord of the manor, and 154 landholders took nine years. The commons comprised High Moors (268 acres), part of Crookes Moor (170), Brincliffe Edge (66), Bents Green (32), Whiteley Wood (28), Greystones Cliff (26), Carter Knowle (24), Little Sheffield Moor (17) and numerous smaller greens. The effect of this enclosure on the landscape is best seen between Bents Green and Ringinglow, where the rectangular patterns of fields divided by stone walls is evident on both sides of the turnpike road. This road was given a standard width and a straight course by the enclosure commissioners. Little Sheffield Moor, by contrast, was used straightaway for building purposes.

The commons of Brightside bierlow, that is mainly the Wicker and Pitsmoor, were enclosed between 1788 and 1795 and immediately built upon. Then, in 1791 an Act was obtained to enclose the commons and wastes of the townships of Upper and Nether Hallam (including Heeley) and the neighbouring township of Stannington, across the Rivelin Valley. The long-drawn out process was not completed until 1805. Enclosure had been proposed in 1787, but had met with opposition, partly because the Crookesmoor racecourse would have to be closed. When the commissioners and surveyors got approval to begin, they met fierce resistance. On 23 July 1791 the Revd James Wilkinson (Vicar and Magistrate), Mr Joseph Ward (Master Cutler), and Mr Vincent Eyre (agent to the Duke of Norfolk and Town Trustee) requested military aid to allow the work to go ahead. They claimed that:

> considerable bodies of disorderly people in this neighbourhood have lately several times assembled in considerable forces with the riotous intention of preventing the Commissioners acting under the authority of an Enclosure Bill ... and not only drove them from the commons, but also menaced them with the greatest personal danger, if they attempted to proceed with the Enclosure, and have also actually burned the farming property and broke the windows of

several houses and menaced the lives and property of the freeholders to enclosure, and openly avowed their intention of laying open the enclosures in the neighbourhood already made ... and burning the houses of all the freeholders who have countenanced the late enclosures.

These were troubled times, and the authorities were fearful of riots similar to those that had recently occurred in Birmingham. As we shall see, Sheffield was becoming a radical town, prone to mass demonstrations in favour of reform. The enclosure went ahead with the help of the troops. The more distant moors in the west were nibbled away at their edges, as at Hollow Meadows, but the greater proportion was preserved by the new owners for grouse shooting; the public were denied access.

Meanwhile, the enclosure of the commons of Ecclesfield and Wadsley had taken place between 1784 and 1789, and those of of Handsworth parish between 1802 and 1805. The last of the Sheffield townships to be enclosed was Attercliffe-cum-Darnall (1810–19), which had 238 acres of commons (including four greens) and 50 acres of open-fields. The old field paths and tracks across the commons were fenced off. A new road across Attercliffe and Darnall commons was given the name of Broughton Lane, for here, in 1792, Spence Broughton's body had been gibbeted after he had been hanged for highway robbery. The gibbet and a few remains of the skeleton were not removed until 1827.

In 1795 the Revd William Macritchie wrote in his *Diary of a Tour through Great Britain*:

J. McIntyre, *Sheffield from Psalter Lane*. This undated (but mid-nineteenth-century) view from Brincliffe Edge shows one of the largest of the many local sandstone quarries, where building stone and cutlers' grindstones were obtained. The spires of St George's, the parish church, St Marie's, and St Paul's rise from the near horizon amidst the chimneys.

The town of Sheffield lies in the heart of finely swelling hills that rise all round it, adorned with well-cultivated fields, beautiful plantations, and enclosures, with a vast number of elegant seats of gentleman, all enjoying the finest situation ... [I dined] at the elegant country-seat of Mr William Shore [Tapton Hill], a man whose grandfather was a common hammerman, and who now enjoys a fortune of some thousands a year. I was a good deal struck with the elegance and luxury of his table ... Adieu to Sheffield. It is a dirty, monotonous town, but surrounded with one of the finest countries in England: romantic dales, sweetly rising hills, plantations, enclosures, and neat gentlemen's seats on every side.

Edward Blore's view of *Sheffield from the Attercliffe Road* (1819) and J. McIntyre's undated *Sheffield from Psalter Lane, Brincliffe Edge* confirm this description of a manufacturing town set in attractive countryside. Attercliffe was still a rural settlement approached along a turnpike road that followed the banks of the River Don. The rugged grindstone quarries at Brincliffe Edge remind us that industrial workers could obtain a living in the rural parts of the parish, near the 'elegant seats' of the gentry. In 1830 William Cobbett noted in his *Rural Rides*, 'The ragged hills all around this town are bespangled with groups of houses inhabited by working cutlers.'

Holmehead Wheel, Rivelin Valley. This photograph, taken about 1900, shows the typical rural nature of the cutlers' grinding wheels in Sheffield's river valleys. The Holmehead Wheel was the first recorded in 1742. In 1794 fifteen men were employed here by Cadman and Co. as grinders at eleven troughs. Some old grindstones act as stepping-stones in the foreground. The ruins of the buildings, wheel pit, weir and dam survive.

Cutlery

In the second half of the eighteenth century, as the population rose to undreamt of heights, the number of workers who were employed in the Hallamshire cutlery trades increased enormously. Even the London cutlers could no longer compete with the huge quantities of knives that were made in Sheffield from Huntsman's cast steel or from local cementation steel. The Hallamshire men became increasingly specialised as forgers, grinders or finishers, or as the manufacturers of particular products, such as razors or surgical instruments. The 'little mester' with his apprentice and a journeyman remained a typical figure, but small partnerships were now common and a few larger firms had been formed. By 1789 journeymen were said to outnumber freemen by as many as ten or twelve to one. The authority of the Cutlers' Company collapsed under the sheer weight of numbers. In 1791 the Company was forced to abandon its customary insistence on a formal seven years' apprenticeship and to admit as freemen, upon the payment of fees, all those who wished to work. In 1814 entry into the cutlery trades was made entirely free.

The break with the past was far from complete, however. Handicraft skills remained the traditional ones that had been passed down from father to son or from master to apprentice, most working units were as small as before, and prices and piece rates varied little. Factors and employers were content with a system by which specialist tasks were performed at agreed prices by outworkers, who provided their own tools and accommodation and in return chose their days and

Shepherd Wheel on the Porter Brook is the sole complete survivor of the scores of cutlers' grinding wheels that were once powered by Sheffield's rivers. Its present appearance dates from the late eighteenth century when Mr Shepherd was the long-term tenant, but it occupies a site that has been used for grinding cutlery since Elizabethan times. It is operated occasionally as a working museum.

PHOTOGRAPH: CARNEG

The huge overshot wheel, made of iron, at the rear of Shepherd Wheel. Overshot wheels were the normal type in the Sheffield region, where the rivers descend quickly from the Pennines. Water was channelled from the Porter Brook along a goit to a large pond, then via a penstock above the wheel.
PHOTOGRAPH: CARNEGIE

One of the many uses of worn-out grinding stones — steps at Shepherd Wheel.
PHOTOGRAPH: CARNEGIE

hours of work. Quality control could be enforced by the refusal of payment for poor work, and when trade was bad the outworkers were left to fend for themselves. Nevertheless, strikes for better wages were organised in 1777, 1787, 1790 and 1796 in the file, table knife, scissor, and spring knife trades, respectively.

During the 1787 strike, Joseph Watkinson, the Master Cutler associated with the new practice of counting thirteen knives to a dozen, was the victim of a vicious lampoon by Joseph Mather, a radical file-cutter and popular song-writer. The chorus to Mather's song went:

Then may the odd knife his great carcass dissect,
Lay open his vitals for men to inspect,
A heart full as black as the infernal gulf,
In that greedy, blood-sucking, bone-scraping wolf.

A new era in industrial relations had begun.

Many Sheffield cutlers were still able to turn their hands to the manufacture of a range of goods. Sketchley's *Directory* of 1774 names the makers of table knives, case knives, butchers' knives, spring knives, pen- and pocket knives, lack-, stag-, seal'd- and spotted-penknives, and various other 'spotted' wares whose scales of horn were burnt to imitate the appearance of the more expensive tortoiseshell. The great variety of Sheffield's products was illustrated in Joseph Smith's *Explanation or Key, to the Various Manufactories of Sheffield, with Engravings of Each Article* (1816). The enormous variety of choice that was offered to customers by the

"SHEPHERD'S WHEEL,"
GRINDING CUTLERY BY WATER POWER,
SHEFFIELD, ENGLAND.

No I.

Shepherd Wheel. Men are shown sitting astride their 'horsing' in the traditional position adopted by Hallamshire grinders. (The grinders of Thiers, central France, lay flat on their stomachs, with the wheel at a lower level.) The grinding wheels are powered by the huge overshot wheel. The grindstones were made from local coal-measure sandstone. Shepherd Wheel was divided into two buildings, known as 'hulls'.

mid-nineteenth century is revealed by surviving artefacts and the illustrations in the pattern books of local firms, now forming part of the Hawley Collection at the University of Sheffield.

By the late eighteenth century the River Don had an average of three water-powered sites per mile, the Loxley and Sheaf had four, the Porter five, and the Rivelin six. Moreover, many of these sites had recently been enlarged to accommodate more grinders. Dams had been widened and water wheels designed for greater efficiency. An anonymous survey of the water mills on the local rivers in 1794 shows how every available site had been occupied. Sheffield's industrial development was firmly based on water power. Its concentration of water-powered sites was without parallel in the rest of Britain.

One of the wheels on the Porter Brook in 1794 was rented by a Mr Shepherd, who was there long enough for his name to become permanently attached to the site. Its earlier history probably goes back to at least 1584. In 1794 Shepherd Wheel consisted of ten grinders' troughs, which were presumably arranged in the two buildings that now form an industrial museum. Thirty years later, it passed to the Hinde family, three generations of whom rented the property until the 1920s or early 1930s, when its working life ended. The water wheel is of the overshot type, 18 ft in diameter and 6 ft wide. Its spokes, hub and rims are made of cast iron, but the 'buckets' which retain the water are of wrought iron with elm or oak 'back-boards'. The power that is generated comes from the fall of water from the pentrough to the bottom of the wheel. Some 18 or 20 grindstones and several glazing wheels can be turned at an amazing speed when the water wheel rotates. Shepherd Wheel was probably used for grinding knives of all kinds. The grinding troughs were filled with water when working, so that the revolving grindstones were kept wet enough to prevent burn marks on the knife blades. Forks, needles, brace bits and spindles were ground dry, however. The grinder crouched over the grindstone by sitting astride a wooden seat or 'horsing', which was chained to the floor. The stone revolved away from the grinder (except in the scythe trade), and threw up large quantities of 'swarf' (a wet mixture of tiny particles of sandstone and steel) against a board. A typical grindstone was 3 ft diameter when new, but would last only from four to eight weeks. The dangers of contracting 'grinders' asthma' and of rheumatism in the wet conditions are apparent. After grinding, the blades were dried and then glazed on a wheel which was covered by a strip of leather impressed with emery or silver sand and covered with tallow fat. The glazing process protected the blades from rust and gave them a smooth appearance, which was then improved by polish-

lay Wheels Forge. he old methods of scythe production were still in use at he outbreak of the econd World War. ere, a forger and a striker are shown forging the grist roove) in the back f a scythe blade to make it rigid. The Sheffield district pecially the parish of Norton) was an important national centre of scythe aking from at least the sixteenth century.

Water-powered til[t]
hammers at
Abbeydale Industr[ial]
Hamlet.
PHOTOGRAPH: CARNEGIE

ing. Shepherd Wheel ceased to work commercially in the 1930s. The City Council voted for its demolition in 1957, but it was saved and restored by the Council for the Conservation of Sheffield Antiquities (now the South Yorkshire Trades Historical Society) and opened as a working museum in 1962.

The advantages of water power over manual labour in trades other than grinding were obvious to the Revd William Bagshaw, after a visit to Smithywood Tilt at Norton on the river Sheaf in 1793. He wrote in his diary: 'Mr B[iggin] can there make at his forge with two men about twelve to fifteen dozen of scythes in the course of a day. At a common smithy two men can only make about half a dozen scythes a day, i.e. prepare them for the grindstone'. These advantages are immediately apparent at a working day at Abbeydale Industrial Hamlet, when water is poured from the pentrough on to the giant wheel and the tilt and plating hammers are set to work.

The anonymous list of 1794 provides our first evidence that rotary steam engines were used to supplement the water power at some of the wheels, such was the demand for space at a trough amongst the grinders. Probably the first firm in the Sheffield 'light trades' to employ steam power was that of Bailey, Proctor & Turner, opticians and manufacturers of

right An advertising board from the Sheffield Metal and Wire Company on display at Abbeydale Industrial Hamlet.

PHOTOGRAPH: CARNEGIE

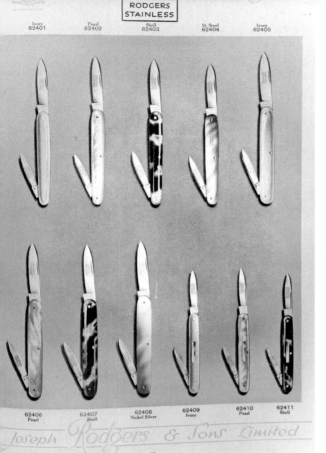

Joseph Rodgers & Sons Limited. A page from one of their catalogues illustrates a range of penknives, for which the firm were world famous. By the 1850s Rodgers' works in Norfolk Street was easily the largest cutlery factory in the world. They had an unbeatable reputation for knives, marked with a star and Maltese cross. Enormous quantities were exported to America.

HAWLEY COLLECTION, UNIVERSITY OF SHEFFIELD

lenses, whose works was sited at the foot of Park Hill on the River Sheaf. Their steam engine was installed in 1786. By 1794 over 300 steam-driven grinding troughs had been built.

By the late eighteenth century London and overseas markets had become far more important than ever before. Some Sheffield firms had warehouses in London and salesmen in America. European customers had also increased in number, but were spread thinly. Cutlery was no longer sold through merchants in London or Hull, and travellers to country fairs and markets were less important than before. In 1792 the editor of the *Sheffield Advertiser* remarked that 'of late years an immense quantity of business heretofore transacted at the great regular marts of the Kingdom now goes on by frequent and immediate correspondence between the manufacturer and the vendor of the shop'. Full-time travelling salesmen or agents selling on commission were now employed by the larger firms.

By 1800 much of the world's cutlery trade, especially that of America and the British Dominions, was dominated by Sheffield. As the British navy ruled the seas, local merchants had ready access to distant markets for quality products made of Huntsman's cast steel. This trade was hit hard by the American War of Independence and by the Napoleonic Wars and the subsequent economic depression, but the opening of the Sheffield Canal in 1819 coincided with general recovery. William Cobbett observed in his *Rural Rides* in 1830 that the Hallamshire cutlers had not suffered to the same extent as the West Riding weavers because the traditional hand skills had not been destroyed by machinery, thus 'the trade of Sheffield has fallen off less in proportion than that of the other manufacturing districts.' The prolonged depression of 1837–43 did, however, hit Sheffield hard, but when times were good the town prospered.

Dramatic changes in the structure of the Sheffield cutlery industry were signalled in 1823 when Messrs Greaves's Sheaf Works was opened at a cost of £50,000, four years after the Sheffield Canal had finally linked the town with the Don Navigation at Tinsley. The employees converted and melted steel in the largest collection of cementation furnaces seen in Sheffield. They made their own tools, and then manufactured razors, penknives and other cutlery wares, especially for the American market. The Sheaf Works was by far the largest business in

The Sheaf Works. Built about 1823 by Messrs Greaves, the Sheaf Works is regarded as Sheffield's first self-contained factory, making its own steel, tools and cutlery. Sited by the new Canal Basin, it later had the advantage of the Sheffield–Manchester railway crossing the site. The recently restored office block is all that remains of the works (see page 99).

Sheffield at that time. The main office block in Maltravers Street, which is all that is left of the works, has recently been renovated as part of the Victoria Quays development and so is once again a local landmark.

Small, backstreet works employing a few hands remained the typical units of production, but by 1850 four other firms had hundreds of workers: Joseph Rodgers & Son's Norfolk Works, George Wostenholm's Washington Works, Mappin's Queen's Cutlery Works, and James Dixon's Cornish Place Works. The firm which, above all others, became internationally renowned for the quality and design of its knives in the nineteenth century was that of Rodgers. The family were cutlers in Hawley Croft by 1724, and the famous mark of the Star and Maltese Cross was confirmed to Joseph Rodgers in 1764. By the later eighteenth

century the firm was beginning to expand in new premises in Norfolk Street. In 1817 they were known as 'merchants, factors, table- and pocket-knife, and razor manufacturers', and by 1840 they employed 520 workers. Under John Rodgers (1779–1859) the firm surpassed all others in quality, range and output, and the brilliance of their marketing. In 1822 they had the then-novel idea of opening a showroom in Norfolk Street, which attracted large numbers of visitors, and they took particular pride in making Exhibition knives. The Year Knife, which was put on display in their new showroom had 1822 blades in the form of a Maltese Cross. The Norfolk Knife, made for the Great Exhibition in Crystal Palace in 1851 and now on display in the Cutlers' Hall, is a spring knife with 75 blades, punches, gimlets and hooks, acid-etched views on each of its blades, and decorative carving on its pearl scales. The skills of Sheffield craftsmen have never been surpassed.

At the time of the national census of 1841, about 60 per cent of British cutlers worked in and around Sheffield. Cutlery manufacture remained a handicraft, or rather a series of crafts, for the trades were sub-divided and much was done (even for the largest firms) by outworkers. An article in *The Penny Magazine* in 1844 observed that 'Nearly all the articles of cutlery made at Sheffield travel about the town several times before they are finished.' The trade was not dominated by large factories. Hallamshire was an industrial district where mutual dependence existed side by side with keen competition. The range of products was wide and firms were quick to respond to changing demand. The outstanding example of this readiness to exploit a new market was the Bowie knife, made in thousands in response to an American craze from the 1830s to the 1860s. American demand for all kinds of Sheffield products remained high until the outbreak of their Civil War. The fortunes of local firms, both big and small, were largely dependent on sales in America.

Steel

Huntsman had made Sheffield internationally famous as a steel-making centre. The industry had expanded so rapidly that by the mid-nineteenth century the Sheffield region manufactured 90 per cent of British steel and nearly half the European output. Cementation ('blister') steel furnaces had increased in size until some had the capacity to produce over 40 tons. Over 200 of them now ejected smoke into the Sheffield atmosphere. The production of high-quality crucible ('cast') steel was on a much smaller scale; although the secrets of Huntsman's methods had become widely understood, the great days of expansion were yet to come. Despite its pre-eminence, the Sheffield steel industry was still a back-yard one. Sheffield steel of both kinds was manufactured almost exclusively from Swedish and Russian bar iron, imported via Hull and the Don Navigation.

The Globe Works. In 1852 John Walters (who had recently won a prize medal at the Great Exhibition) moved his business out of the town centre to the Globe Works, which had been built in 1824 by William Ibbotson, steelmaster. Walters made table knives, spring knives, steel and tools. Bowie knives for the American market were a speciality. Between 1865 and *c*. 1910 the Globe Works was occupied by Unwin & Rodgers.

PHOTOGRAPH: CARNEGIE

Demand for both cementation and crucible steel came largely from the local cutlery and tool industries.

Sketchley's *Directory of Sheffield* (1774) named five 'manufacturers of steel'. Since the 1760s, John Marshall of Millsands had made cast and blister steel and William Parker & Co. had been described as iron and steel manufacturers. The firm of Huntsman's was well established in Attercliffe, Boulsover & Co. were sawmakers and cast steel manufacturers, and Greaves, Loftus & Brightmore of Townhead Cross, were sawmakers and (cementation) steel manufacturers. Beyond the town, Richard Swallow made cementation steel at Attercliffe Forge and Samuel and Aaron Walker made both kinds of steel, as well as iron products, alongside the Don Navigation at Masbrough.

Benjamin Huntsman had been succeeded by his son, William Huntsman (1733–1809), who had served an apprenticeship to a button maker. Sketchley's directory recorded the firm of Huntsman & Asline, button makers, in Jehu Lane. As buttons made of crucible steel did not blister, the business prospered. Buttons formed only a part of the market for Huntsman's 'cast steel', however. Much greater demand came from the makers of tools, dies, and rolls. In Gales and Martin's directory (1787) Huntsman & Asline were listed as steel refiners. Their firm was comparable in size to those of Richard Swallow at Attercliffe Forge and Booth, Binks & Hartop at Brightside Forge, the other major firms in the eastern part of Sheffield parish before the district was transformed by the giant steelworks of the second half of the nineteenth century.

Until then, steel was made by a small group of big firms and a large number of small ones. As we have seen, Greaves's Sheaf Works was opened in 1823. Other firms which grew in size during the prosperous 1840s and 1850s were Sanderson's,

left Butcher's Wheel, Arundel Street. When grinding works were powered by steam, they still kept the old name of 'wheel', rather like the cotton factories were known as 'mills'. The works of William and Samuel Butcher grew into an integrated unit that made files, edge-tools and knives. (See also page 258.)
PHOTOGRAPH: CARNEGIE

Jessop's, Butcher's and Vickers'. The Abbeydale Industrial Hamlet gives a sound idea of the modest size of the typical crucible-steel furnace of this period. So do the engravings in Pawson and Brailsford's, *Illustrated Guide to Sheffield and Neighbourhood* (1862). Even the biggest firms of later years began in a small way. Thus, Thomas Firth started in 1842 with six crucible holes and only a few employees. The owners were usually descended from old Hallamshire families and were managers who knew every part of their business. When William Ibbotson built the Globe Works by the River Don in 1824, he set up home there. As in the cutlery trades, few firms could manage on their own, but were dependent on their competitors for specialist jobs, or 'hire-work'. Even the largest steel firms did not do their own tilting and rolling. Some firms were able to thrive entirely on 'hire-work' and marketing. Hallamshire firms had to be co-operative as well as competitive, sharing their knowledge and skills. They quickly acquired a reputation for adaptability and innovation as a result of this clustering.

In the first half of the nineteenth century the steel industry was dependent on the handicraft skills of its workforce. Progress was not made through the application of scientific knowledge but by the traditional methods of ingenuity, trial and error. A clever, hard-working, risk-taking mechanic could make his fortune, however humble his beginnings. The trade was easy to enter, as Huntsman had shown, and nearly all the capital that was invested came from local sources.

Like the cutlers, the Sheffield steelmakers prospered largely because of the American market. After the Napoleonic Wars American demand for cutlery and edge tools (made from Sheffield steel) soared to new heights. Even when American industry started to make many of its own tools, Sheffield steel was still the raw material. Before 1860 tool steel and files for American machine-shops always came from Sheffield. It has been estimated that in good years a third or more of the town's steel output was sent across

Sir John Brown (1816–96) as an old man. Brown began his business career in the file and cutlery trades, but made his fortune through the manufacture of steel and railway rolling stock. His Atlas Works employed thousands of workers. Endcliffe Hall was built for him in Italianate style in 1865.
SHEFFIELD LIBRARIES, ARCHIVES AND INFORMATION: LOCAL STUDIES

the Atlantic, in addition to the vast trade in cutlery and edge tools. The American market was largely responsible for the remarkable expansion of the Sheffield crucible steel industry between the Napoleonic Wars and the American Civil War. Large fortunes were made from the American trade by the firms of Sanderson, Jessop, Vickers, Greaves, Butcher, and Cammell.

The years of greatest expansion in the manufacture of steel were yet to come, however. In 1837, as Sheffield was being connected to Rotherham by rail, Spear & Jackson, saw makers, moved out of the town to the far end of Savile Street, where they founded their Aetna Works in the middle of fields. They were pioneers of the move to the east end of the parish. The building of railways throughout the world created a demand for crucible steel: for locomotive parts, and for the machine tools to make them. Sheffield firms responded quickly. John Brown of Rockingham Street invented the conical spring buffer and moved to a new site in Furnival Street in 1848, before moving again to a much larger site in Savile Street in 1857. The town centre did not have the space to accommodate large businesses. Savile Street offered space, low rents, and level sites next to the railway, which could import coke and coal and export finished products. By 1840 the Sheffield to Rotherham railway was connected to main lines leading to London, Leeds and Birmingham. Five years later, upon the completion of the Woodhead Tunnel, a direct route to Manchester, Liverpool and America was opened. In 1847 this route was linked to Savile Street by a short, steep incline under Spital Hill. Charles Cammell established the first of the great steel firms in the east end when he built his Cyclops Works on the Sheffield side of Spear

& Jackson in 1846. Cammell had come from Hull as a young man to sell files for Ibbotson Bros and had started a steel and file business. At his Cyclops Works his firm made railway parts, rails and (later) armaments. He became one of the richest men in Sheffield and lived for a time as the squire of Norton Hall. He did not, however, become a benefactor to his adopted town.

Iron

Meanwhile, the scale of operations in the iron industry had also become much bigger. The largest firm of iron manufacturers and coal owners was that of John Booth of the Brushes, William Binks of Darnall, and John Hartop of Brightside, who owned or leased the Park Ironworks and coal mines, the Brightside Forge and Rolling Mill, the Nether Forge, and the Royds Mill and Wheel. John Booth was also a partner of Samuel and Aaron Walker at their Masbrough ironworks and at Beeley Wood tilt and forge. In 1784 Booth, Binks & Hartop installed a steam engine to pump water out of their mines. Four years later they purchased a Boulton & Watt engine for their works. Steam was also used to power William Hartop's Attercliffe Corn Mill.

New slitting mills were built at Attercliffe (1747) and Brightside (1753) and a rolling mill was constructed at Owlerton (by 1753). Under Booth, Binks & Hartop Brightside Forge became a major works and Park Furnace was developed for coke, pig and cast iron. From 1762 Thomas Boulsover rolled steel for saws and fenders at Whiteley Wood, and within a few years the Kenyons forged, rolled and slit iron at Middlewood and at their new Ponds Forge.

Other steam engines had been installed by the close of the eighteenth century; at Gibraltar, by John Parkin, a

left Crucibles at Abbeydale Industrial Hamlet.
PHOTOGRAPH: CARNEGIE

Green Lane Works. H.E.Hoole's Green Lane Works was founded in 1795, for the manufacture of stove grates and fenders. A rebuilding in the mid-nineteenth century included this attractive gateway and clock tower. The works is now occupied by modern workshops and offices and the entrance has been cleaned and re-painted.
PHOTOGRAPH: L. NUTTALL

A HISTORY OF SHEFFIELD

steel caster, and at the Kenyons's iron forge in the Ponds. Steam power gradually became a necessary and significant supplement to the water wheels along the river valleys. Steam began to replace, rather than supplement, the traditional water wheel only from the mid-1820s, when the Vulcan Works and steam rolling mill replaced the old Bennett Wheel. Most of the steam engines were installed at new locations in or close to the town, providing power for wheels, tilts, and slitting or rolling mills. One engine was used for grinding snuff, two others for corn, and one each for cotton spinning and carpet weaving.

The change of fuel in the iron furnaces, from charcoal to coke, cannot be dated precisely. The Walkers were using coke at Masbrough by 1767, Park Furnace used coke from 1786. The old charcoal–iron partnerships, dominated by rural gentlemen, withered in face of this competition. The Walkers became the leading ironmasters in the North of England, Booth, Binks & Hartop flourished, and

Forging press. The plaque on the machine says it was made at John Brown's, c.1911.

Richard Swallow had a large business at Attercliffe Forge until he went bankrupt in 1808. Many smaller iron furnaces were found in the back streets of the town. The market was expanding, for cast iron was needed not just for anvils, kitchen utensils, fenders and so on, but for engineering, machines, tools and construction. Stoves and fenders were the main products of Hoole's Green Lane Works, established in 1795 and rebuilt in the mid-nineteenth century with a clock tower at the entrance. This striking landmark in the Don Valley has recently been cleaned and repainted and now accommodates modern workshops and offices. Another well-known Sheffield firm was founded in Pear Street by David and Dennis Davy. They made sawmills, wagon axles, iron and brass castings, slide lathes, and high-pressure and condensing steam engines. By 1850, when they moved to the Park Iron Works, they were also involved in steel plant production and rolling mill design, a business that made Davy's an internationally known name in the twentieth century.

Tools

Tools had been made in Sheffield for centuries before the industry became internationally famous, but information about the early history of tool making is hard to come by. The local production of tools seems to have been on a modest scale before the middle years of the eighteenth century. Until Huntsman invented crucible steel, Sheffield was a much smaller centre of tool manufacture than were London and Birmingham. Some of the local forges are known to have made saws and no doubt cutlers could easily manufacture chisels and plane blades just as they made files and awl blades before the making of such tools became separate trades. But it was only during the mid-eighteenth century that the manufacture of saws was established as a separate business. The new trade

Mousehole Forge, *c.* 1890. The site was used by a smelting mill in 1628 and acquired its nickname from its secluded position between the rivers Rivelin and Loxley. The works had been converted into a forge by 1664. Three generations of the Bamforth family owned it in the late seventeenth and early eighteenth centuries, and in 1757 it was leased by the ironmaster, John Cockshutt of Wortley Forge. In the late eighteenth century the Armitage family took it over and made it world-famous for its anvils. Hugh Armitage is shown on the left, posing with the hammer. The wrought iron butt of the anvil is being faced with double shear steel. Mousehole Forge closed in 1933 and gradually became derelict until John and Julia Hatfield restored it. It is now a popular venue for charity events such as jazz concerts and Christmas carols.

prospered. By the time of the 1841 census 80 per cent of English saw makers worked in Sheffield.

Tool makers are absent from Sketchley's 1774 directory, but in 1787 Gales and Martin listed twelve firms of edge tool makers in the town and six more just beyond. Even if we add the names of the makers of hammers, saws, scythes, sickles and shears, the numbers are small compared with almost 200 men who were making various kinds of pen- and pocket knives and another 100 who made table knives. The 1797 *Directory* lists twelve edge-tool makers and four joiners'-tool makers compared with more than 270 pen- and pocket-knife makers in the town and its neighbourhood. By then the term 'cutler' was restricted to a knife maker; the manufacture of edge-tool trades had become recognised as a distinct business.

The cutlery firms of the latter years of the eighteenth century rarely had more than two or three partners, whereas the tool-making firms often had up to five, sometimes more. They operated on a larger scale and turned out quite a variety of products. For example, in 1797 the firm of John Sorby & Sons, founded thirty years earlier, were edge-tool and sheep-shear manufacturers in the Wicker. By 1823, when they moved to a new site on Spital Hill, they were merchants and factors, as well as manufacturers of patent sheep-shears, patent augers, edge tools, hammers, hoes, saws, spades and shovels. A similar example is provided by Philip Law, who was named in the 1774 directory as an edge-tool manufacturer of Coal Pit Lane. By 1787 Law had moved to Carver Street. Forty years later, Philip Law & Sons had also become steel merchants and their range of products included saws and files. The woodworking tools of Sheffield firms, notably those of Law,

of Kenyon, and of Newbould, now feature prominently as collectors' items in displays at Colonial Williamsburg, Virginia. The American market was as important for the tool industry as it was for cutlery and steel.

The Abbeydale Industrial Hamlet gives a good idea of the scale of enterprise of a tool-making firm at this time. Visitors can see the dam and three principal water wheels, the tilt forge, grinding shop, crucible steel shop and smithies, and the manager's house, workers' cottages, warehouses, coach house and stables. The Abbeydale Works was one of the largest water-powered sites on the River Sheaf. The site had long been used for industrial purposes when, in 1740, Thomas Goddard took a lease for 21 years in order to make scythes. For nearly two centuries the Abbeydale Works made Crown scythes (which were forged under the tilt hammers) and patent riveted scythes, as well as grass hooks, hay knives, and other agricultural edge tools. A 'sandwich' of two pieces of wrought iron around a piece of crucible steel was forged under the tilt hammer and shaped under the slower plating hammer. The steel was then drawn to a cutting edge and passed to hand forgers for hardening, tempering and grinding.

Many of the features of the museum can be dated. The Goddards enlarged the dam in 1777, built the tilt forge in 1785, and erected three houses by 1795. After 1802 the tenancy passed to a succession of different partnerships. In 1811 a new warehouse and workshops were built, about 1817 a new grinding wheel was installed, in 1829 the works began to make its own crucible steel, in the following year the manager was provided with a new house, and in 1840 the coach house and stables were built. Between 1849 and 1935 Abbeydale Works belonged to the Tyzacks, a family who were making glass in Lorraine during the fifteenth and sixteenth centuries before fleeing to Sussex as Huguenot refugees. One branch eventually moved to Stourbridge, where Benjamin Tyzack, the youngest of five sons, took up scythe making. Benjamin moved first to Cuckney, then to Norton. His son John was a scythe grinder at the Walk Mill (the site of the present Dore railway station) when he died in 1756. The Sheffield Tyzacks are descended from him. The Abbeydale Works declined after 1900, when the Tyzacks concentrated on their Little London works. The site was bought by J. G. Graves in 1935 and donated to the City. After restoration by the Council for the Conservation of Sheffield Antiquities, the museum was opened in 1970.

Other trades

By the early nineteenth century the manufacture of Old Sheffield Plate had become a mature and profitable industry, whose products added much to Sheffield's reputation as a place where high-quality wares were made. Individual units of production were on a larger scale than was normal in the cutlery industry, with men and women working at different processes in up to a dozen rooms. A new era began in 1795, when steam power was installed for the processing of silver and fused plate at the Rolling Mill (formerly the Cooper Wheel) on the River Sheaf. The silver platers became some of the richest men in town. A refining business, founded by John Read about 1760, even made a lot of money

Fred Ellis, soldering a mount to a silver tray, *c.* 1900. The photograph shows a tray and mount cramped together with wire while a blowpipe is used in the final soldering. Pearl ash was used to clean the finished product.

from reclaiming precious metals from the waste and the sweepings of the plated and solid silver trades.

The designs used by the platers followed the styles that were fashionable in silver. At first, rococo effects were favoured, but by the early 1770s the fashion was for the neo-classic style. This was soon followed by decoration executed in relief and by pierced work. Wirework baskets and pierced vessels such as salt cellars were often provided with blue glass liners. The mass-production technique of die-stamping brought a new approach to design. For example, various patterns for the bases, shafts and nozzles of candlesticks could be assembled in different combinations. Items made either of silver plate or of solid silver found a ready market. By the 1770s Sheffield silver and plated goods were sold throughout Britain and in Ireland and parts of Europe. Most Sheffield firms employed a London agent and many also had a warehouse in the capital. Soon afterwards, America and the West Indies became lucrative outlets. The home of George Washington at Mount Vernon, Virginia, contains several examples of Sheffield craftsmanship.

By 1825 Sheffield had about 28 firms manufacturing silver plate. The firm that was acknowledged as supreme for the quality of its wares was not a Sheffield one,

Mrs Cocker, burnishing silver, c.1900. Women wer employed in the silver trades to do the burnishing which produced a bright surface. The methods were unchanged from the eighteenth century. First, the tray was scrubbed with a damp linen rag dipped in white Calais sand, then scoured with a hairbrush, which was also dipped in Calais sand, and washed in water. The burnish in the photograph was constantly dipped into the 'sud pot' of soap and water to stop it marking the silver. A leather strap was used to keep the burnish smooth. The burnish was pressed hard and drawn back and forth across the tray. Finally, a 'blue' or 'blood' stone and wet rouge were use to remove marks.

however, but that of Matthew Boulton, who had begun production at his Soho Works, Birmingham, about 1762. Boulton's chief rival in Sheffield was the firm which had been established in 1784 by Samuel Roberts and George Cadman. Roberts was granted numerous patents for his products and manufacturing techniques between 1790 and 1830. By then, the great days of the industry were numbered. In 1840 the new method of electro-plating was patented by Elkington's of Birmingham. It quickly superseded fused plate and many Sheffield firms turned to the new method. The Old Sheffield Plate industry had lasted about 100 years. No works survives sufficiently to form the basis of an industrial museum, but a fine collection of plated wares is on display in the Weston Park Museum.

It was less to Sheffield's credit that the goods that were made from solid silver or fused plate could be imitated in products that were largely made of tin, dressed up by salesmen as 'Britannia' metal. As we have seen, the origins of this trade are obscure. The first reference to it is in the 1797 directory, when Froggatt, Couldwell & Lean were listed as manufacturers of 'Britannia Metal goods' and

A HISTORY OF SHEFFIELD

as silver platers. The industry expanded during the second decade of the nineteenth century, so that thirteen firms were in business by 1821. Some of them were using steam power to roll their metal. As a cheaper substitute for Old Sheffield Plate, Britannia metal looked the part and sold well in both Britain and America.

The demand for coal had never been greater. It was required, either in its raw form or as coke, not only for fires in the rapidly growing number of houses and cutlers' smithies, but for steel converting, iron manufacture, brick making, lime burning, glass making, brewing, baking, soap boiling, hat making, paper making, dyeing and so on. Local coal varied in quality, even within seams. 'Park hard' coal was preferred by the cutlers, 'Darnall hard' was the best coking coal. The seams ranged from the thin ganister seam in the west, to the five-foot Silkstone seam under the Park and the nine-foot Barnsley bed further east. The old pits had been shallow, but during the time that John Curr, a Durham man, was in charge of the Duke of Norfolk's collieries shafts were sunk to a depth of 120 yards. Curr acquired a national reputation as a colliery engineer. His methods of winding and haulage, which involved inclined planes and 'drawing engines' of

Installation of a steam pumping engine at Nunnery Colliery in the late 1860s. The engine was needed to drain the pit once the company began to mine the Parkgate and Silkstone seams. Wheels and wooden runners are being used to hoist the beam into position. It had been brought from Walker & Eaton's Spital Hill Engineering works by 45 horses. The engine was capable of lifting 1,000 gallons of water each stroke, at the rate of 2½ strokes per minute. It was used until 1933 and demolished in the early 1960s.

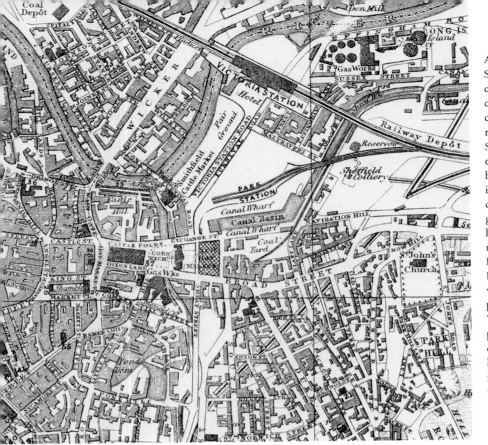

A detail of a map of Sheffield, 1864. The coal yard by the canal basin and the coal depot by the railway indicate how Sheffield's industrial development has benefited from improved communications. A gas works had been built between the railway and the River Don. Park Hill and the Wicker were now densely populated suburbs. The medieval pattern of the central streets, however, remained intact.

AUTHOR COLLECTION

right The Sharrow Snuff Mills of Wilsons [sic] & Co., established on the Porter Brook in the mid eighteenth century. The manager's house was built in brick later in the century. The water-wheel is still in working order and both the goit and dam survive intact. Various nineteenth-century buildings, including the counting house warehouse, stable block and a new mill of c.1885, are arranged around a courtyard. This family-run business became a Limited Company in 1952

PHOTOGRAPH: CARNEGI

his own design, were adopted in many other coalfields. He also thought up ingenious solutions to the problems of ventilation and flooding. His drainage soughs from the Park and Manor Collieries stretched for one-and-a-half and two miles to the Sheaf. The Darnall Colliery was drained by a 1,500-yard long sough across Attercliffe Common to the River Don. Newcomen-type steam engines were installed where the surface terrain was unsuitable or the pits were too deep. The first one appears to have been the 'Fire Engine' on Attercliffe or Darnall Common that was marked on Thomas Jeffreys's map of 1767–72, probably to drain the Greenland Colliery. Another steam engine was installed in 1790 at the Duke of Norfolk's Attercliffe Colliery, a little further north. The opening of the Sheffield Canal in 1819 provided an enormous boost to the local trade. Leather's map of 1823 marks the 'Coal Yard' that the Park Colliery had constructed close to the canal basin. With the coming of canals and railways, the Yorkshire and Derbyshire coalfield was at last able to compete with the North-east coalfield in national markets.

The dramatic developments in many of Sheffield's industries in the late eighteenth and early nineteenth centuries tend to obscure the fact that many old trades continued much as before. The Rawsons, Aldams, Hooles, and others tanned leather at Upperthorpe, Crookes, Little Sheffield, Wardsend and Neepsend in the old way, though in 1758 the Rawsons had converted their Ponds site into a brewery. The industry failed to grow in the nineteenth century, in the way that it did

A HISTORY OF SHEFFIELD

in Walsall or Leeds; only the new tannery at Meersbrook competed successfully. Other trades benefited from the growth of the staple industries. The paper mills along the river valleys, for example, expanded production to meet the increased demand for wrapping paper and stationery.

Meanwhile, the button trade flourished as never before. An inventory of the goods of Thomas Holy, taken in 1758, listed more than a quarter million buttons made of brass, tin, zinc, pewter, horn, glass or pearl, with some lacquered or silvered. Holy sold his wares throughout Yorkshire and in neighbouring counties; his son and grandson sold in national and international markets. A younger Thomas Holy joined Thomas and William Newbould in a major button-manufacturing and international mercantile business. Sketchley's 1774 directory separated fourteen manufacturers into metal- and horn buttonmakers and pro-vides the first reference to 'vigo buttons', which were made of horn; the name may be connected with the town of Vigo in north-west Spain, but the meaning of the term remains mysterious. Gales and Martin's 1787 directory named 23 button manufacturers in or close to town, thirteen of whom used horn. The trade appears to have peaked about that time.

Although brass was commonly used for buttons, only a few brass makers set up business in Sheffield. The town had even fewer pewterers, and the production of white and red lead was confined to the works established in 1759. Demand for its products came from the growing building industry, for white lead was used as a base for paint and putty, and red lead was ideal for priming and waterproofing.

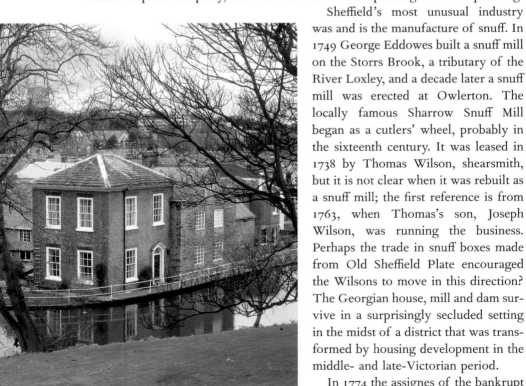

Sheffield's most unusual industry was and is the manufacture of snuff. In 1749 George Eddowes built a snuff mill on the Storrs Brook, a tributary of the River Loxley, and a decade later a snuff mill was erected at Owlerton. The locally famous Sharrow Snuff Mill began as a cutlers' wheel, probably in the sixteenth century. It was leased in 1738 by Thomas Wilson, shearsmith, but it is not clear when it was rebuilt as a snuff mill; the first reference is from 1763, when Thomas's son, Joseph Wilson, was running the business. Perhaps the trade in snuff boxes made from Old Sheffield Plate encouraged the Wilsons to move in this direction? The Georgian house, mill and dam survive in a surprisingly secluded setting in the midst of a district that was transformed by housing development in the middle- and late-Victorian period.

In 1774 the assignes of the bankrupt

William Bower sold his silk mill to Joseph Wells and James Rickards, silk merchants of London. The 80 workers were mainly women and children who operated over 2,500 silk reels and the same number of spindles. By 1789 the works had been converted into a cotton mill by Wells, Heathfield & Co. Two years later, a steam engine was installed to supplement the power provided by the water wheel, but in 1792 the mill suffered the first of two major fires. A second mill, with a steam engine, was built in 1805 on the site of the adjoining Kelham Wheel, but in 1810 the bigger mill was seriously damaged by fire and subsequently largely demolished. The second fire seems to have caused the collapse of the firm, for in 1815 the works, having been rebuilt and made fireproof, was auctioned by the bankers Walkers, Eyre & Stanley. An advertisement in the local newspaper, the *Iris*, on 21 February 1815 offered for sale:

> All that capital new erected cotton factory, situate at Sheffield aforesaid, with the Steam Engine, Clerk's House, and two other Dwelling Houses, Counting House, extensive Warehouse, preparing Rooms, and Smiths' Turners', and other Workshops, thereto adjoining, lately belonging to Messrs Heathfield & Co.

The Mill was said to be six storeys high, 142 ft long, and 29 ft broad inside. A 68 hp Boulton & Watt steam engine had recently been installed and 4,096 spindles and 1,290 mule spindles were at work. The smaller cotton mill had 3,326 spindles, worked by a water wheel and a 20 hp Boulton & Watt engine. In 1829 the larger mill was converted into a workhouse; the smaller mill returned to grinding.

The *Returns of Cotton and other Mills* for 1803 and 1804 record an inspectors' visit to the Sheffield Cotton Mill on 29 November 1803, when all except three of the 129 apprenticed children were found to be well, their rooms airy and clean,

their provisions good, and their morals well attended to. An account of their weekly fare noted that milk pottage was supplied for breakfasts, that either boiled meat, stew, baked puddings, milk pottage or bread and butter were provided for dinners, and that suppers consisted of milk pottage or water gruel.

Young children commonly began work at the age of 11, though some started much earlier at six or seven. In the 1860s some boys of seven or eight regularly worked night shifts of 12 hours in the new east-end steelworks, for boys were cheaper than men. Girls were very rarely employed in iron and steel works or at the grinding wheels, but could obtain employment as file cutters, in the hair seating trade, or in warehouses finishing, wrapping and packing. Girls as well as boys worked in the local coal mines before the 1842 Act, hurrying loaded corves and attending ventilation trap doors. But the usual job for a teenage girl was that of domestic servant. The 1841 census calculated that 71 per cent of Sheffield girls under the age of 20 were employed in this way. Adult women often found work as 'buffer girls' in the silver-plate trade, doing the dirty job of polishing. One firm of platers employed 300 women. Several hundred others found work in the cutlery trades.

In 1843 the Revd J. C. Symons observed that:

> Generally speaking the labour of the child is enforced by the conviction in the child's mind that work is less painful than blows. At the same time I am convinced that there is no great amount of ill-usage of the children, unless by the small cutlers. I do not think inhumanity is a common vice among the Sheffield workmen, who notwithstanding their vices, are generally far from bad-hearted.

The hours of work varied from trade to trade, but could be as many as 12 to 14 a day, with half-an-hour for breakfast, an hour for lunch, and half-an-hour for tea. The monotony was relieved by the continuing tradition of 'Saint Monday' and sometimes 'Saint Tuesday' as well. The Saturday half-holiday became common from the 1840s. Official holidays consisted of half a day on Shrove Tuesday, two half or two whole days at Easter and at Whitsuntide, two half days at the fairs in summer and November, and four to eight days at Christmas. The Christmas holiday was preceded by the hectic activity of 'Bull Week'.

The poor

The workhouse at West Bar Green was visited by Sir F. M. Eden in 1797, as part of a national enquiry. His report in the abridged version of *The State of the Poor* reads:

> There are 148 persons (mostly old and infirm, lunatics, soldiers' wives, or young children) in the Workhouse. Some are employed in spinning for the use of the house. Men who are able to work are sent to various employments in the town. Their earnings are about £170 a year. The Workhouse is situated in an airy part of the town. The staircases are narrow and steep; the lodging rooms about 9ft 6in square with two beds in each, except one which is rather

larger and contains 6 beds. Beds and pillows are filled with chaff. Each house has 2 coarse sheets, a coverlet and a blanket of the woollen manufacture of the house. The number of beds is 43. Two, three, and sometimes even four paupers sleep in a bed.

Bill of fare: Breakfast – every day, water pottage, gravy (forming a sort of soup) and bread. Dinner – Sunday, Tuesday, Thursday beef, bread, broth and potatoes, or cabbage and beer; Monday, Wednesday, Friday, puddings and sauce, and beer; Saturday, cheese, bread and beer. Supper – Sunday, Tuesday, Thursday, broth and bread; Monday, Wednesday, Friday, bread and beer; Saturday, milk pottage and bread. In summer milk pottage is occasionally served for breakfast and supper. The Poor are allowed to carry their breakfasts and suppers into their lodging rooms, but must eat their dinners in the hall, and leave on the table what they cannot consume. 3oz of cheese are allowed on cheese days to grown persons. The dinners at Easter and Whitsuntide are veal, bacon, and plum pudding. The old people dine first; what they leave forms part of the dinner of the children. The food is plentiful and good. There are 972 out-pensioners, any of whom have families. The usual allowance to a pauper with one child is 1s. 6d. a week. There are several public charities in Sheffield, including two schools. In the winter of 1794–95 a subscription was opened for the relief of the Poor and £1,000 subscribed, with which flour was bought and retailed at reduced prices. The Duke of Norfolk likewise distributed £100 in coals ... Wheaten bread is universally used here. Malt liquor and butcher's meat form part of the diet of all ranks. The tradesman, artisan and labourer all live well, and in general industry is a more prominent feature in their conduct than economy. Almost every manufacturer, however, is a member of a friendly society ... Wages of labourers are 2s. a day, with one pint of ale, and half a quartern loaf; masons 2s. 8d. a day, assistants 2s. In the cutlery trade men earn 10s to 30s. a week. Women follow various employments. Those who spin lint earn 6d. a day; washer-women 1s a day and victuals. The demand for labour has decreased since the war began, but as many men have joined the army and navy, those who are able and willing to work may earn a good livelihood. The late rapid rise of the rates has been ascribed to the war, which has thrown many families on the parish, to the stagnation of trade, to the high price of provisions, and by some to the introduction of machinery. In the opinion of such persons it is a national misfortune that a wool spinner can by means of machines do ten times the work he could without them. About 20 removals a year; one or two usually contested. Certificates very rarely granted ... There were 395 ale-houses in 1791.

The workhouse was no longer at the edge of the town, as it had been when it was built, but was now surrounded by houses. As the population grew and the number of paupers increased, the accommodation became insufficient. In 1829 the cotton mill was converted into a workhouse and the old one was taken down. The Poor Law Amendment Act (1834) replaced the arrangements that had been in force since the late sixteenth century by new unions of parishes or townships.

Sir Francis Chantrey (1781–1841). Born in a small farmhouse at Jordanthorpe, Chantrey was apprenticed to a wood carver and gilder in Sheffield High Street. He became a portrait painter in Paradise Square before moving to London. He achieved fame as a sculptor and was knighted in 1835. King George IV paid 300 guineas for his bust. Chantrey was buried at Norton, where he is commemorated by an obelisk at the edge of the churchyard.

SHEFFIELD LIBRARIES ARCHIVES AND INFORMATION: LOCAL STUDIES

A HISTORY OF SHEFFIELD

The Sheffield district was reorganised into two unions in 1837: 'Sheffield' consisted of Sheffield, Brightside, Attercliffe and Handsworth; 'Ecclesall' comprised Ecclesall, Upper and Nether Hallam, Norton, Totley, Dore and Beauchief. The Sheffield Union inherited the workhouse that had once been a cotton mill and the Brightside bierlow workhouse at the top of Rock Street. The Ecclesall Union inherited the Psalter Lane poorhouse and another building at Crookes; in 1843 these were replaced by a new workhouse at Nether Edge, which was later converted into a hospital.

Newspapers

A great deal of miscellaneous material about Sheffield in the late eighteenth and early nineteenth centuries can be obtained from the local newspapers. A hundred years earlier, London papers had been available a few days late at Sheffield inns, the coffee house, and at barbers' shops. Sheffielders were among the subscribers to the *Northampton Mercury* by 1720, but it was not until 1754 that they had a paper of their own. Only a few copies survive of the *Sheffield Weekly Journal*, which Francis Lister of the Market Place published on Tuesdays, for after his death in 1755, it was amalgamated with the *Doncaster Flying Post* ... In 1760 William Ward, also of the Market Place and Sheffield's only printer, started the *Sheffield Public Advertiser*. This survived until 1793, when it was merged with the Tory *Courant* ... The rival radical paper, the *Sheffield Register*, was started in 1787 by Joseph Gales of the Hartshead, who at the height of the political troubles of 1794 fled to America to avoid arrest. His paper changed its name to the *Iris* under the editorship of James Montgomery, previously Gales's assistant.

These papers were largely concerned with national news, culled from London newspapers, but comment on local matters ranged widely. For example, on 5 December 1794 the *Iris* observed that:

> The incessant rains which have generally prevailed for some time past, and the uncommon warmth of the weather, for the season of the year, have occasioned in many parts of the country low fevers and other epidemic complaints. The town of Sheffield continues happily free from any unusual providence of disease. It has often been remarked that infectious distempers are not apt to spread in this place. The smoke, produced by the manufactories, is thought by many persons to be serviceable in this view.

On 5 October 1798 the *Iris* reported that:

> On Monday [17 September] a Cricket Match was played at Stannington, for twenty-two guineas, between players of that place and this town; when the former won the latter by twenty-five notches at three innings – And, on Monday last, at Owler Grove, between the same players, there was another

match, for twenty-two guineas also, when Stannington again beat Sheffield at one inning only.

Much of the information of local interest was contained in the advertisements. For example, on 12 September 1794 the *Iris* advertised:

> Runaway Apprentice – John Grayson, apprenticed to Robert Wilde, tailor, Attercliffe – £1 1s. 0d. reward. The said Apprentice is 5 feet 8 inches high, slender, marked with the small-pox, and sandy-coloured hair; Had on when he went a brown coat, black and red striped waistcoat, and thickset breeches; and had with him a blue coat, buff waistcoat, and velveteen breeches.

New papers were started during the nineteenth century. In 1807 Todd's *Sheffield Mercury*, a Tory newspaper, was launched. Eventually, the *Mercury* and the *Iris* were absorbed into the Tory *Sheffield Times* (1846). From 1819 to 1861 the radical *Sheffield and Rotherham Independent* was published as a weekly by Andrew Bacon, and then as a daily by the Leader family. The first local daily was the *Sheffield Daily Telegraph*, launched in 1855, shortly after the repeal of the Stamp Act. *The Star* was first published in 1885, though under a different name at first.

Politics and religion

Newspapers are a prime source of information about the political strife of the 1790s, when Sheffield became one of the most radical towns in the country. The huge increase in the population had turned Sheffield into a bustling place whose governing bodies seemed increasingly anachronistic. They soon proved inadequate in face of mob violence. In 1791 the Cutlers' Company lost its ancient right to regulate admissions into its trades. In the same year rioters for a time stopped the enclosure of Crookes Moor, until a company of Light Dragoons arrived from Nottingham on 27 July. Excited by their arrival, a large crowd gathered in the town centre. About 9 p.m. a mob of several hundred people attacked the nearest symbol of authority – the town gaol in King Street – breaking its windows and freeing the prisoners. The shout then went up: 'To Broom Hall', the home of Vicar Wilkinson, the town's only magistrate. The mob broke all his windows, smashed part of his furniture, damaged and burned his library, and set his haystacks on fire, before they were dispersed by the Dragoons. Arriving back in town, they broke the windows of the Duke of Norfolk's agent, Vincent Eyre. The following day, more soldiers arrived from York and order was restored. Five rioters who had been arrested were examined a few days later at the Tontine Inn by Col. R. A. Athorpe of Dinnington Hall and committed to York assizes. Four of them were subsequently released, but John Bennett was found guilty of arson and hanged on 7 September. The Town Trust paid £561 expenses in legal costs and compensation for the victims of the riot. Sheffield had never witnessed anything as serious before.

Populous manufacturing towns such as Sheffield still had no Members of Parliament. Some of the inhabitants had the right to vote for county MPs at elections held at York, but the mass of the population were disenfranchised. During the 1790s Sheffielders became articulate in their demand for reform. The Sheffield Society for Constitutional Information held its first meetings in December 1791 and soon forged links with a similar body in London. These two societies were amongst the earliest working-class political organisations in Britain. The Sheffield society grew rapidly, so that by June 1792 eight branches were meeting regularly at different houses and pubs, all on the same evening; a general meeting was held once a month. Skilled cutlers, earning good wages, many of them sober Methodists, formed the core of a membership that rapidly rose to about 2,000. Admission to meetings was by ticket, and good order was maintained, yet an undercurrent of violence cannot be denied. Steel blades for pike-staves were offered to members of the London Constitutional Society. A Sheffield cutler, Henry Hill, made 120–140 steel blades; his claim that they were purely for self defence was not believed by the authorities.

The public mouthpiece for parliamentary reform was Joseph Gales's print works at Hartshead, which published his newspaper, the *Sheffield Register*. In 1791–92 a sixpenny pamphlet edition of Tom Paine's *Rights of Man*, published in two parts, attracted 1,400 subscribers. The song of a Sheffield filecutter, Joseph Mather's, *God Save Great Thomas Paine*, set to the tune of the national anthem, was hugely popular. The situation became tense when working-class Sheffielders began wholeheartedly to applaud the progress of the French Revolution. On 27 November 1792 a public event was organised in the centre of Sheffield to celebrate the victories of the French Revolutionary armies over Austria and Prussia in the Low Countries. A whole ox, paid for by subscription, was roasted throughout the previous night, then drawn through the crowded streets, cut up, and distributed to the poor. The procession lampooned Edmund Burke, author of *Reflections on the French Revolution* and critic of the 'swinish multitude', by depicting him riding on a swine. A caricature painting of Britannia was given an upper part representing Henry Dundas, the Home Secretary, and a lower part showing an ass. Late in 1792 the authorities took the precaution of building a cavalry barracks on the edge of the town, near Shalesmoor. The execution of Louis XVI in January 1793 tempered the local enthusiasm for the French Revolution. When war broke out between Britain and France in February, the public mood changed dramatically.

The hardship of the war years was felt particularly in 1794–95, when high corn prices brought distress to all parts of the country. The campaign for reform was waged with renewed vigour. The government, fearing that any concessions would take Britain down the same path as France, were equally determined on repression. After a public meeting held on Castle Hill on 7 April 1794, Henry Yorke, the principal speaker, was arrested and sentenced to two years imprisonment for conspiracy. Joseph Gales fled to America. In January 1795, James Montgomery, Gales's successor at the *Iris*, was jailed for six months for publishing a song that was critical of the government.

In August 1795 corn prices throughout the country reached record heights. A Corn Committee, led by Dr John Browne, sold grain at low prices in Sheffield, and Henry Hartop of the Attercliffe corn mill became a local hero when he sent

his waggons full of cheap flour into the town. Feelings were running high, when on 4 August 1795 crass action by the authorities turned a trivial incident into a riot. After their evening parade, some privates from the local barracks refused to disperse because they had not been paid, and a crowd gathered to see what would happen. The officer in charge sent for Colonel Athorpe, the magistrate of Dinnington Hall, who was dining at Wentworth Woodhouse. According to Montgomery's account in the *Iris*, Athorpe rode into the amazed crowd brandishing his sword. Two people were killed in the ensuing struggle. Athorpe's acquittal by the subsequent enquiry met with Joseph Mather's fiercest scorn. The eight verses of Mather's song, *The Norfolk Street Riots*, were a bitter attack on what he regarded as corrupt government:

> Corruption tells me homicide
> Is wilful murder justified,
> A striking precedent was tried
> In August, 'ninety-five.

> When arm'd assassins dress'd in blue
> Most wantonly their townsmen slew,
> And magistrates and juries too
> At murder did connive.

Mather referred to Athorpe as 'a madman drunk' and 'the bloody tyrant', but although he was bound over to keep silent for a year, he was not punished. The magistrates recognised his popular status and acted discreetly. They were nevertheless firm in stamping out further political agitation. The Sheffield Society for Constitutional Information never met in public again.

Grain warehouse at Victoria Quay. Built in 1819 at the terminus of the Sheffield Canal, it was cleaned and restored in 1994. Note the hoists in the gables, and the stone-dressed arched openings at ground level.
PHOTOGRAPH: CARNEGIE

right Plaque in the redesigned Town Hall gardens to Samuel Holberry, who was resurrected as a local hero in the 1970s when the Sheffield Labour Party moved sharply left.
PHOTOGRAPH: CARNEGIE

A HISTORY OF SHEFFIELD

Long after the Napoleonic Wars, a new campaign for parliamentary reform, following the disappointment of the Reform Act of 1832, was focused on the six points of a charter of demands. Chartism, as the movement became known, attracted a large number of supporters in Sheffield and other manufacturing towns. In September 1838 a meeting in Paradise Square attracted a huge crowd, when Ebenezer Elliott and Isaac Ironside were the main speakers. Several thousand people packed Paradise Square again in May 1839. By this time, the Chartists had become deeply divided between those, such as Elliott and Ironside, who advocated 'moral force' and those who felt that 'physical force' was necessary. The mood turned ugly, with 'torchlight' meetings on Sky Edge and elsewhere. In January 1840 Samuel Holberry, a Sheffield working man, led an uprising, in which he planned to seize the Town Hall and the Tontine Inn, murder the watchmen and set fire to the houses of the magistrates and other important people. The plot was betrayed, weapons were discovered, and Holberry was imprisoned for four years at York assizes, with shorter sentences for the others. Samuel Holberry became a local hero after his death in prison and a large crowd attended his funeral. The 'moral force' Chartists, led by Ironside, remained strong and were able to attract another huge crowd to Paradise Square on 13 March to express sympathy with the new French revolution- aries. On 16 April 1848 a large crowd met peacefully on Attercliffe Common, and on the following day another mass meeting was held in

Paradise Square. The national movement collapsed after 1848, but the Sheffield Chartists managed to retain their momentum. By November 1849 they held 29 seats on the borough council. They were particularly influential in their efforts to improve the health of the town and the treatment of paupers.

In 1841 Ebenezer Elliott told the Revd J. C. Symons's enquiry into the moral and physical conditions of the young persons employed in the Sheffield trades that neither the churches nor the chapels were well filled, and that educational provision was not keeping pace with the increase in population. He observed gloomily:

> Let any stranger, who happens to have formed a high opinion of the intelligence and morality of the workmen of Sheffield, take a walk on a Sunday morning through the Old Park Wood, or visit the lanes and footpaths adjoining the town, and he will be surprised to meet group after group of boys and young men playing at pitch penny, or fighting their bull-dogs, and insulting every decently dressed passenger.

These were the sort of men, he claimed, who supported 'physical-force' Chartism. They were not the type who attended the Mechanics' Institute.

A survey taken a few years earlier in 1838 by the Revd Thomas Sutton estimated that only one-third of the working-class children of Sheffield received proper instruction. About half the children who were registered could read, but only a quarter could write. In 1843 J. C. Symons reported that 'two-thirds of the working-class children and young persons are growing up in a state of ignorance, and are unable to read'. He thought that not more than 50 per cent attended school regularly and that the quality of the teaching was poor.

The schools that were available ranged from the old Grammar School in Campo Lane and the Boys' Charity School in the north-east corner of the church-yard (founded in 1710 and rebuilt in 1825) to the National, Lancasterian, Ragged, and Sunday schools and a variety of private schools, including small 'dame schools' of uncertain value. The former National School in Carver Street survives intact with its inscription: 'Built by Subscription 1812'. In 1792 the *Sheffield Register* had praised the work of the local Sunday Schools, which had 'greatly improved the morals of the children, as may be seen by their constantly decent and orderly behaviour.' Many parents, however, preferred to send their children to private schools rather than to the rigidly formal and doctrinal denominational schools. Provision for what would later be called secondary and adult education came in the 1830s and 1840s. The Mechanics Institute (1832) and the Owenite Hall of Science (1839) taught practical courses, while the Church of England Educational Institute (1839) and the People's College (1842), founded by the Revd R. S. Bayley, a Congregational minister, provided liberal education. The Collegiate School was opened in 1836 and the Wesleyan Proprietary Grammar School was founded two years later.

The Sunday School movement formed part of the evangelical revival of the late eighteenth and early nineteenth centuries. We have seen that the earliest Methodists faced fierce hostility, but on 15 July 1779 John Wesley 'preached in Paradise Square, to the largest congregation I ever saw on a week-day.' In 1781 he described Sheffielders as 'a lively and affectionate people.' The Methodist advance began in earnest after 1800. According to its inscription, their large new

James Montgomery (1771–1854). Born in Scotland, the son of Moravian missionaries, Montgomery inherited his parents' serious evangelical purpose. He was prominent in national movements for social and educational progress, such as the abolition of the slave trade and the welfare of chimney sweeps, and acquired a national reputation as a poet, hymn writer, essayist and editor. In Sheffield he edited the Radical newspaper, *The Iris*, as a young man and became leader of the local Sunday School movement. Montgomery Hall is named after him.

A HISTORY OF SHEFFIELD

chapel was built in Carver Street in 1804, 'when the nation was engaged in an expensive war, and threatened with extermination by a haughty usurper.' By the time that Brunswick Chapel was built in dignified classical style in 1833 the Wesleyan Methodists had become respectable pillars of society. Methodism was already splintering into different sects, however. The Wesleyan Methodists remained the strongest body, but the Methodist New Connexion (which appealed particularly to the urban poor) broke away in 1797, the Primitive Methodists formed their own organisation in 1812, and Sheffield became the centre of the new Wesleyan Reform movement in 1849. All these denominations attracted strong support in the town and its neighbourhood.

Some of the Old Dissenting congregations responded enthusiastically to the evangelical revival, but others eschewed such enthusiasm and became Unitarian once the central doctrine of that church was made legal in 1813. The Catholics, too, now attracted large numbers to their new church of St Marie's, largely because of Irish immigration. Meanwhile, the Church of England was at last making a determined effort to respond to the growth of industrial towns such as Sheffield. The old parish church was heavily restored in the 1790s and again in 1842, and Sheffield benefited from the 'Million Act' (1818), which provided state funds for new Anglican churches where provision was woefully inadequate. Four 'Million Act Churches' – St George, St Philip, St Mary, and Christ Church, Attercliffe – were built in Sheffield during the 1820s, each in the neo-Gothic style that had become the height of fashion for ecclesiastical buildings. In the 1840s the ancient parish of Sheffield was at last divided up, into 25 new ecclesiastical districts.

Fulwood Old Unitarian Chapel, built in 1729 from a bequest of William Ronksley, schoolmaster and author of children's text books. The parsonage was attached in 1754, and the small school-room (left) soon afterwards.

National School, Carver Street. The Church of England and the non-conformist chapels were the main providers of elementary education before the Education Act of 1870. In 1817 the National Society for the Education of the Poor in the Principles of the Established Church throughout England and Wales took over the schools that had previously been built by the SPCK and began their own programme of building. The inscription on the National School in Carver Street informs us that it was built by subscription in 1812.

PHOTOGRAPH: CARNEGIE

The former Carver Street Methodist Church. Built in 1804 on the western edge of the town, this Wesleyan Methodist chapel soon became one of the leading nonconformist meeting houses in Sheffield. Its congregation numbered 766 in 1851.

PHOTOGRAPH: CARNEGIE

  A HISTORY OF SHEFFIELD

On 29 March 1851 a national census of church attendance was held for the first and only time. Its findings provided little comfort for the faithful, for well over half the population of England and Wales attended neither church or chapel. The shock to the established church was compounded by the revelation that about half of those who did attend religious services preferred those of the Nonconformist chapels. In the West Riding of Yorkshire the proportion of Nonconformists was even higher. The great majority of Sheffielders never attended any religious service, except those of baptism, marriage and burial. The enormous number of pubs proved a far greater attraction for many.

All Saints Church, Ecclesall. The medieval lords of the sub-manor of Ecclesall had a chapel-of-ease, served by canons of Beauchief Abbey. This was rebuilt by Puritans in the 1620s. Then in 1789 work began on a new church at a different site. This in turn was almost completely rebuilt in the form seen here in 1843 and extended to the east in 1908 (partly obscured in this photograph by the trees to the right).

PHOTOGRAPH: CARNEGIE

The highest attendances at the various churches and chapels in Sheffield on census day were as follows [the dates in brackets are the dates of the buildings]:

Church of England

Sheffield, St Peter: 1200

Sheffield, St Paul: 375

Sheffield, St James perpetual curacy: [no return]

Sheffield, St George: 1300

Sheffield, St Philip (1828): 650

Sheffield, St Mary (1830): 422

Sheffield, Hospital Chapel: [no return]

Moorfields, St Jude: 60

Hollis Croft: 20–50

Eldon Street, St Jude (1849): 120

Carver Street National School (1851): 260 [including Sunday School scholars]

Wicker, Trinity (1848): 800

Crookes, St Thomas (1840): 108

Pitsmoor, Christ Church (1850): 164

Fulwood, Christ Church (1828): 127

Ranmoor, St John the Evangelist (1838–40): 1000

Beauchief Abbey: 20

Norton, St James: 166

Ecclesall, All Saints: 270

Ecclesall Union Dining Hall and Chapel [i.e. Nether Edge Workhouse]: 105

Attercliffe, Christ Church (1826): 138

Darnall, Holy Trinity (1845): 48

Brightside bierlow, licensed room: c.70

Heeley, Christ Church (1848): 280

Gleadless (1838): 150

Handsworth, St Mary: 230

Independent or Congregationalist

Nether Chapel (1715, rebuilt 1827): 243

Lee Croft Chapel (c.1785): 169

Howard Street Chapel (1790): 290

Garden Street Chapel (before 1800): 140

Queen Street Chapel (before 1800): 454

Westfield Terrace, Mount Zion Chapel (1834): 345

Fulwood Chapel (1729): 33

Attercliffe Zion Chapel (rebuilt 1805): 126

Attercliffe Salem Chapel (1828): 60

Brightside school (c.1818): 42

Handsworth Woodhouse Zion Chapel (1850): 47

Gleadless, Bethel Chapel (c.1820): 35

Unitarian

Upper Chapel (1700, rebuilt 1848): 500

Baptist

Townhead Street Chapel (Particular; 1814): 264

Eldon Street school room (General): 95

General Baptist Chapel [minister at Spring Lane] (1842): 252

Port Mahon Chapel (1839): 360

Quaker

Meeting House Lane (before 1800): 136

Handsworth Woodhouse (before 1800): 52

Wesleyan Methodist

Norfolk Street Chapel (1780, enlarged 1823): 600

Wesleyan Chapel [minister at Surrey Street] (1830–31): 500

Shalesmoor, Ebenezer Wesleyan Chapel (1823): 340

Carver Street Chapel (1804): 766

London Road, Brunswick Chapel (1834): 502

Wesley College Chapel (1840): 400

Manor Chapel or school: 25

Park Wesleyan Chapel (1830): 481

Wicker, Stanley Street Chapel (1831): 30

Bridgehouses Chapel (1833): 261

Grimesthorpe Chapel (1833): 35

Attercliffe Chapel: 40

Darnall Chapel (1822): 40

Handsworth Chapel (1814): 70

Handsworth Woodhouse Chapel (1841): 52

Hollinsend Chapel (before 1820): 20

Heeley Chapel (1826): 50

Totley Chapel (1848): 52

Hallam Chapel (1783): 45

Crookes Chapel (1836): 129

Owlerton Chapel (1822): 170

Abbeydale (expelled Wesleyans), dwelling house: 40

Sharrow Vale (Wesleyan Methodists expelled; 1845): 60

Handsworth, Reform Preaching Room (1850): 80

Richmond, a house: 40

Methodist New Connexion

Scotland Street Chapel (before 1800): 550

South Street Chapel (1827): 446

Walkley Chapel (1819): 42

Attercliffe Chapel (1836): 90

Hankridge school room (1845; 'erecting new building Talbot Street'): 45

Primitive Methodist

Bethel Chapel (1836): 1550

Hollinsend Lane, dwelling house (1850): 16

Roman Catholic

St Marie's (1847–50): 2000

Victoria Street: 250

Other denominations

St Luke Episcopal Chapel, Dyers Hill (1851): 25

Christians, Meeting Room (c.1840): 60

Israelites, Meeting Room, Paradise Square (before 1800): 27

Evangelists Room, holding the faith of the One Holy Catholic and Apostolic Church (1850): [no return]

The Church of Jesus Christ of Latter Day saints, lately a dwelling house: 46

The 1841 Census for Sheffield

The pattern of surnames in Sheffield on the eve of the greater mobility brought about by the railways can be captured by an analysis of the 1841 census, the first to provide full details of the names of all the inhabitants. The 55 most common surnames in the parish of Sheffield, each of them possessed by more than 300 people, were as follows [in their most popular spellings]:

> Smith (1,624), Taylor (1,022), Wilson (925), Walker (678), Hall (660), Turner (628), Shaw (605), Wright (586), Johnson (580), Ward (573), Thompson (572), Rodgers (571), Brown (567), Haigh (563), Jackson (541), Parkin (531), Green (521), Marshall (503), White (486), Lee (485), Barker (466), Clark (452), Roberts (450), Robinson (443), Hobson (434), Morton (429), Wilkinson (418), Wood (405), Booth (400), Wragg (397), Ellis (394), Fox (392), Gregory (388), Wild (386), Greaves (376), Hill (373), Lindley (366), Crookes (364), Harrison (364), Cooper (356), Marsden (353), Pearson (351), Brammall (345), Stephenson (338), Webster (337), Holmes (336), Allen (335), Bradshaw (324), Elliott (323), Hudson (318), Furness (317), Parker (314), Sykes (313), Staniforth (307), and Foster (300).

The list is headed by the most common names in England. Some of these names are ranked differently than in other places, however. Hall is not quite so common elsewhere, nor is Rodgers (especially in the the Sheffield version of the usual spelling). Parkin and Wragg are northern names, and so are surnames derived from various place-names, such as Morton, Lindley, Marsden, Brammall and

Bradshaw. Some of the local locative surnames – notably Crookes and Staniforth – were formed in Sheffield in the Middle Ages. Other common surnames that were coined locally from minor place-names several centuries earlier include: Broomhead (168), Bullas (93), Creswick (101), Dungworth (172), Hawksworth (160), Hawley (139), Houseley (46), Osgathorpe (19), Shirtcliffe (80), Swinden (113), and Worrall (96). The distinctive surnames Crapper (51), Hattersley (167), Scargill (13), and Shemeld (88), were also recorded in the local poll tax returns of 1379 and are well known today.

The origins of families that moved from neighbouring counties to settle in Sheffield are also revealed by surnames of this type. By 1841 some of these families had lived in Sheffield for two or three centuries and had become numerous. Surnames which had been derived from places further north in the West Riding of Yorkshire included Armitage (203), Barnsley (42), Broadhead (104), Burkinshaw (191), Cawthorne (67), Copley (126), Crossland (122), Gledhill (92), Hinchcliffe (177), Holdsworth (58), Hoyland (147), Littlewood (148), Lockwood (122), and Sorsby (98). Families which hailed from Lancashire included Broadbent (32), Clegg (80), Dearden (77), Lomas (124), Ogden (103), Platts (206), Rowbotham (124), Schofield (131), Wardle (65), and Wolstenholme (202). Cheshire names ranged from Bradbury (134), and Brammall (345), to Marples (160), Staffordshire ones from Plant (78), and Salt (39), to Bagnall (33), and Derbyshire surnames from Bagshaw (210), Bamforth (99), Bolsover (59), Bowden (60), Cartledge (96), Charlesworth (162), Darwent (146), Eyre (239), Froggatt (133), Glossop (224), Heathcote (83), and Needham (224), to Newbould (115). The fewer examples from Nottinghamshire included Bingham (245), Boot (37), and Clarbrough (24). The distances that some recent migrants had travelled were greater than in previous centuries – 327 Sheffielders had surnames beginning with M^c and 82 had names starting with O' – but on the whole the catchment area was similar to what it always had been. Soon, however, this old pattern was affected by the building of large steelworks in the east end of Sheffield. The chance of finding work brought migrants from the midlands and the south of England, and a few from overseas.

THE REV? JOSEPH HUNTER F.

presented to him by Sir R.C.Hoare Bar.

Joseph Hunter (1783–1861). The eminent antiquary of Hallamshire and South Yorkshire. A cutler's apprentice, he later trained for the ministry and became the minister of the Unitarian church at Bath. In 1833 he moved to the Public Record Office, where he became an assistant keeper five years later. A prolific and careful scholar, Hunter laid the foundations for the study of the history of the Sheffield area

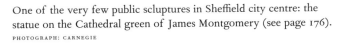

One of the very few public sculptures in Sheffield city centre: the statue on the Cathedral green of James Montgomery (see page 176).
PHOTOGRAPH: CARNEGIE

A HISTORY OF SHEFFIELD

St John's Church, Ranmoor. The finest of Sheffield's Victorian churches, St John's was designed by local architect, E.M.Gibbs in a Gothic Revival style and opened in 1879, but all except the tower and spire burned down in 1887. Rebuilding was achieved by the following year.

PHOTOGRAPH: CARNEGIE

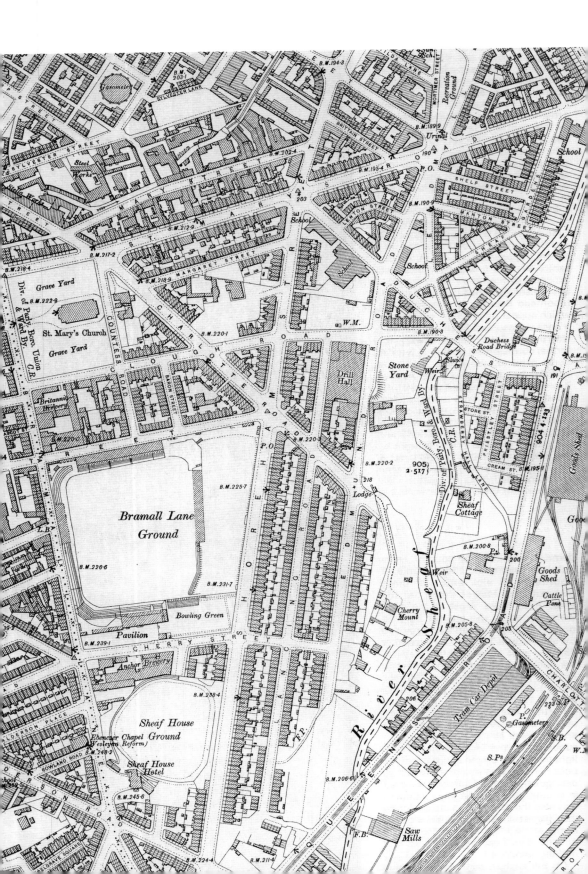

CHAPTER 5

Steel city and cutlery capital

DURING THE REIGN OF QUEEN VICTORIA Sheffield acquired much of the character that it retains today. The central streets were remodelled as a commercial centre, giant new steelworks were erected in the east end, rows upon rows of red-brick, terraced houses were built in the working-class suburbs, and the middle classes retreated to the west, away from the smoke and the grime. The population of the borough soared to new heights, at a speed that had never been achieved before and which would never be matched again. In 1851 the new borough contained 135,310 inhabitants; by 1901 the number had grown to 380,793, or to well over 400,000 if newly incorporated areas are added. In 1893 Sheffield had been given the status of a city in recognition of its growth and the international reputation of its products. By 1911 the population had overtaken that of Leeds, making Sheffield the most populous place in Yorkshire and the fifth city in England, behind only London, Birmingham, Manchester and Liverpool.

The central urban township (that shown on the eighteenth-century maps of Gosling and Fairbank) was nearly full by the middle of the nineteenth century. In 1851 the town had 83,447 people (compared with 10,121 in 1736); by 1901 the inhabitants numbered 90,398. The spread of the town westwards and north-westwards beyond its ancient boundaries explains much of the early rise of the population of the neighbouring townships, but by the end of the century new middle-class estates and working-class suburbs had contributed to the increase. Ecclesall bierlow had 24,552 inhabitants in 1851, compared with 83,543 fifty years later, while the population of Nether Hallam had risen considerably from 8,897 in 1851 to 78,111 in 1901. Upper Hallam had only 1,499 inhabitants in 1851 and the population had risen only slowly to 3,846 in 1901. The suburbs of this westerly township are mostly twentieth century in character. During the second half of the nineteenth century the population of the east end rose dramatically,

The Bramall Lane district, from the Ordnance Survey map of 1905. St Mary's was one of the churches built in the 1820s at the edge of the expanding town. It still stood near the southern limit of Sheffield when the cricket ground on Bramall Lane was opened on 30 April 1855. First-class cricket was played here until 1973. The Sheffield United Football Club have used it since 1889. The Victorian street patterns remain familiar and much of the terraced housing is still in use. Charlotte Road had not then been linked across the river valley. The railway line heads north to the 1870s predecessor of the Midland station. Duchess Road School was one of the largest old board schools that had recently become known as council schools. At the time of this map it had 1,189 pupils on roll with separate accommodation for boys and girls.
AUTHOR

especially near the new steelworks. The population of Brightside bierlow rose from 12,042 in 1851 to 73,088 in 1901, while that of Attercliffe-cum-Darnall climbed from 4,873 in 1851 to 51,807 in 1901. By then, the division between the middle-class west end of the city and the working-class east end was pronounced.

Much of this population increase was the result of earlier marriages and therefore more children, but a lot of it was due to immigration. In the east end especially, young immigrants came from the surrounding rural areas to live in new terraced houses and to work in a completely alien environment. At the time of the 1851 census 36.3 per cent (and 49 per cent of those aged over 20) were born outside the borough boundary, but most of the incomers had travelled no further than the immigrants of previous centuries; 21.5 per cent of the population had been born elsewhere in Yorkshire or Derbyshire, and 5.6 per cent had been born in Leicestershire, Lincolnshire or Nottinghamshire; only 3.3 per cent of Sheffield's population were Irish. The borough had some Scots, but few Welsh; the only other distinctive group of immigrants were a small number of Germans, mainly pork butchers and watchmakers, or cutlers. More Irish people settled in Sheffield during the next few decades. They came mostly from western and central Ireland and congregated in the north-western part of the central township, where in 1861 some enumerators' districts contained as many as 25 per cent Irish residents (if English-born children of Irish parents are counted). The Irish in Sheffield were never as numerous as those in Leeds or the industrial towns of Lancashire. Nor did Sheffield have a large Jewish colony such as settled in Leeds later in the century; in 1900 the city had only about 600 Jews. Meanwhile, large

The Cyclops Works. Charles Cammell & Co.'s Cyclops Works in Savile Street was one of the first of the enormous new steelworks that were laid out in the flat fields by the River Don to the east of the town centre during the 1840s. The rural situation of the new works is shown very well in this view. Cammell and others took advantage of the new processes in steelmaking and the coming of the railways. The smoke from the cementation and crucible steel furnace added to the pollution that was such a feature of Sheffield until modern times.

numbers of Sheffielders emigrated, particularly to the United States of America, where the native cutlery industry offered employment. An unknown proportion of these emigrants eventually returned, but many settled overseas permanently.

Steel

During the second half of the nineteenth century, steel surpassed cutlery as the major industry of Sheffield. For the first time, the manufacturers of steel ceased to look primarily to the cutlery industry for their customers. The new steelworks responded to international demands for railway stock and later for armaments. At first, the steel that was produced in the east end of Sheffield was made in crucible and cementation furnaces, but from the 1860s it was largely manufactured by new methods, starting with the Bessemer converter. These new developments enabled Sheffield to retain its position as the world's most famous steel-manufacturing centre, a position that it had held since Huntsman had perfected the art of making cast steel in crucibles.

The owners of the east-end steelworks were practical men, experienced in the local trades, whose social ambitions were generally limited to a desire to appear

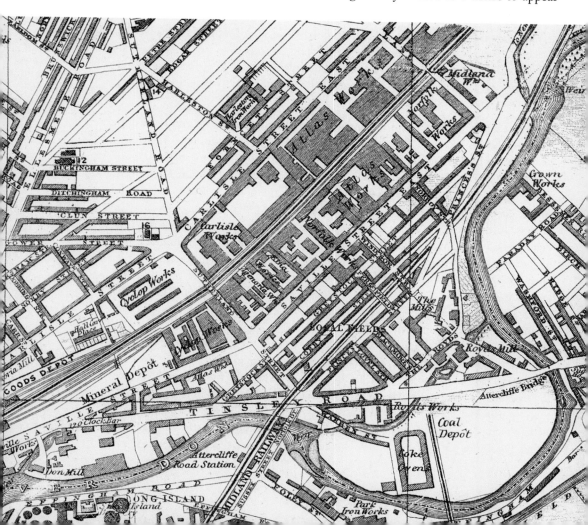

important in Sheffield. The pioneers were Charles Cammell (1810–79), Edward Vickers (1804–97) and his sons, Thomas Firth (1789–1850) and his sons, Sir John Brown (1816–96), and Thomas Jessop (1804–87).

As we have seen, Charles Cammell had erected his Cyclops Works in Savile Street in 1846, next to Spear & Jackson's Aetna Works. (The owners of these large enterprises in the east end named their works after volcanoes, such as Etna and Hecla, or after giant figures from mythology, such as Cyclops or Atlas.) The next major firm in Savile Street was Firth's, whose Norfolk Works had been founded near the town centre in 1840. Thomas Firth had moved to Sheffield from Pontefract and had risen to the position of head melter for Sanderson's crucible-steel business in West Street. Between 1851 and 1855 the business founded by Thomas and his five sons was re-sited at the other side of the Aetna Works from the Cyclops Works. The leading figures in the firm were Mark (the salesman) and Thomas, junior (the melter). An advertisement of 1862 described Firth's as:

Mark Firth (1819–80). Steel manufacturer, Mayor, Master Cutler, and philanthropist, in 1875 he gave Firth Park to the public and in 1879 founded Firth College, the forerunner of the University.

> Manufacturers of Genuine Double Refined Cast Steel for Axes, Edge Tools, Saws, Files, Machinery, and for every other purpose; also genuine blistered steel, shear, German, faggot, spring, &c, improved cast steel for locomotive railway & carriage springs, and manufacturers of every description of files, saws, & edge tools, warranted.

In 1863 Thomas Firth & Sons expanded by building an extensive gun works on a site further to the east. Guns and projectiles soon formed the most important part of their business.

Unlike Charles Cammell, the Firths were public benefactors. Mark Firth lived at the top of Wilkinson Street before he built a large house at Ranmoor, which he named Oakbrook. He served as Master Cutler from 1867 to 1869 and as Mayor in 1875. In that year, he entertained the Prince of Wales, who had come to open Firth Park, which Mark had laid out for public use in half the grounds of the former Page Hall estate, a mile or so from the Norfolk Works. In 1879, upon the opening of Firth College, Prince Leopold and John Ruskin were amongst his guests at Oakbrook. The Firths also built chapels and almshouses. The family had a high profile in Sheffield, but their works never reached the size of their mighty neighbours in the east end.

John Brown, the son of a Sheffield slater, was apprenticed to a firm of merchants before he became a salesman. In 1844 he began to make steel in Orchard Street, and later in Furnival Street. In 1856 he moved his firm from the town centre to Savile Street and began to build his enormous Atlas Works. Within a few years, these works had spread north of the railway line into Carlisle Street. By 1864 Brown's employed 3,300 men, nearly as many as Cammell's. A drawing of the Atlas Works in 1865 shows not only cementation and crucible furnaces but

puddling furnaces, where wrought iron was made for plate, and steel was puddled for other purposes. In 1860 John Brown had been the first Sheffield steel man to adopt the Bessemer process. In the same year, he began to build his large mansion at Endcliffe, where he was visited by the Prime Minister, Lord Palmerston, and by the Lords of the Admiralty and various members of the local nobility. In 1867 he erected the huge All Saints' Church in Brightside (now demolished). John Brown served as Master Cutler from 1865 to 1867 and was active on the Town Council; he became Mayor in 1863 and the first chairman of the Sheffield School Board in 1870. Brown was knighted in 1867, but in 1871 was forced to resign by his fellow directors, when armour-plate orders fell well below the level of his investment programme. He lost most of his fortune and left the area, dying in Kent in 1896.

Two generations of John Vickerses had been corn millers at Millsands before Edward Vickers (1804–97) turned from corn milling to steelmaking on the same site. By 1863 his business was expanding so quickly that he decided to move east to Brightside Lane, where he built his River Don Works. A drawing of 1879 shows an enormous works with the largest crucible steel capacity in the world. Edward's sons, Tom and Albert, turned the firm into the country's biggest manufacturer of armaments before the First World War. Tom served as Master Cutler in 1872, but both he and Albert eventually moved to London.

The other large steelworks in the middle years of the nineteenth century was Jessop's. William Jessop made steel in Furnival Street until about 1840, when he took over the site of the old Brightside Forge. In the 1850s Jessop's had ten cementation steel furnaces and 120 crucible steel holes. They made steel principally for the American market. William's son, Thomas, became Master Cutler in 1863 and Mayor the following year; and his name is commemorated by the Jessop Hospital for Women, which he paid for. He died at Endcliffe Grange in 1887. His son, William, succeeded him as chairman of the firm, but preferred country life to managing a large steelworks.

More than a century after Huntsman had perfected his crucible steel, a new method revolutionised the industry. This was Henry Bessemer's converter, an egg-shaped furnace which was open at one end so that for about thirty minutes air could be blasted into molten pig iron, causing it to burn with fierce intensity. The oxygen in the blast rapidly burnt the carbon and other elements and thus converted the iron into steel. No fuel was required. Steel could now be made in much greater quantities, at about a fifth of its previous price. Bessemer's steel was quickly in demand for railways, ships, bridges, and other heavy engineering work.

Bessemer announced his invention in London in 1856. Two years later, he moved to Sheffield to open the Bessemer Steel Works in Carlisle Street, with the avowed intention of stimulating others to follow his example. Sheffield steel-makers soon began to take out licences that allowed them to install their own converters. John Brown was the first in 1860, Charles Cammell followed in 1861, and Samuel Fox of Stocksbridge began in 1862. The scale of production was far larger than in the crucible furnaces. The age of bulk-steel manufacture had begun. By 1870 more steel was produced in Britain by the Bessemer process than in

Bessemer converter, Kelham Island Industrial Museum. Henry Bessemer's invention of the converter in 1856 was quickly taken up by the steel-masters in Sheffield's east end. Steel could now be produced quickly and in large quantities. The process was crucial to the industrial development of Sheffield. The converter at the museum entrance is one of the last pair to be used in Britain – at Workington, where production ceased in 1975.

crucible pots. By 1880 the UK production of Bessemer steel amounted to almost a million tons, whereas about 100,000 tons of cast steel was made in crucibles. The crucible process was not abandoned, however, for it produced steel of a higher quality than did Bessemer's converter. The Bessemer process replaced wrought iron, and allowed Brown's and Cammell's to build up a very profitable trade in rails, but it was unsuitable for cutlery and edge tools and the more critical applications.

By 1870 William Siemens, in south Wales, had fully developed a process whereby cast iron and scrap material were melted in an open hearth, under a slag

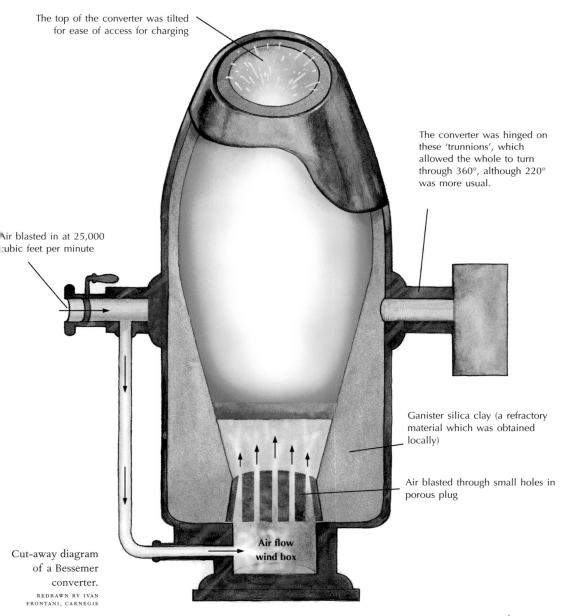

The top of the converter was tilted for ease of access for charging

The converter was hinged on these 'trunnions', which allowed the whole to turn through 360°, although 220° was more usual.

Air blasted in at 25,000 cubic feet per minute

Ganister silica clay (a refractory material which was obtained locally)

Air blasted through small holes in porous plug

Air flow wind box

Cut-away diagram of a Bessemer converter.

REDRAWN BY IVAN FRONTANI, CARNEGIE

to which iron ore was added. Carbon was thereby burnt and the iron converted into steel. The Siemens open-hearth process was slower than Bessemer's method, but it had the advantage that molten steel could be analysed and modified during the melt. The steel that was produced was therefore of a better quality than Bessemer's. It thus gradually became the accepted method for the manufacture of guns and for special forgings for ship shafting, power transmission, and other heavy engineering applications. Sheffield firms were among the first to use the process. They adopted it as quickly as they had the Bessemer converter ten years previously. Whereas the Bessemer process could convert up to 25 tons of pig iron into steel in half an hour; the Siemens furnace eventually reached a capacity of 100 tons or more, albeit in a 'heat' that took ten to twelve hours. By 1879 Vickers's had installed ten open-hearth furnaces, Cammell's had between six and eight, and the total production of open-hearth steel in Sheffield was well over 20,000 tons. By the end of the century, the Siemens process had largely replaced other processes, except that firms such as Hadfield's and Edgar Allen's retained the converter, or variants of it, for making steel for castings, and crucible steel was still preferred by the cutlers and tool makers.

All the Sheffield steelworks that were early users of the Bessemer process had an adjacent rail mill. John Brown made his first rails in 1860 and for a time was the largest rail maker in the world. In 1861 Charles Cammell started the same trade. In 1871 George Brown (a nephew of John's) founded Brown, Bayley & Dixon, in Attercliffe, in order to manufacture Bessemer steel and rails. Fortunes were made from the world-wide demand for railways. By 1873 the Sheffield district was able to make about a quarter of a million tons of rails per annum. America, in particular, was a major customer for Sheffield steel. It has been estimated that in 1871 Brown's and Cammell's alone exported to the United States about three times the whole domestic American output.

All the early steelworks that were built in the Lower Don Valley during the middle decades of the nineteenth century were located in Brightside bierlow. Many of the employees lived in the Wicker, which was within walking distance of the steelworks. Only a small proportion of those who worked in the Savile Street and Brightside Lane steelworks lived on the Attercliffe side of the valley. Even in 1868 Attercliffe could still be described as a village. Huntsman's and Sanderson's works were relatively small, and the owners continued to live in fine houses in the village, unlike the Brightside steelmasters who preferred the western suburbs and who had no interest in creating communities based on their works. Coal miners and cutlers were more numerous than steelworkers in the 1851 census for the township of Attercliffe-cum-Darnall. But the population of the township doubled between 1861 and 1871, and then grew even more rapidly. By the end of the century, the villages of Attercliffe and Darnall had been changed out of all recognition.

The skilled workers in the east end steelworks, especially the crucible melters, came from the town centre, where the industry had long been established. Puddlers were attracted from Staffordshire and other ironworking districts. Bricklayers, joiners and furnace builders were also recruited, together with a large labour force of unskilled workers. Many young men came in search of higher wages from agricultural counties, especially Nottinghamshire and Lincolnshire. They found rooms as lodgers or in boarding houses and when trade was bad they returned to their native villages. The new settlements around the steelworks soon acquired their own sense of community. The steelmasters did not own the houses of their workers and made no attempt at 'social control'. The immigrants searched out former neighbours and acquaintances and formed clusters in certain streets and family groups at work. They even continued the old practice of celebrating 'Saint Monday' as a day off, when routine maintenance work could be carried out at the works.

The good times came to an end in the 1870s, though they soon returned. The boom in railway building in Britain finished in 1873, and by 1876 the export trade in rails to America had collapsed. Increased competition from other steel-producing regions exposed Sheffield's weakness in being so far away from supplies of pig iron and from its markets. By 1878 the biggest Bessemer works in the country was in Barrow-in-Furness. The Americans and the Germans had quickly adopted the Bessemer and the Siemens processes, and when (in 1879) Thomas Gilchrist invented the 'basic' process which eliminated phosphorous, the Americans were able to use massive reserves of iron ore which had previously been useless. By 1890 both America and Germany had overtaken Britain in terms of total output. Sheffield could no longer claim to be the world capital of steel-making as far as tonnage was concerned, but it maintained its role as the leading centre of the manufacture of special steels. The local steelworks continued to expand in order to meet the increased demand for armaments and steel castings. Brown's decided to stop producing rails and to turn instead to armaments and to engineering products which were of such high value that freight costs were not an important consideration. In the late nineteenth and early twentieth centuries, Sheffield's skilled craftsmen invented and perfected many of the alloy steels for which the city became famous. At the same time, the traditional Sheffield methods were the only ones that could produce tool steel of sufficient quality. More and more Sheffield tools were required in all the industrial parts of the world, in order to work the bulk steels into shape.

From the 1860s onwards the arms trade accounted for much of the expansion of the Sheffield steel industry. As the science of explosives and the technology of guns developed, the demand for steel forgings, armour-plate and projectiles increased. The Bessemer and Siemens bulk steelmaking processes provided the means. Firms had to be large in terms of capacity, work-force and capital invest-ment, but high-risk ventures could be very profitable. In 1859–60 John Brown pioneered the commercial production of armour-plate in the United Kingdom; by 1867 three-quarters of the British Navy ironclads were defended by armour-plate made at Brown's Atlas Works. Brown's and Cammell's acquired almost a monopoly of the British armour-plate trade, Firth's were prominent in the manu-facture of projectiles and guns, in 1880 Hadfield's began the manufacture of shells, and in time Vickers's became pre-eminent in supplying all types of ordnance. These Sheffield firms became national names in the middle and late

Victorian period. They were amongst the largest companies in the country. The Lower Don Valley was the scene of continuous experiments and intense competition, as firms within walking distance of each other battled to make armour-plate that could not be penetrated by shells, or shells that could effectively tear into the defence provided by armour-plate. Sheffielders were to reap a bitter harvest from this arms race, on the Western Front in the First World War.

Meanwhile, the Sheffield cementation and crucible steel industry had reached a peak of *c.*130,000 tons per annum by about 1870, but twenty years later production had fallen by two-thirds. Competition from bulk steel, general depression, and the severe consequences of American tariffs were only partly offset by increased demand for tool steel. Even the largest firms, such as Vickers's and Brown's, kept an interest in the Huntsman method, however, and some smaller firms still managed to make satisfactory profits. The man with the most unlikely background for a Sheffield crucible steel maker was undoubtedly Edgar Allen (1837–1915), who was born in London in poor circumstances, an illegitimate descendant of a wealthy Russian family. His linguistic ability enabled him to sell steel and tools on the Continent for Ibbotson Bros. In 1868 he began his own business making hand-cut files, some tool steel, and circular saws. Crucible steel-making soon became his major concern. About the same time, a number of

Grimesthorpe Works. The No. 2 Steel Foundry at Cammell's Grimesthorpe Works specialised in the manufacture of ordnance. Casting sand is piled up in the foreground. The east end steelworks made fortunes out of the arms race leading up to the First World War.
SHEFFIELD LIBRARIES, ARCHIVES AND INFORMATION: LOCAL STUDIES

German steelmakers and toolmakers settled in Sheffield. They included Henry Seebohm and George Dieckstahl, who both arrived in 1865, and Wilhelm Kayser and Joseph Jonas, who came later. Many of the manufacturers of special steels were small, family-controlled firms, with only a modest amount of capital, businesses such as those of John Vessey, J. J. Saville, Swift Levick & Sons, Arthur Lee, and George Senior of Ponds Forge. These new ventures flourished alongside such established firms as Huntsman's, Sanderson's, Butcher's, Bedford's, and Marsh Bros, all of which continued to do well.

The sixty years between 1860 and 1920 were a time of great ingenuity in the production of special steels. Most of the major alloy steels — those which owed their remarkable properties to elements other than carbon — were discovered before the First World War. Before 1860 steel had been made by rule-of-thumb methods, and even by 1880 science had made little impact on steelmaking. In the late nineteenth century, however, the directors of the east-end steelworks recognised that research and development were crucial to commercial success. It has

The River Don engine at Kelham Island Industrial Museum. Built in 1905 by Davy Brothers to drive the armour plate rolling mill at Cammell's Grimesthorpe Works, this 12,000 horse power steam engine was worked until 1978 when it was moved to the museum.

been claimed that Sheffield turned itself into perhaps the most advanced science-based steel centre in the world, with a sustained programme of innovation in alloy steels.

One of the most important discoveries was made by another outsider, however. In 1870 Robert Mushet, of the Forest of Dean, found that if powdered tungsten was added to the crucible melt, the result was a much harder and better-cutting tool steel. Mushet licensed his method to Samuel Osborn, whose Clyde Steel & Iron Works in the Wicker produced steel and tools. 'Mushet' tool steel was an immediate winner.

Robert Hadfield's discovery of manganese steel in 1882 was of even greater importance. His father, Robert Hadfield (1832–88), a close relative of John Brown, was a local rate-collector who in 1872 had opened a steel foundry in Newhall Road, Attercliffe, which he named the Hecla Works. Robert Hadfield (1858–1940) joined his father and began his experiments at an early age in a small furnace at home. He was only 24 when he discovered that steel with 12½ per cent manganese content hardened with use. This new alloy had numerous applications. Hadfield's discovery ranks with that of Benjamin Huntsman in creating a new branch of the Sheffield steel industry. His metallurgical brilliance was matched by his entrepreneurial skills. He became chairman of the family business upon his father's death and developed it into one of the largest steel firms in Britain, concentrating particularly on armaments; Hadfield's shells were considered the best. The firm had insufficient room to expand at Newhall Road, so in 1897 he built a new works which he called East Hecla, just over the boundary in Tinsley, on the site now occupied by the Meadowhall Shopping Centre. Robert Hadfield was considered an enlightened employer, but he lived far away from his works, at Whirlow and in London. He became Master Cutler in 1899, received a knighthood in 1908, and was made a Fellow of the Royal Society in the following year.

The other famous name in special steels is that of Harry Brearley (1871–1948), a man with a working-class background and little formal education who found employment at the Brown-Firth Research Laboratory. While working in his lab in 1912 he discovered a low-carbon steel containing about 12 per cent chromium which resisted corrosion. This he first called 'rustless steel', but the name that caught on was 'stainless steel'. The usefulness of this discovery for the Sheffield cutlery industry soon became apparent.

Sheffield therefore remained the leading international centre for special steels. It had also become one of the greatest producers of guns, projectiles and armour-plate that the world had ever known. The arms race up to the First World War filled the order books of Sheffield's leading steel firms. The technical competition between guns and armour-plate intensified as the forged-steel shells of Hadfield's and Firth's penetrated the homogeneous all-steel armour-plate of Vickers's, Brown's, and Cammell's. Hadfield's research and development kept

Sir Robert Hadfield (1858–1940). Hadfield's discoveries of manganese steel in 1882 and other alloys soon afterwards were instrumental in preserving Sheffield's position as the steel capital of the world in the late nineteenth century. His firm in the east end of the city was leading producer of shells in the arms race leading up to the First World War.

their shells in the lead before the First World War. The five leading Sheffield steel producers in 1914 – Vickers's, Brown's, Cammell's, Hadfield's, and Firth's – grew enormously as a result of the armaments trade. Vickers's ranked amongst the top ten industrial firms in Britain in terms of capital and amongst the top fifteen in the size of its workforce. Brown's also came in the top-twenty UK companies. But some firms no longer confined their activities to Sheffield. By 1914 Vickers's employed 22,000 people, of whom only 6,000 worked in Sheffield, mostly at the River Don Works.

The period leading up to the First World War was a time when many steel firms merged into even larger companies. Small firms continued to thrive, however, for the new special steels had created entirely new industries in Sheffield. Many of the engineering firms whose names became locally famous were founded between 1860 and 1900, for example Ambrose Shardlow (*c.*1869), W. S. Laycock (1880), Thos. W. Ward (1878), and Aurora Steel & Iron Gearing Co. (*c.*1900).

Sheffield's expertise in steel manufacture and engineering did not lead to success in the motor car industry, however. Nine types of car were made in Sheffield before and just after the First World War. The Sheffield Simplex, a high-quality, prestigious car was made between 1906 and 1922 at Tinsley, and the Richardson car was made at Aizlewood Road between 1919 and 1921, but the Charron

Harry Brearley (1871–1948). Born in a poor working-class district of Sheffield and largely self-taught, Brearley became internationally famous as the discoverer of stainless steel at the Brown-Firth Research Laboratory in 1912. His autobiography, *Knotted String*, was published in 1941.
SHEFFIELD LIBRARIES, ARCHIVES AND INFORMATION: LOCAL STUDIES

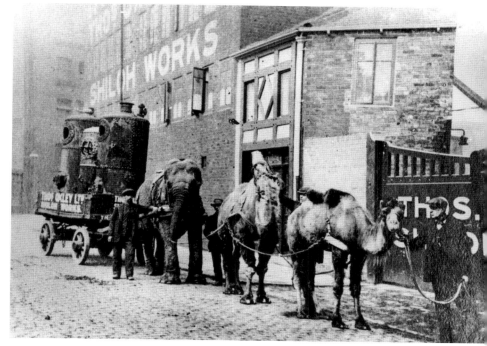

Two camels and an elephant on war service for Thomas Oxley Ltd, Shiloh Wheel, Stanley Street, 1914.
SHEFFIELD LIBRARIES, ARCHIVES AND INFORMATION: LOCAL STUDIES

The Richardson car
was made between
1919 and 1921 as a
cheap, light vehicle
by the firm run by
Charles and Ernest
Richardson in
Aizlewood Road.
About 500 cars wer
made, but very few
survive.

The Sheffield
Simplex car was
made between 1906
and 1922 as a high-
quality, luxury
vehicle. The com-
pany moved from
London to Sheffield
in 1906, when Earl
Fitzwilliam, a
company director,
built a factory at
Tinsley. Of the
17,000 cars that wer
made, only three
survive.

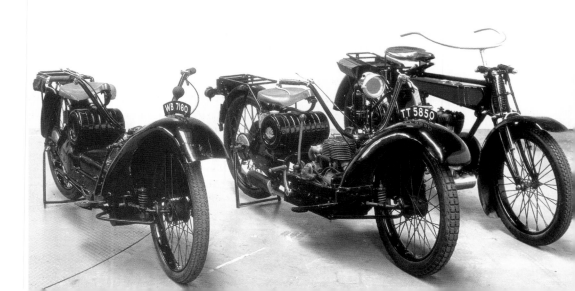

Wicker Arches form the most substantial part of the 40 arches which carried the great viaduct of the Manchester, Sheffield & Lincolnshire Railway 660 yards across the Don Valley to Victoria Station. Designed by Weightman & Hadfield and built under the supervision of the engineer, John Fowler, the project was completed in 1848. The stone came from Wharncliffe Crags. The central span is 72 feet wide and effectively divides the city centre from the industrial East End.

PHOTOGRAPH: CARNEGIE

Model B (285cc) (*far left*) and Model C (348cc) (*centre*) Ner-a-Car motor cycles 1926, designed in America and made under licence in the UK by Sheffield Simplex. (*right*) Wilkin motorcycle 1922, produced by Wilkin Motors Ltd of Onslow Road. A super lightweight motorcycle, the Wilkin was a comfortable and efficient solo touring bike.

PHOTOGRAPH CARNEGIE: COURTESY OF SHEFFIELD INDUSTRIAL MUSEUMS TRUST

Laycock, Hallamshire, Cavendish, La Plata and other cars had even shorter lives. At least seven Sheffield cars still exist: three Sheffield Simplex, two Charron Laycocks and two Richardsons. A Charron Laycock and a Sheffield Simplex are on display at Kelham Island Industrial Museum.

The demand for guns, shells, and armour-plated ships during the First World War encouraged Sheffield's firms to expand to an even greater size and to install electric-arc furnaces. By 1915 up to 25,000 tons of steel a week left Sheffield for use by the Allied forces. Those men who were not called upon to fight earned high wages, especially when they were on overtime. From 1915 women were recruited in large numbers, especially in the workshops where millions of shells were produced. Firth's Templeborough Works employed 5,000 women. All the works, large and small, were at full stretch, earning high profits. The tool steel trade was also very busy. But the firms that had been founded by Germans were looked at with hostile eyes. Sir Joseph Jonas was a victim of hysteria that stripped him of his knighthood. Seebohm & Dieckstahl of the Wicker changed its name to Balfour Darwin and opened a new works on Broughton Lane.

Cutlery

The triumphant success of the new breed of steelmasters came at a time when the Cutlers' Company, having lost its old authority over the cutlery trades, was searching for a new role. In 1860 the steelmakers were admitted into membership. Several of them went on to serve as Master Cutler. Steel had overtaken cutlery as Sheffield's major industry, but the cutlery trades nevertheless remained buoyant. During the 1860s and 1870s Sheffield was still the world's main producer of cutlery. By the end of the century, such was its triumph over its native competitors that virtually all the United Kingdom's knifemakers worked in Sheffield.

Vicker's East Gun Shop. The workforce at one of the units of Vicker's steelworks at Brightside in September 1913, eleven months before the outbreak of the First World War. At that time, Vickers employed 22,000 men in different parts of the country.
HAWLEY COLLECTION, UNIVERSITY OF SHEFFIELD

WELCOMED IN 1895 DOUBLY WELCOME IN 1919.

Royal visit to Cammell Laird works, 1919, by King George V and Queen Mary.
SHEFFIELD INDUSTRIAL MUSEUMS TRUST

It seemed that the handicraft skills of Hallamshire craftsmen would ensure their invincibility. They won the prize medals at industrial exhibitions and their order books were full. The threat posed by mechanisation was scoffed at.

The cutlers' workshops and factories were sited in the central township, as they always had been, and at Crookes, Walkley, Heeley and some of the other villages that were becoming merged with the town as houses and businesses spread outwards. These centres of the 'light trades' were very different in their character and in the occupational structure of their inhabitants from the new east-end communities that were principally involved in the 'heavy trades'. In the 1851 census the village of Crookes contained: 1 awl-blade maker, 4 cutlers, 1 edge tool grinder, 3 file cutters, 1 file moulder, 1 grinder, 1 joiners' tool forger, 5 joiners' tool makers, 2 pen-blade forgers, 9 pen-knife grinders, 2 razor grinders, 1 razor-scale presser, 1 razor maker, 1 saw dresser, 3 saw grinders, 2 saw makers, 3 scale cutters, 1 silver polisher, 1 silver plater, 1 silver smith, 13 spring-knife cutlers, 3 spring-blade grinders, 11 table-blade forgers, 45 table-blade grinders, and 3 table-knife cutlers, but only 3 steel melters. The 1881 census for Crookes recorded an increased number of specialist jobs in the 'light trades'. It also noted 19 male and two female file cutters, eight sheep-shear grinders (where none had existed in 1851), and 36 men who worked in the silver trades, compared with only three men thirty years earlier.

By the time of the 1851 census the new steelworks in Brightside bierlow had not made an impact on the inhabitants of Darnall. The village had 178 coal miners (39 per cent of the work-force), and 92 men (20 per cent) who worked in the

Hardening table blades. Mr Reaney at work, c. 1902, forging a blade in the time-honoured manner on his 'stithy and stock'. Behind him is the projecting handle of the bellows that kept the fire bright in his hearth.

'light trades', compared with only six steel and iron workers (1 per cent). By 1881 the occupational structure had changed dramatically. Darnall now had 270 coal miners (24 per cent), 197 steel and iron workers (17 per cent), and 190 railway waggon and carriage makers (17 per cent), compared with 98 men (9 per cent) in the cutlery and allied trades. The 'light trades' provided employment for similar numbers as before, but the greatly expanded work-force had found jobs in the steelworks and the mines.

   The cutlery industry remained dependent on the handicraft skills of thousands of outworkers in small workshops. Cutlery factories which employed more than 500 workers were still exceptional, and even they relied on outworkers. The distinction between masters and men was not as obvious in Sheffield as it was in other industrial towns. The masters came from relatively modest backgrounds, often from families that had been involved in the local trades for generations. But the independent 'little-mester' had his problems. His working hours and working conditions were not regulated by parliamentary legislation, and in time of depression he found himself in a poor bargaining position with the factors and the factory owners. He was often simply an outworker with little control over his business affairs.

   When trade was good, however, the 'little mester' continued to do well. He was well fed and well housed compared with artisans and labourers in other parts of England. He could justly take great pride in his skills, which kept Sheffield

Forging table knife blades. William Carr and 'Old Kirk' are shown at their trades in the Suffolk Works, *c.*1902, using machines which had recently been installed. The photograph was designed to illustrate the advantages of modern methods over traditional hand skills.

ahead of its international competitors. The 'light trades' were unaffected by the processes that had transformed the 'heavy trades' of the east end. The business leaders shared their workers' determination to continue in the old ways, confident that the quality of their products would enable them to withstand the competition of the cheap, mass-produced knives of the mechanised factories of America and Europe. The Hallamshire cutlery industry became complacent and failed to modernise.

Those owners who did try to introduce machines faced the hostility of a workforce that resisted change and which was effectively unionised. The first attempts to install machinery were made during the 1860s. The great filemakers' strike, which began on 24 February 1866, started as a dispute over wages, but it soon became clear that fear of machinery taking jobs was the principal motivation of the 4,000 strikers. The strike collapsed in May, after sixteen weeks. The grinders used physical intimidation to force their fellow workers into a trade union. The customary method, known as 'rattening', involved the removal of a non-unionist's wheel bands and tools. Employers turned a blind eye to the practice. But in the 1850s and 1860s more violent methods were used. Charges of

Scissor making, c. 1902. A scissor maker setting blades, probably at the works of E. M. Oakes & Co., Solly Street. Scissor making was already well established as a local craft when the Cutlers' Company was founded in 1624. The traditional methods of manufacture (forging, hardening, grinding, polishing and assembly) continued into the twentieth century.
HAWLEY COLLECTION, UNIVERSITY OF SHEFFIELD

gunpowder were placed in chimney stacks and grinding troughs, a saw grinder was shot at in 1854, a file grinder was a victim of a gunpowder explosion in 1857, a saw grinder was murdered in 1859, and other grinders were assaulted. In 1861 an innocent person was killed in a gunpowder attack on the house of a fender grinder in Acorn Street. These attacks excited little local interest until the disturbances associated with the file strike of 1866 brought trade unions into the public limelight. On 8 October that year the home of a saw grinder in Hereford Street was shattered by a gunpowder explosion. William Leng, proprietor of the *Sheffield Telegraph*, started a fierce debate and agitated for a full-scale investigation into the 'outrages' committed by trade unions, especially those in Sheffield and Manchester. The Government agreed with him, and early in 1867 appointed a Royal Commission of Inquiry. Its public hearings, which were held almost daily for five weeks, caused great excitement in Sheffield. The truth eventually emerged that the 'outrages' had been organised by the treasurer of the Associated Trades of Sheffield, William Broadhead, landlord of the Royal George Inn in Carver Street. As all the witnesses had been examined under indemnity, Broadhead was not charged. He emigrated to America in 1869, but returned in later life. Many union members, particularly the saw grinders, defended him, and continued with the less violent forms of 'rattening'. One of the outcomes of the enquiry was the Trade Union Act (1871), which legalised unions and thus removed the need for secrecy.

Competition from abroad intensified with the adoption of cheap Bessemer-steel blades and handles made of artificial materials. The cutlery industry in Connecticut and Massachusetts expanded rapidly after the American Civil War. Sheffield emigrants played a part in this expansion, both as businessmen and as workers, but the chief reason for American success was a willingness to innovate. The American knives were of poorer quality than Hallamshire wares, but they were cheaper. During the 1870s Sheffield firms found it increasingly difficult to sell in the American market. The introduction of the McKinley tariff in 1890 signalled the end of what had been a very lucrative trade. Meanwhile in Germany, the cutlery firms of Solingen also converted their works to mass-production methods; they were especially successful in the market for pocket knives. Sheffielders continued to resist machines. In 1873 an American visitor to the firm of Joseph Rodgers reported that, 'They pride themselves on the age of their establishment and on the fact that they do not use improved machinery.' Only a few firms made a determined effort to change, but even in the 1890s no cutlery factory in Sheffield was completely mechanised. As long as Britain ruled the waves and had an empire, Sheffield goods could be sold in the colonies. The loss of the American market was a severe blow but was not fatal. Before the First World War, few Sheffield cutlers were concerned about the future prosperity of their business. The 1911 census revealed that the 'light trades' still employed about 35,000 people, only 5,000 fewer than those who worked in the 'heavy trades'.

The principal cutlery firm during the second half of the nineteenth century remained that of Joseph Rodgers & Sons. Upon the death of John Rodgers in 1859, the business continued under the direction of his nephews, particularly

Robert Newbould. By 1870 the firm employed 1,200 workmen and had offices and warehouses in London, New York, Montreal, Toronto, New Orleans, Havana, Bombay and Calcutta. Rodgers's was the largest cutlery business in the world. In the first decade of the twentieth century the firm produced, every year, an estimated 1,600,000 pen- and pocket knives, 1,450,000 table knives, butchers' knives, etc., 500,000 razors, 144,000 scissors, and 35,000 pairs of carvers. The firm rightly claimed to be 'Manufacturers of Every Description of Cutlery and Silver and Plated Goods'.

Rodgers's reigned supreme, but another Sheffield firm became almost as well known in America. The Wolstenholmes had taken their surname from a small place in the parish of Rochdale, but in the middle of the fifteenth century they had crossed the Pennines and had settled in the parish of Dronfield. George Wolstenholme (born 1717) was apprenticed to a cutler in Stannington and eventually set up as a 'little mester'. His grandson, George, moved to Sheffield, where in 1815 he built the Rockingham Works. The next George (1800–76) short-ened his name to Wostenholm to use on his knives. After completing an apprenticeship with his father, he obtained his freedom in 1826 and took the trademark I*XL (a pun on 'I excel'). George Wostenholm was a practical cutler, a brilliant salesman and a ruthless and autocratic employer, whom some considered a bad-tempered workaholic. No-one doubted his sheer determination to build a business that emphasised quality and which was geared to the American market. He crossed the Atlantic thirty times in the pursuit of orders, and in America travelled as far west as San Francisco. In 1848 he bought a factory in Wellington Street and re-named it Washington Works because of his American connections. Here, his workers made pocket-, hunting- and Bowie knives and razors. Unlike Rodgers's and some other firms, Wostenholm's never ventured into the production of silver- and electro-plate and table cutlery.

The firm expanded rapidly during the heyday of the American trade. In 1855 Wostenholm's employed 650 men, women and children. The Washington Works was the second largest cutlery factory in Sheffield and the I*XL mark was renowned. George Wostenholm turned some of his enormous energy into creating the Kenwood estate at Sharrow, modelled on country estates that he had seen in upstate New York. He was married three times but had no children to succeed him. He sold his firm to his business associates in 1875, the year before his death. His Washington Works was demolished in 1976.

The third largest cutlery works in Victorian Sheffield (and therefore in the world) was the Queen's Cutlery Works of Mappin Bros, which employed about 300–400 workers in the 1860s. The Mappins were descended from a foreign immigrant who had settled in Sheffield in the 1590s. The family did not prosper until the nineteenth century, when several of them became rich. Joseph Mappin, an engraver in Fargate, had two sons: John Newton Mappin, who made his fortune

George Wostenholm (1800–76). The photograph was taken in New York in 1856, the year he became Master Cutler. The American market was vital to his success in establishing his Washington Works as a great cutlery manufactory, second only to that of Joseph Rodgers. Wostenholm laid out his Kenwood estate at Nether Edge on the model of towns which he had seen in New England. His works has been demolished, but his home survives as a hotel.

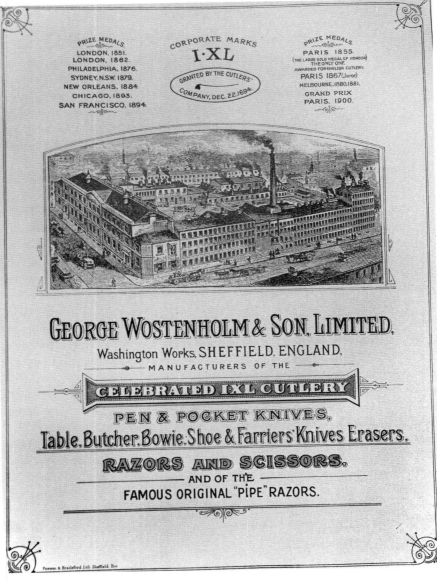

GEORGE WOSTENHOLM & SON, LIMITED,

Washington Works, SHEFFIELD, ENGLAND,

MANUFACTURERS OF THE

CELEBRATED IXL CUTLERY

PEN & POCKET KNIVES,

Table, Butcher, Bowie, Shoe & Farriers' Knives Erasers,

RAZORS AND SCISSORS,

AND OF THE

FAMOUS ORIGINAL "PIPE" RAZORS.

George Wostenholm & Son Limited. This early twentieth-century catalogue depicts the Washington Works founded by George Wostenholm in 1848. It was less a modern factory than a large collection of workshops of the old type. Production was geared to the American trade (hence the name of the works), with an emphasis on knives and razors. Good quality pocket-knives, hunting-knives and Bowie-knives were the firm's speciality.

HAWLEY COLLECTION,
UNIVERSITY OF SHEFFIELD

as a brewer and who bequeathed his art collection and the Mappin Art Gallery to Sheffield, and Joseph Mappin, who started his own cutlery business in Norfolk Street and Mulberry Street. Joseph's son, Frederick Thorpe Mappin (1821–1910) succeeded his father, and through his ability and energy built a large business in knives, razors and plated wares. In 1851 he opened the Queen's Cutlery Works, next to Rodgers's Norfolk Street Works (on the site now occupied by the Central Post Office). It has been well described as more a collection of workshops than a factory. The firm was re-named Mappin Bros in 1851. Eight years later, Frederick left to become the senior partner in Thomas Turton & Sons, steel- and-tool makers, until 1885. He was also a director of the Midland Railway from 1869

to 1900 and was a Liberal MP for East Retford (1880–85) and for Hallamshire (1885–1906). Honours were showered upon him. He became Mayor in 1877, a baronet in 1886, and Sheffield's first honorary freeman in 1900. His support for education led him to found the Technical School and to help establish the University, where he was the first senior pro-chancellor. When he died in 1910 he left a fortune of nearly £1 million, far more than any Sheffielder had left before. He gave eighty pictures to the Mappin Art Gallery. Meanwhile, his younger brother, John Newton Mappin (1835–1913) had started his own electro-plating and cutlery business with his brother-in-law, George Webb. Their works was sited in Norfolk Street, opposite St Paul's churchyard. There they made silver and plated salvers, dish-covers, entree dishes, carvers, dinner- and dessert knives, and some pocket knives. The emphasis was on quality and artistic design. Mappin & Webb's remains a household name for high-class jewellery and silverware, though it is no longer connected with Sheffield.

From the 1840s onwards, many Sheffield cutlery firms (with the notable exception of Wostenholm's) turned to the manufacture of silver- and electro-plate goods. They could adapt readily enough to the production of dessert knives, lemon saws, silver carving sets, fish carvers and silver fruit knives for middle- and upper-class households. They went on to supply tea- and coffee services, claret jugs, cruet sets, cups, salvers, trays, cake baskets and entree dishes. By the late nineteenth century the dominant firms in this trade were Walker & Hall, Dixon's, Hutton's, and Mappin & Webb.

Walker & Hall were established about 1845 by George Walker, a table-knife forger, who had learned the new electro-plate technology in Birmingham, and his two partners. In 1848 Henry Hall of Worcester joined the partnership, and five years later the firm was re-named Walker & Hall. Their Electro Works was situated in Howard Street. Hall's nephew, John Bingham, became a partner in 1852 and took full control when Hall retired in 1873. He served as Master Cutler twice, was a prominent Conservative on the borough council, and was knighted in 1884. John Bingham and his brother Charles developed the firm so successfully

Heeley Silver-Rolling Mills and Wire Mills. Men and boys are shown at work rolling and pressing during the 1920s or 1930s. Rolling improved the durability of silver-plated goods. The Heeley works was established in the 1890s on three acres of land by Guernsey Road, conveniently close to the railway. J. Newton Mappin was the first chairman and four of the other eight directors were Mappins. They claimed to have installed 'every modern improvement devised by mechanical science.'

that it was the largest employer in the cutlery trades by the First World War, with 2,000 workers. Though Walker & Hall's main line was in plated goods, they also made steel table knives of the best quality. Their factory remained a prominent Sheffield landmark until its demolition in 1965.

The most impressive cutlery factory that still stands in Sheffield is the former Cornish Place Works of James Dixon & Sons, by the River Don in Neepsend. For years its blackened exterior was a reminder of the days of 'Smoky Sheffield', when factories looked far less attractive than they do in the illustrations used for advertising purposes. It has recently been cleaned and converted into apartments. Although Dixon's made a wide range of cutlery, they were principally makers of plated and silver goods. The firm was founded in 1805 in Silver Street as Dixon & Smith, makers of Britannia metalware, pewterware and Old Sheffield Plate. In 1822 James Dixon, the founder, set up on his own in Cornish Place on the banks of River Don. His sons and grandsons expanded the business, selling their wares

Harry Wood, hand chasing a silver tray, *c.* 1900. The tray was kept in shape by embedding it in warm pitch, which sets hard when it cools. The required pattern was traced and pricked on paper, then sprinkled with chalk and rubbed over the surface of the tray. A steel pointer was then used to mark the pattern, and a series of delicate punches was employed to indent the finer features.

HAWLEY COLLECTION, UNIVERSITY OF SHEFFIELD

throughout Britain and in America and the colonies. Dixon's reached their peak in 1914. Demand for their products never recovered from the impact of the First World War on the market for luxury goods.

William Hutton & Sons began as silversmiths in Birmingham. In 1832 William Carr Hutton (1803–65) moved to Sheffield to manufacture goods made from silver- and British-Plate (an alloy of copper, zinc and nickel). As early as 1843 he licensed Elkington's electro-plate process. Herbert Hutton (1843–1904), the youngest of his five sons, became the leading figure in the Sheffield part of the business in the late nineteenth century, the other brothers moving to Birmingham, London and overseas. In 1885 Hutton's moved into the large building that still fronts on to West Street. There they made a wide variety of luxury silverware and plated knives of various kinds. Before the First World War, the firm employed over 900 people, but it closed soon afterwards, in the 1920s.

One of the firms that was prepared to mechanise and which survived the First World War was that of Needham, Veall & Tyzack. The firm's origins go back to John Taylor who started a small business in pen, pocket and sports knives in

The façade of the Cornish Place Works on Green Lane. The factory extended back to the banks of the River Don in a wedge-shaped piece of land between Ball Street and Cornish Street. This part of the works dates from the 1850s. At its peak in the late nineteenth century, the works employed over 1,000 workers.
PHOTOGRAPH: CARNEGIE

St Philip's Road about 1820. In 1838 Taylor was awarded the 'Eye Witness' corporate mark, which is still used by his successors. By 1856 the business had been taken over by a cutler and shopkeeper, Thomas Brown Needham. About twenty years later, Needham was joined by James Veall at the factory in Milton Street which is still used by the firm. Walter Tyzack joined the partnership in 1879. By the 1890s the work-force numbered several hundreds. Needham, Veall & Tyzack were a traditional cutlery business who made pen- and pocket knives, table knives, butchers' knives, carvers, scissors, pruning shears, and razors, but one that was prepared to move with the times.

Many other firms deserve to be mentioned by name. They include J. & J. Beal of the Red Hill Works, Brookes & Crookes (the winners of gold medals), George Butler & Co. (active since the seventeenth century), Cadman's, John Clarke & Son of the Mowbray Works, Deakin's Tiger Works in West Street, Thomas Ellin & Co. of the Sylvester Works, Joseph Elliot & Sons of Hollis Croft, Harrison Bros & Howson (whose large Alpha Works in Carver Street survives in part, though adapted for other uses), George Ibberson & Co. of Rockingham Street, Martin, Hall & Co. (large-scale manufacturers of silver- and electro-plated goods), Nowill's (whose mark was awarded in 1700), Thomas Turner & Co. at the Suffolk Works, Unwin & Rodgers of the Rockingham Works, and John Waters & Co. of the Globe Works.

The first stainless steel knives appeared in the autumn of 1914, two years after Brearley's invention, just as war broke out. The impact of the war on the Sheffield cutlery trades was uneven. The luxury market was affected badly, so many of the larger firms suffered, but other manufacturers benefited from the sudden demand for bayonets, army knives and razors. The makers of surgical instruments were also hard-pressed to meet their orders, and some firms turned part of their resources to making swords. In the long run, the basic structure of the cutlery industry was not much altered by the war. The knife trade remained dominated by a large number of small firms, whose craftsmen stuck determinedly to the old methods of which they were so proud.

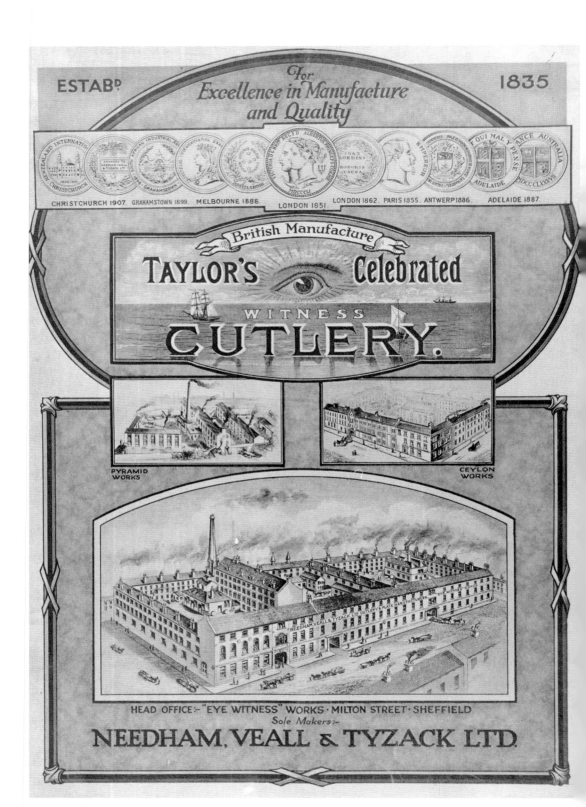

  A HISTORY OF SHEFFIELD

Tool-making and other industries

The Sheffield tool industry had grown from a modest size in the mid-eighteenth century to world leadership by the late nineteenth century. It had the inestimable advantage of ready access to supplies of crucible steel. Some of the most prominent tool-making firms made their own steel and often had an interest in the manufacture of cutlery as well. Two old-established firms may be quoted as examples. The history of Marsh Bros as a cutlery firm can be traced back to 1631. Between 1780 and 1815 they made spring knives at Park Hill, before moving to Castle Hill and then to Porter Street, finally settling at their Ponds Works in 1828. There, they made steel, saws, files, many different types of edge tools, and all types of knives and razors, priding themselves on the quality of their products. During the 1840s and 1850s they sold large quantities of their goods in America, where they had permanent representatives in Philadelphia and New York. By 1862 they employed about 250 people. High American tariffs affected them so badly, however, that in the 1890s they stopped making knives in order to concentrate on special tool steels and the making of tools for the engineering trades. They survived as an independent steel-and-tool maker until the 1960s.

The Butcher brothers, William (*c.*1791–1870) and Samuel (*c.*1797–1869), inherited a cutlery business that went back to 1725. By 1819 they were making a wide variety of steel goods in Eyre Lane. Their success in America enabled them to expand considerably between 1830 and 1860, when they were manufacturing steel at the Philadelphia Works, Neepsend, and files, razors, chisels, planes and high-quality table cutlery, pocket knives, and Bowie knives in their Arundel Street factory (known as Butcher's Wheel). At that time, their workforce numbered 1,000. Neither of the brothers had heirs and so the business declined rapidly after their deaths. At their peak, Butcher's had a very high reputation.

THE

FOURTH EDITION.

SHEFFIELD STANDARD LIST,

ILLUSTRATED,

CONTAINING PRICES & PATTERNS OF

MACHINERY, FILES, RASPS, SAWS, JOINERS TOOLS,

LIGHT & HEAVY EDGE TOOLS,

LANCASHIRE TOOLS, MACHINISTS PLUMBERS & TINMENS TOOLS,

Spades, Shears, Anvils, Bellows, Wire and other

SHEFFIELD GOODS,

NOTE.— THE PRICES OF THE CUTLERS' COMPANY HAVE BEEN STRICTLY ADHERED TO IN THE FOLLOWING LIST.

SHEFFIELD.

DRAWN, ENGRAVED, PRINTED, AND PUBLISHED BY R.T. BARRAS, 27, HIGH STREET.

1864.

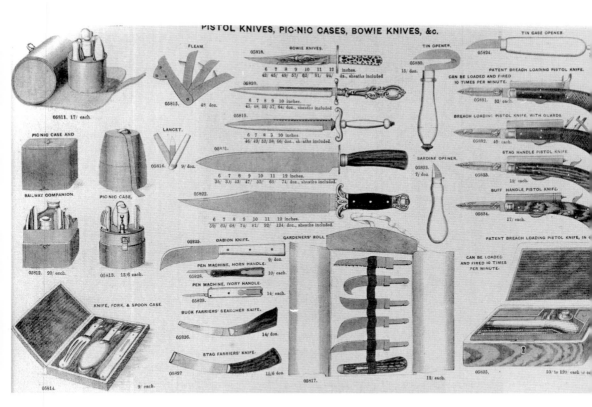

By the early 1870s, the number of Sheffield tool firms numbered well over 250. Most of them were small-scale businesses, but several larger firms employed 200–400 men. The file trade was of prime importance. One of the oldest firms, going back well into the eighteenth century, was that of W. K. & C. Peace, who made their own crucible steel. They moved from Neepsend to larger premises in Mowbray Street about 1854. They too prospered from American orders. A newer business was that of George Barnsley, who was first listed in a Sheffield directory of 1837 as a file manufacturer in Wheeldon Street. By 1852 he had moved to Cornish Street, where he made steel, files, shoe knives and butcher's knives; later on, he also made saws. Saws were the main concern of some other well-known firms of toolmakers. By 1880, Spear & Jackson's Aetna Works in Savile Street employed over 800 workers, who made saws, files and edge tools, all from the firm's own steel. Another famous firm was that of Thomas Turton & Sons, who took over part of the business of Greaves's Sheaf Works in 1850. They described themselves as 'Merchants & Manufacturers of Steel, Files, Saws, Edge Tools, & Every Description of Cutlery, also Locomotive & Railway Carriage Springs'.

Other firms prospered by concentrating on joiners' tools. David Flather started a joiners' tool-manufacturing business in 1817. After moving to Fargate and Hollis Croft, he settled in Solly Street. By 1859 David Flather & Sons were also making engineers' tools and saws. Five years later, they were listed in a directory as steelmakers and file manufacturers. The steelmaking business became the separate company of W. T. Flather; the older business lasted until well after the Second

Page 45 of *The Sheffield Standard List*, fourth edition (1864) shows the typical layout of the catalogue. The local products shown here include Bowie Knives. The knives are priced in shillings either individually or wholesale.

Turner, Naylor & Co. Limited, Tool-makers: centenary catalogue, 1910, depicting their Northern Tool Works, John Street; (inset) a catalogue aimed at the important American market, 1909. The firm had been founded as Sorby, Turner and Skidmore in the Wicker by 1821. In 1871 they changed their name to Turner, Naylor and Co. of Castle Hill and Darnall and eight years later to the Northern Tool Works. The firm went out of business in 1963.

HAWLEY COLLECTION, UNIVERSITY OF SHEFFIELD

TURNER, NAYLOR & CO.
LIMITED.

PRICE LIST
OF
AMERICAN
TOOLS.

TRADE MARK.

ESTABLISHED 1810.

SHEFFIELD.

1909

TURNER, NAYLOR & CO LTD
LATE SORBY & TURNER,
MANUFACTURERS OF
LIGHT & HEAVY EDGE TOOLS,
ENGINEERS' TOOLS,

Steel
**
Sheep-
Shears,
**
Joiners'-
Tools,

Files,
**
Saws,
**
Augers,
**
Hammers,
**
&c.

Established 1810

TRADE

CENTENARY "**1910**" CATALOGUE
TRADE
"I. SORBY"
MARK.

TRADE

MARK.

TRADE
I.
SORBY
MARK

THE NORTHERN TOOL WORKS,
SHEFFIELD.

Telephone No. 200.   Telegraphic Address—"Punch," Sheffield.

at Stationers' Hall.   WM. TOWNSEND AND SONS, PRINTERS, SHEFFIELD,

---

World War. William Marples, who may have been descended from Robert Marples, Sheffield's first recorded sawmaker (1747), was making joiners' tools by 1833. Within four years he had moved to Broomspring Lane, where he also made skates, braces and bits. By 1859 he had moved again, to Westfield Terrace, where he made joiners' tools, edge tools and files. By the 1870s William Marples & Sons had expanded their business almost back into Rockingham Street. They had also become merchants with a London office. Another manufacturer in the same line of business, Aaron Hildick, had a distinctive Staffordshire surname. In the 1860s he made plane irons and other edge tools in the Wicker. By 1871 his firm had moved to Bridge Street, and in 1902, as business prospered, they moved again to Rutland Road.

Tyzack's were the leading manufacturers of scythes, at their Little London Works and at Abbeydale. Charles Skelton, whose Sheafbank Works opened in Heeley in 1870 became the chief manufacturer of shovels and garden tools. James Chesterman led the way with measuring equipment. He moved from London to Sheffield in 1820 to work as a silversmith and in the following year invented a method of using a spring to make an automatic rewinding tape. In 1842 Chesterman's produced the first long steel-measuring tape and the first woven metallic tape. After their Nursery Street works had been destroyed in the Sheffield Flood of 1864, the firm moved to new premises in Plum Street off Ecclesall Road. (In 1963 they were amalgamated with the measuring-tools company of John Rabone & Sons of Birmingham.)

Sheffield business was dominated by its manufacturers of steel, cutlery and tools, but a few men made their fortunes from other trades. An outstanding example is George Bassett (1818–86), who moved to Sheffield from Ashover about 1842 when he acquired a confectioner's business in Broad Street. Pawson & Brailsford's *Illustrated Guide to Sheffield* (1862) advertises a large business making 'lozenges, liquorice, comfits, pastilles, ju-jubes, acid drops, candied peel and orange marmalade'. George Bassett was a respected Methodist who became Mayor in 1876. An obituary in 1886 described him as 'the foremost confectionery manufacturer in England'. The celebrated Liquorice Allsorts came later, in 1899.

Another well-known Sheffield name was that of William Batchelor, who in 1895 began to sell tea from part of a Methodist chapel in Stanley Street. In 1912 he started to sell dried peas in packets instead of using the customary method of

F.G. Pearson's, fork manufacturer. The interior of Hope Works, Furnace Hill, near West Bar in the early twentieth century. A stack of finished forks, without their handles, can be seen in the centre foreground.

Alderman George Bassett, an immigrant from Derbyshire who established a successful confectionery business and became Mayor of Sheffield in 1876.

In 1912 William Batchelor expanded his tea business in Stanley Street by selling dried peas in packets, instead of selling them loose in sacks. In 1937 the company built this works near Wadsley Bridge station. The peas came by rail from Lincolnshire and Nottingham- shire and were pro- cessed by soaking, cooking, colouring and canning.

selling them loose over the counter in sacks. Batchelor's Peas became known throughout the land, especially after 1937 when the company moved to a new site at Wadsley Bridge to process peas from Lincolnshire and Nottinghamshire.

By the mid-1850s the tanneries at Crookes, Walkley and Philadelphia had been closed and the only tanyards left in Sheffield were those at Upperthorpe, Neepsend and Woodhouse. The industry had failed to adapt to new methods along the lines of the tanneries in Walsall and Leeds. Just one firm went against the trend: that of Francis Colley & Sons of the Meersbrook Tannery. Colley started as a currier and then as a leather merchant in Market Street. His large tannery at Meersbrook was established in the 1870s at the junction of Valley Road and Chesterfield Road. It closed in 1906, but the inscription 'Meersbrook Tannery' still adorns a building that was part of the works.

Fortunes were to be made out of the brewing industry, for Sheffield had an enormous number of pubs. At the time of the 1831 census, when the town was still comparatively small, the Sheffield district had about 1,500 licensed premises. The heavy, hot nature of steelmaking made the workers in the east end legendary beer drinkers. Sheffield's oldest brewery, and one of the largest, was that of Thos. Rawson & Co. of Pond Street, founded in 1758. Another early enterprise was that of Proctor & Co.'s Exchange Brewery, established in the Market Place in 1820. Twenty years later, Edward and Robert Tennant took over this business and in 1852 moved to the banks of the Don by Lady's Bridge. By the end of the century the Exchange was Sheffield's largest brewery. The second largest was the

PHOTO NO. 9. SERIAL NO. 182. AMONG INDUSTRIES RANGING FROM THE MANUFACTURE OF SNUFF TO CARDBOARD BOXES, ARE INCLUDED THE CANNING OF FRUIT AND VEGETABLES. (PHOTO: BY COURTESY OF BATCHELOR'S PEAS LTD., A LOCAL CANNING FACTORY.) (INSET). DIRECT FROM THE CAN.

nearby Lady's Bridge Brewery of Duncan Gilmour & Co., founded by a Scot in 1831. (They merged with Tetley's in 1954 and the old Gilmour Brewery in Bridge Street became the site of Sheffield Magistrate's Court.)

By the 1880s Sheffield had 30 breweries. They included those of Thos. Berry & Co. of Moorhead, founded in 1824, Thos Marrian & Co. of Burton Weir, begun about 1830 by an immigrant from Birmingham, A. H. Smith's Don Brewery, in Penistone Road to the east of St Philip's Church, founded early in the nineteenth century and acquired by William Smith of Barnes Hall, Ecclesfield, in 1832, William Whitmarsh's mid-nineteenth-century brewery, which fronted on to South Street, Earl Street and Porter Street, and Richard Truswell's Brewery in Eyre Street. William Stones began modestly in the 1840s and opened his Cannon Brewery in Rutland Road in 1865. The history of Ward's, Sheffield's other well-known former brewery, is more complicated. It was preceded in Ecclesall Road by William Bradley's Soho Brewery. Bradley's partner, John Newton Mappin, left by 1849 upon acquiring the Masbrough Old Brewery. The Soho and the nearby Albion Brewery were merged by George Wright in the 1880s and taken over by Septimus Henry Ward in 1890. Two other firms in different branches of the drinks business were established in the nineteenth century. Hay & Son, wine merchants of Norfolk Street, were founded In 1829, and British Syphon traces its origins back to J. F. Eardley, a pharmaceutical chemist who began manufacturing soda water in 1880 and soft drinks in 1899.

Tilt hammers, Clay Wheels Forge. This photograph, taken about 1940, shows huge water-powered hammers being used for forging and plating scythe blades. The forge took its name from the Clay family. It has been demolished, but Clay Wheels Lane survives as a road name at Wadsley Bridge. Similar hammers can be seen at the Abbeydale Industrial Museum.

Breweries were among the many works that added to Sheffield's smoky atmosphere. The tremendous demand for coal for both industrial and domestic purposes encouraged coalowners to sink deeper mines. A great pumping engine that long remained a local landmark was installed at Nunnery Colliery in the late 1860s. Large numbers of miners lived nearby in the Park, the Wicker, Attercliffe and Darnall. Although Sheffield lay on the western edge of the South Yorkshire coalfield, and the industry was overshadowed by the metal trades, coal mining was a major source of local employment. Numerous photographs survive from the times of the bitter strikes over wages in 1893 and 1912, when shallow seams and old workings were outcropped by strikers on land remarkably close to houses in various parts of the east end.

The majority of married women did not go out to work but struggled to keep their homes and clothes clean amidst the grime. Dr Frederick Barry's *Report on an Epidemic of Small-Pox at Sheffield During 1887–88* made light of women's

Sheffield from Lady's Bridge (1875). This view by an unknown artist shows a crowd of people crossing Lady's Bridge towards Tennants' Exchange Brewery. In the nineteenth century over-abstraction of water from the river for a wide variety of uses left insufficient for the dilution of waste, a problem that was referred to as 'negative pollution' by the Yorkshire engineer Malcolm McCulloch Paterson when he was giving evidence to a parliamentary committee in 1896. A century earlier, the Wicker had still been a green space; by the time of this painting, it was full of the smoke and noise of industry.

work, claiming that 'comparatively few women are employed in factories, and as the houses are as a rule small, and their domestic duties occupy no large fraction of their time, they have ample leisure for visiting their friends'. Women no doubt had a different point of view. Domestic service remained the chief occupation of unmarried girls. The 1851 and 1881 census returns for Crookes show how increasing numbers of women worked at paid jobs: the numbers of domestic servants rose from 14 to 54, laundresses from 11 to 30, charwomen from two to 13, dressmakers from nine to 22, and silver polishers from none to eight. Most of these jobs were no doubt obtained in the middle-class suburbs nearby. The 1901 census for the whole of Sheffield shows that 24 per cent of the local work-force was female, with 34 per cent of them in domestic service and 20 per cent in the light metalworking trades. Nearly a quarter of these working women were married or widowed.

The town centre

Early Victorian Sheffield lacked the dignified public buildings, the wide streets and elegant squares, the fine houses and wealthy shops that were normally found in the centres of other large towns, even those which had recently risen to prominence because of their industries. Sheffield had not greatly improved by 1875, when J. M. Wilson wrote in *The Imperial Gazetteer*:

> Some of the old streets are small, narrow and irregularly built; some of even the new streets are disfigured by forges, furnaces, and other ungainly buildings;

Norfolk Market Hall, shown here in an old print, was opened in December 1851, on the site of the Tontine Inn at the cost of £40,000 as a general retail market. It was demolished in 1959.

spacious squares or other large open edificed areas are totally a-wanting; and the dwelling houses of the merchants and manufacturers are almost all in the outskirts or in the country; so that the town as a whole, especially with its clouds of smoke, cannot be called attractive. Yet it has good shops, good public buildings and some very fine suburbs; is well-paved, well-drained, and well-supplied with water; has undergone much recent improvement in its street-architecture; and possesses some imposing semi-public edifices, such as a stately great hotel adjoining the Victoria railway station, and the extensive premises of the Messrs. Rodgers in the renaissance style, both erected in 1861.

The major Victorian buildings that were erected in Sheffield were mostly the work of the architectural practices of three generations of Hadfields and three

generations of Flocktons. Their achievements rank with those of contemporary provincial practices elsewhere. The Board Schools designed by Charles John Innocent in the 1870s and 1880s form another fine series of buildings by a local architect. Only occasionally were London architects commissioned to design public buildings, most notably when E. W. Mountford won the open competition in 1891 for a new Town Hall.

Sheffield's first Town Hall had been a modest building by the gates of the churchyard at the top of High Street. In 1808 a new and much larger Town Hall had been erected by the Town Trustees on the corner of Castle Street and Waingate. This has gradually been enlarged into the present County Court building. When the new Town Council were elected in 1843 they had to hire somewhere to meet. It took the best part of half a century for the council to decide that Sheffield needed a grand Town Hall that could stand comparison with those of other northern boroughs. E. W. Mountford's free northern Renaissance

design, rich in details, won the competition and on 21 May 1897 the new building was opened by Queen Victoria. By then, Sheffield had been a city for four years.

As lord of the manor, the Duke of Norfolk retained control of Sheffield's markets until 1899, when he sold his rights to the Corporation. During the second half of the nineteenth century he commissioned his fellow Catholics, the Hadfields, to design a series of market halls. The first was the Norfolk Market, the principal public market, which Weightman & Hadfield designed in 1851 in Tuscan style; it fronted on to Haymarket until its demolition in 1959. At the same time, the Market Hall that had been erected in 1784, fronting on to High Street, was re-designed. Next came the Shambles, which was remodelled in 1855–56 by Weightman, Hadfield & Goldie to become the Fitzalan Market. The most ambitious project, however, was the large Corn Exchange, designed in a Tudor Gothic style in 1881 to replace the Exchange of 1830. The vast central hall was destroyed by fire in 1947 and the surrounding offices were demolished in 1964; the site is now occupied by the Park Square traffic roundabout.

When the Midland Railway was cut through the Ponds in the 1860s, not far from these markets, the railway company agreed to construct Commercial Street in compensation. In 1875 the Sheffield United Gaslight Company built their splendid offices there, the finest commercial building in Sheffield, designed by M. E. Hadfield & Son in the style of a Venetian palazzo. The Midland Railway's station was built in 1870, and extended in 1905 just in time for the royal visit, when King Edward VII and Queen Alexandra came to open the University. The much plainer Victoria Station had

opened in 1851. The adjacent Victoria Hotel, which was built ten years later, long remained the finest hotel in Sheffield.

Sheffield never became a regional commercial centre on the scale of Manchester or Leeds, but by the end of the nineteenth century its central streets contained four-, five- or even six-storey blocks of shops and offices, hotels and banks, cafes and restaurants. For many years, the largest of these was Cole Bros's draper's shop, begun in 1869, which gradually spread from 'Cole's Corner' at the bottom of Church Street back along Fargate. The Victorian choice of style ranged widely from the Tudor Gothic to the classical. Few of Sheffield's shops and offices are outstanding as individual buildings, but collectively they proclaim Sheffield's town centre as prosperous late-Victorian. Two of the best were designed by Charles Hadfield: Parade Chambers in High Street (1883–85) and Cairns Chambers in Church Street (1894–96). They are both built of red brick with stone dressings in the Tudor style and have interesting details. By contrast, the Cutlers' Hall and the neighbouring banks in Church Street are formal and 'correct' in their classicism, conveying an air of reliability and assurance.

In the 1860s the Corporation began to acquire new powers with which to transform the lay-out and the public health of the town. Bye-laws prohibiting the building of back-to-back houses were passed in 1864 and a main sewerage and drainage system was installed in 1866–86. The most important of the various street-improvement schemes was that of 1875, which launched a major

Fargate (left) and Church Street (right) from High Street, looking towards the original Cole Brothers shop. Generations of Sheffielders met their friends at 'Cole's Corner'.

Parade Chambers, High Street, designed by Charles Hadfield in 1883–85 for Pawson & Brailsford, printers and stationers, in Tudor Gothic style. The decorative stone carvings are by Frank Tory, who trained at Lambeth School of Art and came to Sheffield in 1880. The upper rooms were let as offices.

PHOTOGRAPH: CARNEGIE

'Some of the old streets are small, narrow and irregularly built; some of even the new streets are disfigured by forges, furnaces, and other ungainly buildings ... Yet it has good shops, good public buildings and some very fine suburbs.'

J.M. WILSON, 1875

programme to widen High Street, Fargate, Pinstone Street, Surrey Street, Cambridge Street, Leopold Street and other streets in the city centre. Over half a million pounds was spent in the acquisition of property during the next decade. Work began on Fargate in the 1880s, but the whole programme took 25 years to complete.

A long period of wrangling over property boundaries and compensation delayed the beginning of work on High Street until 1895. All the buildings on the south side of the street were then demolished in order to widen the road to twice its width. The old High Street had been too narrow for horse trams to pass through. Most of the new buildings that were erected on the south side of the street in the late 1890s were destroyed during the blitz in 1940, but they are remembered from old photographs. The most striking was John Walsh's department store, which was opened in 1900. Walsh was an Irishman who had learned his trade at Cockayne's in Angel Street. In 1875 he had opened a modest shop, selling baby linen and ladies' outfitting, on the north side of High Street. He grasped the opportunity presented by the widening scheme to erect a much larger shop. His new building was all steel and glass on the ground floor, but the upper floors were masked by Huddersfield stone. By 1925 Walsh's employed 600 staff, some of whom lived in the top-floor dormitories.

John Walsh was also responsible for the Central Chambers and High Court on

the opposite side of High Street. Another attractive building, with a glass-fronted arcade, was Cockayne's draper's shop, which was erected in Angel Street in 1897. The original shop on the same site had been built by earlier members of the family in 1829. The 1897 shop was destroyed in the blitz, and was replaced by the present building in the mid-1950s. Further down the hill, the old timber-framed houses in Snig Hill were demolished when the street was widened in 1900. Other buildings had meanwhile been cleared on the other side of the old Market Place to make the open space of Fitzalan Square (The Duke of Norfolk's middle name was Fitzalan). The Post Office there was finished in 1910.

The district to the west of Church Street and Fargate was radically re-designed in the second half of the nineteenth century. The area had become a typical mixture of houses and industrial buildings, including a gas works and a steel works, but after 1875 a wide new street whose name commemorates the visit of Queen Victoria's son, Leopold, cut a swathe through it. Here were built the Education Offices, Firth College, the Medical School, the Central School, and a new Assay Office. Around the corner in Barker's Pool (on the site of the present Cole's department store), the Albert Hall, noted for its magnificent French organ, was opened in 1873.)

Beyond Barker's Pool, the Water Company's offices in Division Street was built in classical style in 1867 to the designs of Flockton & Gibbs. (The front of the building was preserved when the National Union of Mineworkers' Headquarters was built in the 1980s.) Coal Pit Lane had been re-named Cambridge Street when the Duke of Cambridge had laid the foundation stone for the Crimean War

airns Chambers, designed by Charles
adfield as solicitors' offices, 1894-96, in
udor Gothic style. Frank Tory's carvings
clude a portrait of the first Earl Cairns,
rmer Lord Chancellor.

OTOGRAPH: CARNEGIE

The Water Company Headquarters. The Water Company's offices in
Division Street were built in classical style by the Sheffield firm of
Flockton & Gibbs in 1867. The front was preserved when the
National Union of Mineworkers built their headquarters here in the
1980s. The building has recently been converted into a café and
restaurant.

PHOTOGRAPH: L. NUTTALL

Tramway reconstruction, Pinstone Street, 1909. The narrow central streets of Sheffield were widened to twice their original width at the close of the nineteenth century, partly to accommodate the new electric trams. The work in progress seems to have caused far less disruption than the preparations for the Supertrams in the 1990s. The old tram (bottom right) makes a nice contrast to the new covered ones (whose drivers still need warm clothing). Pinstone Street had replaced the older route to the Moor via Barker's Pool and Coal Pit Lane (Cambridge Street).

memorial at Moorhead. The road ceased to be the most popular route down to the Moor when Pinstone Street was widened under the 1875 Improvement Act. From 1905 Queen Victoria's statue stood prominently on a column at Moorhead, but in 1930 it was moved to Endcliffe Park. The obelisk in Town Hall Square that commemorated the 1887 Jubilee had been removed to the park in 1903.

In 1897, the year that the new Town Hall was opened, *The Builder* carried a report on 'The Architecture of our Large Provincial Towns, X. Sheffield'. Its reporter was not impressed. He thought that:

> The streets of the older part are, with few exceptions, narrow and irregular ... For its size and importance Sheffield does not seem to be very well supplied generally with buildings of good architectural character. It is true that a great part of the area, in fact the whole, except a few streets in the centre, the western suburb, and small districts on the north and north-west, is taken up

by factories and workmen's dwellings; but the number of churches, chapels, and schools is enormous, and they, at least, give the architect a chance which might often have been turned to better account.

We do not know when Sheffield was first described as 'the largest village in the world', but its decidedly provincial character is summed up by its architecture. A much-quoted extract from Dr Frederick Barry's *Report on an Epidemic of Small-Pox at Sheffield During 1887–88* claimed that:

> The Population of Sheffield is, for so large a town, unique in its character, in fact it more closely resembles that of a village than of a town, for over wide areas each person appears to be acquainted with every other, and to be interested with that other's concerns, a state of things leading to an amount of intercommunication such as is not, I believe, met with in other towns of similar size.

Western suburbs

In the eighteenth century, the houses of the leading townsmen had occupied the central streets of Sheffield. From the 1820s onwards the middle classes had moved out of the town into the new western suburbs. The process was completed during the reign of Victoria. By then, the houses of the principal streets had been replaced by shops, banks and offices.

The middle classes had first moved west towards Broomhill, but Sheffield's expanding industries moved in that direction too. The new West Street and Portobello Street soon accommodated steelworks and cutlery businesses as well as houses. Industry did not get as far as Glossop Road, however. Professional people and successful businessmen set up homes and consulting rooms thereabouts, away from the smoke and the grime. In time, the Mappin Art Gallery and the University helped to give the district a genteel air.

Another residential area that was attractive to the middle classes lay within the old hunting park on the slopes of the hill rising from the east bank of the River

The Mappin Art Gallery. Opened in 1887 to house paintings left to the borough by John Newton Mappin, the Art Gallery was built on to Weston Park Museum, which dates from 1875. The interior of the Art Gallery was badly damaged by bombs in the Second World War and was reconstructed in the 1950s and 1960s. It is now undergoing extensive restoration.

PHOTOGRAPH: L. NUTTALL

Queen's Tower in 1995. Built in Norfolk Park for Samuel Roberts, silverware manufacturer, in 1837, Queen's Tower was designed in a Tudor Gothic style by M.E.Hadfield, a leading Sheffield architect. The name and style commemorated Mary, Queen of Scots, who had been imprisoned nearby in the Manor Lodge. In its neglected condition and secluded position amongst modern housing, Queen's Tower seemed even more romantic. It was converted into flats in 2003–4.

PHOTOGRAPH: L. NUTTALL

Sheaf. Park Hill was a working-class district, with some of the worst slums in Sheffield, but only a short distance away to the south, the Duke of Norfolk had reclaimed and landscaped some industrial land to create his private Norfolk Park. In 1856–58 The Farm, near the bottom of Granville Road, had been converted into a residence for the duke when he visited Sheffield. The roads leading to Norfolk Park attracted well-to-do middle-class houses, set in spacious gardens. Here too was the remarkable Queen's Tower that M. E. Hadfield designed in Tudor Gothic style in 1837, so that Samuel Roberts, the silversmith, could indulge his fantasies about the imprisonment of Mary, Queen of Scots. Queen's Tower survives, but The Farm was demolished in 1967. Norfolk Park was opened to the public in 1847, though it remained in the ownership of the Duke of Norfolk until 1909. It became the place where the Sheffield Sunday School Union held its Whit Sings, and where in 1897 Queen Victoria was welcomed by 50,000 children.

Endcliffe Hall, Sheffield.

Clarkehouse Lane, leading to the Botanical Gardens, was a desirable place to live in the mid nineteenth century. The Broomhall estate was being developed to the south, but Endcliffe Vale was still countryside. An 1864 map marks the route as a lane rather than as Clarkhouse Road.

PHOTOGRAPH: CARNEGIE

From the 1830s onwards, the more prosperous of Sheffield's inhabitants moved further west to build villas on the south-facing slopes of Broomhill, Broomhall, Ranmoor, Fulwood, Ecclesall, Nether Edge and Abbeydale. The Mount at Broomhill was unusual in being designed by William Flockton as a row of eight houses linked by a monumental classical façade. Endcliffe Crescent was more typical in being laid out with twelve pairs of semi-detached stone houses, all having long drives and well-wooded gardens. During the 1840s the growing professional and managerial classes favoured Collegiate Crescent and neighbouring parts of the well-wooded Broomhall Park estate, where no commercial development was allowed. Lodges still stand at the former gated entrances to the private roads there.

Much grander houses were built a short distance further west. John Brown commissioned Flockton & Abbott to build Endcliffe Hall as a grand Italianate mansion with a sumptuous interior; it was completed in 1865. A little way up the hill, Flockton's designed another Italianate house for Mark Firth, which he named Oakbrook. Soon afterwards, in 1864–65, M. E. Hadfield & Son designed Thornbury for Frederick Thorpe Mappin. The buildings are now used (respectively) by the Territorial Army (since 1916), as a Catholic school, and as a private hospital.

left Endcliffe Hall, built between 1863 and 1865 by architects Flockton & Abbott, for Sir John Brown.

SHEFFIELD LIBRARIES, ARCHIVES AND INFORMATION: LOCAL STUDIES

The most carefully planned development was that at Nether Edge. A William Fairbank map of 1795 marks just a few farms in that part of Ecclesall bierlow: Nether Edge, Upper Edge and Machon Bank. The Ecclesall Union Workhouse was built at Nether Edge in 1843. This was the district that George Wostenholm, the cutlery manufacturer, was to transform into a model estate based on the towns that he had admired in America. Wostenholm first bought land at Cherry Tree

Nether Edge Tram No. 185 at Moorhead. The original monument at the top of The Moor was erected in honour of those who had fought in the Crimean War. It was later topped with a statue of Queen Victoria. The tram is one of the early ones with the driver and the passengers on the upper deck exposed to the weather. From 1911 all trams were completely covered.

SHEFFIELD LIBRARIES, ARCHIVES AND INFORMATION: LOCAL STUDIES

Hill in 1835 and soon decided to build not only a house but a suburb. He named his house Kenwood after a New England town and employed Robert Marnock to design curving, tree-lined avenues and a variety of stone-built houses. The people who came to live there had to sign covenants which were designed to keep the area purely residential. The detached houses were given large plots in Kenwood Bank, Kenwood Road and Rundle Road, part of Wostenholm Road, and the upper slopes of Brincliffe. Semi-detached houses of various sizes were provided with smaller plots in Kenwood Park Road, Thornsett Road and Steade Road. About 1853, the rest of the Upper and Nether Edge estates were purchased by the Montgomery Land Society, which had been set up by George Wostenholm and Thomas Steade, a builder. The society laid out streets from Glen Road and Byron Road up the hillside as far as Brincliffe Edge and named them Rupert Road, Ashland Road, Nether Edge Road, Oak Hill Road and Edge Hill Road. On them they built a mixture of larger and smaller houses. The character of this district remains largely unaltered (except for the volume of modern traffic). Wostenholm's house is now a hotel, but the building and its grounds are much better preserved than Abbeydale House, the home that John Rodgers, an even greater manufacturer of cutlery than Wostenholm, built in 1850.

Life in the western suburbs was made easier by the introduction of horse buses. The hilly routes that needed four horses were rarely profitable, but the success of other routes encouraged the laying of tram lines in the 1870s. Thus, a line from Moorhead to Heeley was opened in 1876. The abolition of tolls on the turnpike roads was a further encouragement. The last toll bar was that at Hunter's Bar, which ceased to levy tolls after 31 October 1884. The gateposts of this bar have been re-erected in the traffic island at the bottom of Brocco Bank.

In 1896 the Corporation took over the horse-drawn trams. Their first electric tram ran from the city boundary at Tinsley into the town centre on 5 September 1899. Old photographs show how a journey in a tram gradually became more comfortable, not least for the driver. In 1903 covered trams were introduced, in 1907 the driver was protected from the elements by glass, and from 1911 trams were totally enclosed. Trams provided cheap transport, which enabled the working and middle classes to live away from their places of work. They brought people into the town centre for shopping and entertainment and took them to the edges of the town to watch football and cricket. As yet, motor vehicles had made little impact. Reuben Thompson started the first taxi service in Sheffield in 1905, and a sign of renewed interest in road construction came in the same year when the Rivelin Valley road was constructed from Malin Bridge to Rivelin Bridge Post Office, where it joined the turnpike road.

The expansion of the city beyond its traditional boundaries led to administrative changes that recognised the new realities. In 1901 the ancient parish of Norton, which bordered Sheffield at Heeley Bridge, was incorporated within the city. For the first time in its history, Sheffield now included territory that had once formed part of the county of Derbyshire, the diocese of Lichfield and Coventry, and the Anglo-Saxon kingdom of Mercia. In the same year the city also expanded northwards to take in Hillsborough and Southey, and eastwards to include part of Tinsley. In 1912 Blackburn was brought into Sheffield, in 1914 the lower end of the Rivelin and Loxley valleys was incorporated, in 1921 Handsworth, Tinsley and the southern part of Ecclesfield parish were absorbed, and in 1929–34 Dore and Totley were included. By then, most of the inhabitants of Sheffield were hard pressed to say exactly where the city's boundaries extended.

Kenwood Hall. Built in 1844 for George Wostenholm in Tudor Gothic style to designs by the leading local architect, William Flockton. The grounds were laid out by Robert Marnock, who had previously designed the Botanical Gardens. The house was named after a town that Wostenholm had visited in New York State.

below J.Pennell, *Fog, Steam and Smoke on the River Don* (*c*.1909). This was 'Smoky Sheffield' at its worst. It is impossible to recognise any buildings other than the central churches, whose spires are lit by the only shaft of sunlight that penetrated this grim scene.

Working-class housing and public health

A report on the 'Condition of our Chief Towns – Sheffield' in *The Builder*, on 21 September 1861, deliberately sought out the worst aspects of the borough and presented them in a vivid light:

> The narrow streets rise and fall in the most irregular manner ... A thick pulverous haze is spread over the city, which the sun even in the dog days is unable to penetrate, save by a lurid glaze, and which has the effect of imparting to the green hills and golden corn-fields in the high distance the ghostly appearance of being whitened as with snow ... The three rivers sluggishly flowing through the town are made the conduits of all imaginable filth, and at one particular spot ... positively run blood. These rivers ... are polluted with dirt, dust, dung, and carrion, the embankments are ragged and ruined; here and there overhung with privies; and often the site of ash and offal heaps – most desolate and sickening objects ... Sheffield ... is a town where authority is so divided ... that virtually there is no authority at all.

The reporter was appalled at what he found in the Ponds:

> A plank bridge over the Sheaf here shows dead dogs and cats floating on the slimy waters, and a terrible condition of the partially-walled banks, through outlets in which fluents of excremental slush ooze into the river. It is 26 feet

wide at this point, and has all the appearance of having once been a vast covered sewer ... The ponds themselves are lakes of slush. Here a heterogeneous
mass of scabby-looking cottages, isolated dung-heaps and isolated privies, and
detached and semi-detached petty factories, large timber-yards ... and large
factories ... lie and jostle against each other ... In the streets channels are cut
in the pavements to convey the fluid wash from every house across the foot-
ways into the flowing gutters ... while clothes are hanging out to dry across
comparatively wide streets ... We step to a scene that baffles description – a
district of slaughter-sheds for nearly the whole of Sheffield, beginning with a
boiling-house for tripe, and thence slippery with gory slime and drippings from
the ash-pit of the tenements ... above. Pailfuls of blood soak down on the surface of the ground and into the ground through the wretched paving of the
Slaughter-lane, and percolate from slaughter-house to slaughter-house, till the
blood oozingly finds its way, together with faecal matter, into the river. The
sheds themselves are generally so rickety that the removal of the shambles to
an extra-mural site could be effected with but little loss of property; but their
ill condition adds to the ghastliness of the scene.

'The three rivers sluggishly flowing through the town ... are polluted with dirt, dust, dung, and carrion.'

THE BUILDER, 1861

He concluded that:

The rest of these investigations prove that, although Sheffield possesses a
medal of honour conferred at the hands of the Emperor of the French, it is
as devoid of the decencies of civilisation as it was in the Dark Ages.

This was Sheffield at its very worst. The authorities had not yet responded to the
public health problems posed by explosive population growth. The spaces in the
older part of the town had all been filled in and many of the former dwelling
houses had been converted into workshops and factories. Steam engines in the
cutlery works made the air even more polluted than before. Sewage disposal
became a major problem when houses were built in low-lying, ill-drained areas
that previous generations had instinctively avoided. The situation had deterio-
rated rapidly in the 1850s. Throughout the second half of the nineteenth century
death rates in Sheffield from contagious and infectious diseases were amongst the
highest in the country.

G. L. Saunders's investigation into local death rates reported in 1861 that:

In the poorer streets the worst forms of disease are also found in excess, such
as scrofula, syphilis, phthisis, hydrocephalus, fevers, etc ... Intemperance in
Sheffield affects the population as greatly as in any other manufacturing town,
and the temptations to drunkenness meet the working man constantly in the
most striking form. With *thirteen hundred and three* drinking shops, it can
scarcely be wondered at that 979 persons [844 males and 135 females] should
be taken up for drunkenness in 1859.

The worst slums were in the Ponds and in other low-lying districts on the
banks of the Don near Lady's Bridge and in the Wicker, but some better-drained
areas where houses were densely packed, such as Park Hill and the courts leading

off Fargate, Snig Hill and Townhead, were almost as bad. The houses of the Irish immigrants in the eighteenth-century streets of north-west Sheffield had a particularly poor reputation. But this is not the whole picture. In other working-class districts, such as the area between West Street and Division Street, the houses were solidly built and reasonably spaced out. On the whole, Sheffield was still not as bad as most other industrial towns, especially those that housed many of their inhabitants in cellars.

Before electric trams provided cheap transport at the end of the century, families lived close to the man's place of work. The usual accommodation on offer was a back-to-back brick house in a terrace. By 1864, when a Corporation bye-law prohibited the erection of further buildings of this type, Sheffield had 38,000 back-to-backs. Most of these had been built in blocks of from ten to fifteen houses, as speculative enterprises by local tradesmen who had invested up to £10,000. These landlords were more interested in getting a return for their capital than undertaking necessary maintenance work, let alone improvements. Sheffield's back-to-back houses were generally two or sometimes three storeys high. They were built of brick with sliding-sash windows and had a frontage of about 12 feet and a ground floor area of around 150 square feet. The entrance led straight into the downstairs room, which was usually stone-flagged and had a fire-range and a side-oven. Sometimes, the upper floor extended over the tunnels which provided access to the courts or yards at the rear, where the shared privies stood.

The east end steelworkers lived in slightly better-quality houses than those which were available nearer the town centre, for most of them were built after the 1864 bye-law which prohibited the further building of back-to-backs arranged around courts. For this reason, death rates were lower in the east end. The typical houses that were erected in Brightside, Carbrook, and on the hill sides above Carlisle Street, from New Grimesthorpe to Burngreave and Pitsmoor, were built by small speculative builders in rows of two-storey brick terraces. The houses were squeezed tightly together, right up to the steelworks, but their density was still lower than that of houses in the centre of Sheffield. The new settlement pattern of works, houses and public buildings that had been established in the east end by 1890 was to last without major change until the 1960s.

Co-operative building societies formed by respectable artisans had been established in Sheffield from about 1830. Their schemes were admirable, though they involved only a tiny proportion of the population; the majority of the working class continued to rent their accommodation. By 1849 only two estates had been successfully completed by building societies: Birkendale and Hall Carr. In that year two new societies were formed to build houses for their members at Walkley, Crookes and Heeley. By the mid-1860s most of their 76 plots had been built upon. Many of the houses that were erected by members at Walkley, in a variety of individual styles, still stand amidst generous-sized gardens.

Sheffield's smoke problem got worse and worse as industrial and domestic chimneys multiplied. John Murray's *Hand-book for travellers in Yorkshire* (1867) judged that:

'Although Sheffield possesses a medal of honour conferred at the hands of the Emperor of the French, it is as devoid of the decencies of civilisation as it was in the Dark Ages.'

THE BUILDER, 1861

Sheffield, with the exception of Leeds, the largest and most important town in Yorkshire, is beyond all question the blackest, dirtiest, and least agreeable. It is indeed impossible to walk through the streets without suffering from the dense clouds of smoke constantly pouring from great open furnaces in and around the town.

Harvey Littlejohn's *Report on the causes and prevention of smoke from manufacturing chimneys* (1897) noted that:

There are over 600 tall chimneys to which about 850 steam boiler furnaces are attached, while there are 138 chimneys into which the smoke from 266 steam boiler furnaces, together with 383 metallurgical furnaces is discharged, and, lastly, there are 965 chimneys discharging smoke from metallurgical furnaces alone.

Littlejohn's figures were under-estimates, for they did not include 'a considerable number of steel-melting, cupola, and other small furnaces', nor the effects of domestic fires.

A vivid impression of a visit to Sheffield at the end of the nineteenth century is contained in J. S. Fletcher, *A Picturesque History of Yorkshire* (1899):

Under smoke and rain, Sheffield is suggestive of nothing so much as of the popular conception of the infernal regions. From the chimneys, great volumes of smoke pour their listless way towards a forbidding sky; out of the furnaces shoot forth great tongues of flame which relieve the sombreness of the scene and illuminate it at the same time; in the streets there is a substratum of dust

I. Shaw, *Botanical Gardens* (c. 1850). The Botanical Gardens, opened in 1836 by a private company, were laid out to the designs of Robert Marnock, who became the first curator. The view shows Joseph Paxton's glasshouse and the entrance arch. National Lottery funds have recently been obtained to restore the site to its former glory.

and mud; in the atmosphere a choking something that appears to take a firm grip of one's throat. The aspect of the northern fringe of Sheffield on such a day is terrifying, the black heaps of refuse, the rows of cheerless-looking houses, the thousand and one signs of grinding industrial life, the inky waters of river and canal, the general darkness and dirt of the whole scene serves but to create feelings of repugnance and even horror.

Fletcher concluded: 'The prevailing characteristic of the place is utility – stern, hard, and practical.'

The local authorities were powerless to do anything about the smoke and were slow to respond to the challenge of improving public health. After the passing of the Interment Act (1853), the three churchyards and other town burial grounds were closed. The General Cemetery had been opened in 1836 at Sharrow, in what was still rural seclusion. The City Road Cemetery was opened in 1881.

The Public Health Act (1872) was the turning point. Report after report left no doubt as to what needed to be done to improve the worst parts of the town. Some privies were shared by more than sixty persons. One reporter counted 28 decomposing dogs in the river at Ball Street Bridge. A new drainage system,

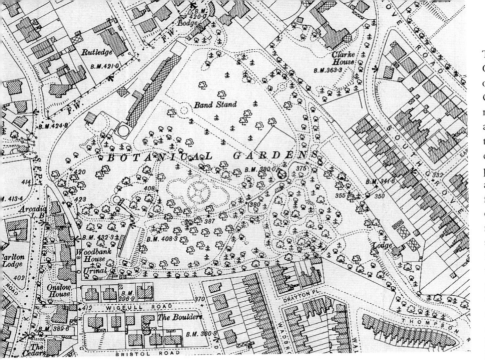

The Botanical Gardens: a section of the 1903 Ordnance Survey map. In the middle and later decades of the nineteenth century Sheffield's prosperous business and professional families moved out of town into the new western suburbs. In 1836 the Botanical Gardens were opened by a private company at what was then the western limit of development. Robert Marnock designed lawns, arbours, shrubberies and walks. A bandstand was the focal point for concerts. The gardens were taken over by the Town Trustees in 1897. The gardens are now open to all.

which the town council had sanctioned in 1866, had done little to alleviate the problems. Fear of the return of cholera in 1871 concentrated minds, but it was not until 1884 that the Corporation began to install an effective sewage disposal system at Blackburn Meadows; the work took two years to complete. Even then, privy middens remained commonplace. In 1888 Sheffield had just over 4,300 water closets, compared with nearly 37,000 privies. Nevertheless, much progress had been made by December 1883, when a survey showed that although some quarters were still filthy and neglected, they were no longer characteristic of the whole of the working-class residential districts. The remaining slums were in the Crofts, Smithfield, Cotton Mill Walk, Pond Hill, the Park, Westbar and Green Lane.

A considerable improvement in the environment was achieved by the provision of public open spaces. Norfolk Park and Firth Park had led the way. In 1875 Weston Park became the first open space in Sheffield to be bought by the town council for public use. Further west, the Botanical gardens, which had been created in 1836 under private ownership, were opened to the public in 1898. Between 1886 and 1890 the council also purchased Meersbrook Park, Endcliffe Woods and Hillsborough Park. By the end of the century the city had 112 hectares of public parks and 19 hectares of recreation grounds. Their bowling greens, boating ponds and band concerts were enormously popular.

By the 1890s gas lighting in houses was fairly common. The provision of pure drinking water was still not entirely satisfactory, however. Demand for water was constantly rising as the population and industry grew and as public health became a matter of increasing concern. Sheffield had ample facilities for collecting and storing water within its boundaries. Between 1830 and 1887 the supply of potable water to the town was the responsibility of the Company of the Proprietors of the Sheffield Waterworks. As we have seen, this company constructed reservoirs

The Sheffield Flood, 1864. The destruction caused by the breach of the Dale Dyke reservoir in March 1864 is revealed by this photograph of one of the water-powered works that were devastated by the full force of the flood water. Harrison's tilt and wheel on the river Loxley was otherwise known as Storrs Bridge Wheel. It was first recorded in 1720. John Harrison, a Sheffield cutler, had taken a lease in 1785. By 1794 he had a tilt and four grinding troughs. Benjamin Tingle was the owner at the time of the flood and John and George Dixon were his tenants.

at Redmires and Crookesmoor and laid connecting aqueducts and mains to house-holders who paid a water rate. An Act of 1853 authorised further reservoirs in the Loxley Valley at Agden, Dale Dyke and Strines. The imperfect construction of the Dale Dyke reservoir was the cause of the greatest natural disaster in Sheffield's history. On the night of 11 March 1864 the embankment of the reservoir collapsed and 114 million cubic feet of water roared down towards Sheffield. Within forty minutes the dam was almost empty. The flood waters poured along the Don Valley, wreaking havoc as they went. During that terrible night, 240 people and 693 animals were drowned, about 100 buildings and 15 bridges were destroyed, and approximately 4,000 houses were damaged.

The Dale Dyke reservoir was rebuilt in the 1870s and new reservoirs were constructed at Agden (1871) and Strines (1875). By 1876 the company stored sufficient water to supply half a million people. The west end of Sheffield had been connected to supplies in 1864–65, Walkley and surrounding districts in 1867–68, and Crookes in 1870–71, but many working-class houses remained unconnected and had to rely on communal standpipes that their landlords had placed in the yards. The Water Company was widely judged to have failed to provide an adequate service. The Corporation finally bought them out in 1888.

The Corporation did not set out to build more reservoirs until they became alarmed at the prospect of neighbouring water authorities taking the resources of the Little Don and the Derwent. During the 1890s Sheffield entered partnerships with other local authorities in order to to share these supplies. The main emphasis, however, was on improvements in the form of inter-connecting mains, filtration plants, sanitary supplies, and the gradual replacement of standpipes by individual house taps.

Further improvements in public health came with the building of specialist hospitals to reinforce the work of the General Infirmary, the Royal Hospital and the hospitals that had grown out of the workhouses at Nether Edge and Firvale. In 1872 Middlewood Hospital for the mentally ill had been built in spacious grounds to the north of the town. In 1878 the Women's Hospital that had been founded in Figtree Lane in 1864 was rebuilt in Leavygreave Road at the sole expense of Thomas Jessop and re-named the Jessop Hospital for Women The Children's Hospital gradually assumed its present character between 1889 and 1903 and the Hospital for Crippled Children (later King Edward VII Orthopaedic) was opened at an isolated site in the Rivelin Valley in 1916. Meanwhile, the Royal Hospital was rebuilt between 1892 and 1915. Private donors also founded almshouses for the elderly to add to the provision at the Shrewsbury Hospital and the Hollis Hospital (which in 1903 moved to its present site at Whirlow). The most notable of the new foundations were Mark Firth's Gothic almshouses at Nether Green (1869–70), J. B. Mitchell-Withers's Gothic Licensed Victuallers' Asylum in Abbeydale (1878) and the George Woofindin almshouses at Hunter's Bar (1898), which were designed as a block of cottages.

During the second half of the nineteenth century the real earnings of the working-class families of Sheffield improved considerably and the hours of work were reduced, except for those men who were employed on 12-hour shifts to keep the steel furnaces in continuous production. Despite periods of unemployment when trade was bad, the skilled workers – the respectable artisans – were more prosperous than before. John Wilson was stating a common opinion when he wrote in 1899, 'I believe the workmen as a whole … were never better fed, better clothed, or better housed, than they are at present.'

When Sheffield was made a city in 1893 some of the well-known suburbs of today hardly existed. The rows of terraced house at Hunter's Bar and Greystones had not yet appeared, Ecclesall Church stood in the countryside, Fulwood, Stumperlow and Lodge Moor were tiny settlements. The house-building boom of the late 1890s and early 1900s was particularly noticeable in the working- and lower middle-class suburbs that grew up alongside the new tram routes: Meersbrook, Woodseats, Norton, Sharrow, Abbeydale, Millhouses, Walkley, Crookes, Hillsborough, Firvale, Tinsley, Darnall and Intake. The Sheffield tram system had been taken over by the Corporation in 1896 and electrified between 1899 and 1902. The last routes – to Middlewood and Crookes – were opened in 1913.

The new houses were sometimes built of stone, or were at least stone-fronted. They were mostly rented, as before. Meanwhile, the Corporation had acquired new powers that enabled them to launch a programme of slum clearance and rebuilding. A start was made in 1904 with the Crofts. This notorious group of courts was bounded by Lee Croft, Campo Lane, Townhead Street, Tenter Street and Silver Street Head. Other properties in West Bar Green and Silver Street

The aspect of the northern fringe of Sheffield … is terrifying, the black heaps of refuse, the rows of cheerless-looking houses, the thousand and one signs of grinding industrial life, the inky waters of river and canal, the general darkness and dirt of the whole scene serves but to create feelings of repugnance and even horror.'

J. S. FLETCHER, 1899

A HISTORY OF SHEFFIELD

were cleared at the same time. About 1,250 people had to be re-housed. New streets were laid out on the cleared sites and new buildings erected, including Sheffield's first 124 flats. Between 1891 and 1901 about 40 of another 300 houses that had been condemned were demolished and the rest closed or repaired.

In 1900 the Corporation began an imaginative scheme at High Wincobank: the first working men's garden suburb in Sheffield. By 1906 41 homes had been completed; by 1919 the estate comprised 617 houses. High Wincobank attracted much publicity and was praised by the leaders of the Garden City Movement. Sheffield was recognised as a pioneer of housing reform and one of the first cities to use the permissive planning powers of the Housing and Planning Act (1909). Even so, the slum problem remained acute. In 1914 nearly 17,000 families still lived in back-to-backs and another 8,000 families lived in houses which required some attention to make them fit for human habitation. Sheffield had more privy middens than any other city in Britain. At the outbreak of the First World War, 11,000 privy middens still served 16,600 of Sheffield's 107,000 houses. Clearly, much remained to be done to bring thousands of homes up to a decent standard.

Entertainment and aspirations

The pub culture of heavy drinking in Sheffield was often remarked upon and frequently denounced. From 1872, the magistrates used new powers to limit the number of licences so as to try to bring the problem under control. Like other Victorian towns, Sheffield had its temperance movement, linked particularly to the chapels, with numerous societies, a Temperance Hall in Townhead Street, and a prominent advocate in Alderman Sir William Clegg, English international football player, prominent citizen, Liberal councillor and chairman of the Education Committee. The temperance movement helped to curb some of the worst excesses of heavy drinking, with their ruinous effects on family life, but

Tug of war team,
*c.*1910.

Decorations for the visit of the Prince and Princess of Wales, 1875. On the occasion of royal visits in 1875, 1897 and 1905 it was the custom to erect temporary arches in Gothic or Classical style , made of wood and plaster board. This one was erected by the bridge over the River Don in Blonk Street. As on all such occasions, much time was spent waiting for something to happen.

failed to impress those who found that heavy labour in the steel industry was thirsty work.

The advocates of temperance were amongst those who welcomed the rise of participation and spectator sport as an outlet for energies. Late-Victorian Sheffield became noted for its professional football and cricket teams and for its hundreds of clubs, ranging from pub sides to teams that competed in the Bible Class League. Swimmers were first catered for by the swimming and Turkish baths in Glossop Road, which were opened as a private venture in 1836. The Corporation built its first public swimming baths in 1869. They took over the Glossop Road baths in 1895 and extended them in 1908–14. Cross-country running was encouraged by

The Yorkshire County Cricket Team (1875). This is the earliest known photograph of the county cricket team. It was taken before a game with Surrey at Bramall Lane, Sheffield, in June 1875. The Yorkshire C.C.C. had been founded at a meeting in Sheffield in 1863. Bramall Lane had replaced earlier cricket grounds at Darnall and Hyde Park.

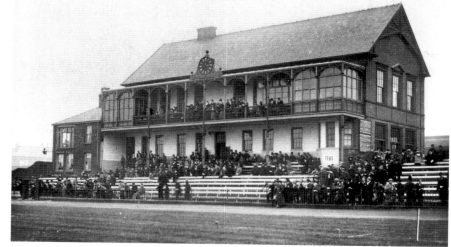

the Sheffield United Harriers, and cycling by a number of clubs, notably the Sharrow Club, founded in 1887. In the following year, the first 'Sheffield Cyclists' Charity Tournament' at Bramall Lane attracted 15,000 spectators. Meanwhile, cheap excursion tickets on the railways enabled Sheffielders to get out into the surrounding countryside, to walk or climb in the Peak District or to fish in Lincolnshire. Joseph Morris's *Little Guide to the West Riding* (1911) thought that: 'no great town in England is situated so immediately on the border of such wild and beautiful scenery'. The Sheffield Clarion Ramblers, founded in 1900 by G. H. B. Ward, soon became one of the best-known walking clubs in the north of England. Ward was a socialist whose life-long ambition was to promote a sense of fellowship between man and nature, and who battled long and hard to make the grouse-shooting moors accessible to the working-classes of the surrounding industrial cities.

Sheffield United Football Club, 1890-91. The United Football Club were remarkably successful in the years immediately after their formation in 1889. Their golden period was between 1897 and 1901, a few years after this early photograph was taken.

This new interest in sport and physical recreation began about the middle of the nineteenth century, when Saturday half-holidays shortened the working week. Cricket was the first popular passion. As early as 1771 a Sheffield team had been assembled to play Nottingham. The Hallam Club (with York, the oldest club in the north of England) was founded by 1804. A large cricket ground at Darnall was the chief venue for matches until an even better ground was laid out at Hyde Park in 1826. Professional challenge matches attracted large crowds; in 1846, for example, an All-England XI was watched by 16,000 spectators at Hyde Park. The authorities welcomed such peaceful activities. When the Sheffield Cricket Club was founded in 1854, the chairman at the inaugural meeting was Michael Ellison, agent to the Duke of Norfolk. The following year, Ellison was instrumental in obtaining a new site in Bramall Lane at the southern edge of the town for the Sheffield United Cricket Club. Sheffield can claim a special place in the history of cricket, for it was here that the Yorkshire County Cricket Club was founded in 1863. In the late nineteenth century, large crowds came to see their matches at Bramall Lane.

Football developed later than cricket as a spectator sport, but by the end of the century it had become the more popular of the two. Sheffield played a leading role in the development of football. Many of the rules of the game that were gradually adopted by the Football Association were those of Sheffield F.C., the club that was founded in 1857 and which is recognised as the oldest in the world. When the Football League was formed in 1888, a new era of professionalism began and Sheffield F.C. got left behind. In its place, two new Sheffield clubs soon gained popular support. In 1867 the Wednesday Cricket Club (founded in 1820) decided to keep their members together in the winter by playing football at their Olive Grove Ground, on the south-eastern edge of the town; in 1899 they moved to Hillsborough. At Bramall Lane in 1889, the United Cricket Club also formed a football club. United and Wednesday were successful sides in the late nineteenth century, especially United, who were Football League champions in 1898, runners up twice in the next five years, FA Cup winners in 1899, and finalists in 1901.

The theatres and music halls in the town centre offered different forms of mass entertainment. The popularity of theatrical performances and music hall turns in the second half of the nineteenth century encouraged theatre owners to improve their buildings and to erect new ones. A succession of theatres have occupied the area where the Crucible and Lyceum theatres now stand. The Theatre Royal succeeded the eighteenth-century Theatre in Norfolk Street, until it was destroyed by fire in 1935, together with the adjacent Assembly Rooms. The Alexandra Theatre at the end of Blonk Street was opened in 1865 on the site of the Adelphi Music Hall, with a capacity of

right Alexandra Theatre c. 1900. Thomas Youdan opened the Alexandra Theatre in Blonk Street in 1865 on the site of the Adelphi Music Hall, for performances of grand opera and pantomime. The theatre could seat 4,000 customers. It was demolished in 1914 when the road was widened.
SHEFFIELD LIBRARIES, ARCHIVES AND INFORMATION: LOCAL STUDIES

left The Old Surrey Theatre, West Bar. Music halls were built in the West Bar district in the 1850s and 1860s. The Surrey Theatre started as a casino and dancing room in 1851 and was gradually extended by Thomas Youdan into a large music hall, theatre, ballroom, museum and picture gallery. It was consumed by fire in 1865. In 1881 the Union Offices and Vestry Offices were built on the site.
SHEFFIELD LIBRARIES, ARCHIVES AND INFORMATION: LOCAL STUDIES

4,000 seats for the performance of grand opera and pantomime; it was demolished in 1914 when the Corporation widened the streets at the bottom of the Victoria Station approach. The Empire Palace in Charles Street was opened in 1895 with a facade of an eye-catching mixture of oriental styles. The Alhambra at Attercliffe, later known as the Palace, was built in 1898 in a similar, light-hearted Moorish style. The City Theatre of 1890 was remodelled as the Lyceum in 1897, with exuberant rococo plasterwork; it is the only one of the old theatres of Sheffield to survive.

From 1896 existing theatres and halls were used as cinemas. The Empire Palace staged the first cinematic demonstration. The first purpose-built cinema in Sheffield was the Picture Palace in Union Street, opened in 1910 and demolished in 1964. Early cinemas took the styles of the Empire and the Alhambra to extremes. The Electra, opened in 1911 in Fitzalan Square, is remembered by its later name of the News Theatre. Cinema House in Fargate and the Coliseum at Spital Hill were opened in 1913. The Landsdowne Cinema, which was opened in London Road in the following year, survives intact, its miniature pagoda still a landmark.

The Sheffield Musical Society had been founded about 1750, when the cult of the Handelian oratorio was starting to take hold of choirs. Sheffield developed a strong choral tradition, with performances given both in concert halls and in churches and chapels. The Music Hall in Surrey Street, which was opened in 1824 on the site of the present Central Library, became the main venue for concerts, public meetings and art exhibitions over the next 50 years. In 1873 the Albert

The central library, Surrey Street.

Hall, which stood where John Lewis's department store is now, opened as the new Music Hall. Large orchestral and choral concerts were given here until the First World War, when it was converted into a cinema; it was destroyed by fire, together with its famous French organ, in 1937. Sheffield choirs gained a high reputation under the direction of Sir Henry Coward (1849–1944), a self-taught musician who had started his working life as an apprentice cutler. As conductor, chorus-master, composer, and director of festivals and Whit Sings, he was the guiding spirit of Sheffield music during his long life.

Nineteenth-century Sheffield produced only one artist of national repute

in Sir Francis Chantrey (1781–1841), sculptor and studio painter, but it had a number of talented figures of lesser repute. The School of Design, founded in 1843 to encourage artisans, changed its name to the School of Art in 1857 and began to provide a general art education in its premises in Arundel Street. The forerunner of the present Faculty of Art and Design at Sheffield Hallam University, it enrolled hundreds of students over the generations. Godfrey Sykes (1825–66) and William Ibbitt (1805–69) studied there. The work of amateurs was encouraged by the Sheffield Society of Artists, which held its first exhibition in 1875, and by the opening of the Mappin Art Gallery in 1887, next to the Weston Park Museum. In the same year (1875) as this museum was founded, John Ruskin opened his St George Museum in Walkley to educate and inspire the working classes. Ruskin was attracted by the handicraft skills of Sheffield cutlers, but appalled by the grime and smoke of the town. His museum was moved to Meersbrook in 1889 and now forms part of the Millennium Galleries.

In 1856 Sheffield was the first town in Yorkshire to establish a public library, in Surrey Street. Six branch libraries were erected in the suburbs between 1870 and 1905, but this early enthusiasm was not maintained and by the end of the century Sheffield had a poor reputation for its library provision. Meanwhile, facilities for higher education had been provided by private donors. The Medical School, which had been opened in Surrey Street in 1829, was transferred to new premises in Leopold Street in 1888. On the opposite side of the road stood Firth College, which Mark Firth had founded in 1879 after the success of the Cambridge University Extension Movement lectures in Sheffield. The college cost Firth £20,000 and was formally opened by Prince Leopold. Another important educational institution was the Sheffield Technical School, which began classes in St George's Square in 1886, largely at the instigation of Frederick Thorpe Mappin. In 1897 the Medical School, Firth College and the Technical School were merged to form the University College of Sheffield. In 1905 the college was granted full University status, with W. M. Hicks, the former Principal of Firth College as its first Vice-Chancellor. The opening of the new buildings at Western

A HISTORY OF SHEFFIELD

Springfield Board School. One of the finest of the schools that were erected by the Education Board, it was designed in 1875 by C. J. Innocent and Thomas Brown. The school was enlarged in 1891–92 to include a playground on the roof and again in 1897. The architects called their style 'English Domestic Gothic'. Innocent's son was the author of *The Development of English Building Construction* (1916), a famous, pioneering study of vernacular architecture.

PHOTOGRAPH: CARNEGIE

Bank by King Edward VII, accompanied by Queen Alexandra, was a major event, witnessed by huge crowds.

Meanwhile, the provision of elementary education had improved considerably. From 1846 child monitors had been gradually replaced by pupil-teachers, but the minimum age of apprenticeship to that position was not raised to 14 until 1877. By the 1860s nearly all the headteachers of the voluntary schools in the borough were ex-pupil teachers who had secured a certificate through part-time study. The churches and chapels continued to build schools throughout the 1870s, but were eventually unable to compete with the new board schools that were paid for out of the local rates. In 1870 the first School Board was elected to provide elementary education for children aged between five and thirteen. C. J. Innocent and his partner Thomas Brown were responsible for 19 of the 22 schools that were completed between 1873 and 1881. These were designed in an imaginative variety of 'English Domestic Gothic' styles, and remain some of Sheffield's finest Victorian public buildings.

The board schools catered for large numbers of pupils.

By 1892 Sheffield had 23 schools with over 1,000 pupils, including four that had over 1,500. Irregular attendance was a problem, but it made class sizes more manageable. The Central Higher Grade School (1880), divided into separate sections for boys and girls, provided a technical education that was considered suitable for an industrial city; it quickly established a sound reputation and achieved full secondary status in 1906. Meanwhile, private education was provided by the Westbourne Preparatory School (1885) and the Birkdale Preparatory School (1905). The Sheffield Girls' High School was established in Surrey Street in 1878, and six years later moved to Rutland Park. In 1902 the government abolished elected School Boards and Sheffield City Council became one of Britain's 330 Local Educational Authorities, with powers to provide secondary as well as elementary education. The new LEA acted quickly. In 1904 they merged Wesley College and the Sheffield Grammar School to form the King Edward VII School, and raised the age limit for the Central Secondary school to 16. The following year, they established the Sheffield Training College, one of the first municipal training colleges for teachers, on the site of the former Sheffield Collegiate School, which had been founded in 1836.

State provision of education took away the need for Sunday Schools to teach reading and writing and allowed them to concentrate on religious instruction. The Sheffield Sunday School Union was established in Queen Street Congregational Church in 1812. When Montgomery Hall, its new headquarters in Surrey Street, was opened in 1886, a crowd of 70,000 gathered in Norfolk Park to watch the processions of 25,000 teachers and scholars from 118 schools. The SSSU's first annual Whit Walk and Sing in Norfolk Park was held in 1857.

The middle and later years of the nineteenth century saw a determined and sustained effort on the part of the various denominations to provide many more

King Edward VII School. Built in 1837–40 as the Wesley Proprietary Grammar School, later the Wesley College, this remarkably ambitious building was one of William Flockton's most successful designs. When Sheffield became a local education authority the college was amalgamated with another school and opened as the King Edward VII School in 1906.
PHOTOGRAPH: CARNEGIE

St Marie's Cathedral. The Roman Catholic Cathedral, dedicated in 1850, was designed by Sheffield architect, M.E.Hadfield, in the Decorated style of the fourteenth century. It occupies the site of the early eighteenth-century Catholic chapel that stood to the rear of Lord's House, the house built in Fargate for the steward of the Duke of Norfolk.
PHOTOGRAPH: CARNEGIE

right Detail of St Marie's Cathedral, showing a sculpture of the Annunciation by Thomas Earp's studio. The cathedral had an estimated congregation of 2,000 soon after it opened.
PHOTOGRAPH: CARNEGIE

churches and chapels for the rapidly growing population. The favoured style, even for the chapels, was now the Gothic, particularly elaborate geometric and decorated forms. Nearly all these buildings were designed by local firms of architects. The old parish church was altered in 1842 and 1856–57, and again in 1880, when the galleries were removed, the nave was extended and new transepts were built. The finest of Sheffield's Victorian churches are undoubtedly St John's, Ranmoor (1887), designed by E. M. Gibbs, and St Marie's, now the Roman Catholic Cathedral, designed by M. E. Hadfield and erected between 1847 and 1850.

A local census of church attendance

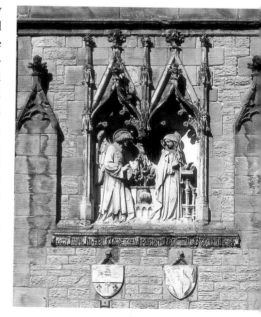

The city centre, 1903. The memory of the castle and the medieval market town is preserved in the names and winding courses of the central streets. Victorian market halls occupy much of the space descending to the River Sheaf, which has been culverted almost as far as its confluence with the Don. The canal basin, opened in 1819, penetrated into the heart of Sheffield. Rows of terraced houses (bottom right) climb up to Park Hill, within the former medieval deer park. Lady's Bridge once marked the northern limit of the town but now leads to dense rows of houses and industrial premises. The Victoria Railway Station and the Wicker Arches were completed in 1848, linking Sheffield with Manchester. Sheffield's industrial East End lies immediately beyond.

The Sheffield City
Battalion. Upon the
outbreak of the First
World War, a
Sheffield City
Battalion of
volunteers was
formed at Sheffield
University. It
attracted 900
recruits from staff,
students and others
in the city during its
first two days. The
photograph shows
training at Bramall
Lane shortly after
the outbreak of war,
before a training
camp was
established at
Redmires.

in 1881 showed that over the previous thirty years the congregations of the Church of England had risen from 14,881 to 33,835 and that their proportion of the total number of worshippers had increased. However, these figures must be set against the substantial rise of the local population during those decades. By 1881 the Anglicans had 50 churches in Sheffield, all of them evangelicalistic or low church in outlook. Despite this considerable growth, the Church of England still attracted fewer worshippers than the various dissenting sects. Sheffield had long been a stronghold of Nonconformity; now it had become a Methodist borough.

Well-educated chapel members were prominent in the affairs of the town. The Congregationalists were active Liberals and the Unitarians provided mayors, aldermen, Masters Cutler and magistrates. Sheffield's industrial and commercial life was dominated by a web of Wesleyan, New Connexion and Free Methodist families. The Wesleyans of Carver Street vied with the Unitarians of Upper Chapel as the leaders of progressive thought in the town. Park, Norfolk Street and Brunswick chapels also attracted huge congregations. In 1908 the Norfolk Street chapel was replaced by Victoria Hall, a large building with 1,800 seats which supported the largest Methodist congregation in the north of England until well into the 1950s. The Methodist New Connexion was also strong in Sheffield; its five chapels of 1851 had become twelve by 1881. Alexander Kilham, the founder of the denomination in 1797, had been the first minister in the Scotland Street chapel. The Firths were the New Connexion's best-known Sheffield members. The Primitive Methodists had started slowly, but by 1881 they had 25 chapels in the working-class quarters of the borough. The United Methodist Free Churches joined forces in 1857. Those Methodists who preferred to go their separate way formed the Wesleyan Reform Union, which had had 15 chapels by 1881. The Congregationalists had 22 chapels, the Baptists only six. At the other end of the social spectrum, the Sheffield branch of the Salvation Army was formed in 1879 and by 1894 had moved to a prime site on Pinstone Street.

Church- and chapel-goers played a large part in local politics. The

Nonconformist denominations were influential in promoting the 'respectability' of the Victorian working class, with its emphasis on regular work, education, thrift and temperate drinking. The workers in the traditional 'light trades' supported the Liberals. The unusual structure of Sheffield industry encouraged the skilled artisan who was independent both at work and in his political and religious beliefs; a high number of sick clubs kept their members off the Poor Law. The unskilled immigrants in the 'heavy trades' of the east end of the borough formed a new type of working class. It was here in the 1890s that Sheffield's first socialists began to gain support.

Until about 1860 Sheffield was strongly Liberal and Radical. During the next few decades, however, as council business came to have much more relevance to the lives of the electors, the dominance of the old groups waned and elections to the town council and to parliament became keenly contested. From the late 1870s Liberal–Conservative rivalry became marked. In 1880, after nearly half a century of Liberal control of the two-member Sheffield parliamentary constituency, the Conservatives gained their first MP. Neither party was able to sustain a commanding majority in the borough council during the 1880s and early 1890s, but for most of that time the Conservatives held a narrow lead. William Leng, the crusading proprietor of the *Sheffield Telegraph* from 1864 until his death in 1902, championed the Conservative cause amongst the skilled working class by advocating 'economy with efficiency' in municipal government; he was rewarded with a knighthood. Conservative dominance at this time enabled Henry

Peace celebrations, 1919. The end of the First World War was widely celebrated with street parties. This one was held in Curson Road, Crookes.

A HISTORY OF SHEFFIELD

Fitzalan Howard (1847–1917), the 15th Duke of Norfolk, to be Sheffield's last Mayor and first Lord Mayor; he was also the city's first Honorary Freeman, the University's first chancellor, and the last Duke of Norfolk to have influence in Sheffield's affairs. The duke was one of Britain's twenty richest landowners; half of his income came from his estates in Sheffield. The Liberals lacked coherent policies and generally voted as individuals. As many of them were small business-men, they too favoured economy. Support for the 'Lib-Lab' ticket increased in

The Civic War Memorial, Barker's Pool commemorates the 5,000 local men who were killed in the First World War. Designed by C.D. Carus Wilson and unveiled in 1925, its 90-feet high steel mast rises from a bronze base. Four soldiers stand in remembrance with bowed heads and reversed rifles.
PHOTOGRAPH: CARNEGIE

the early 1900s, but Labour did not make much headway on its own before the extension of the franchise in 1918. No women had the vote at parliamentary elections before 1918, but some were able to vote in certain types of local elections. Women from Liberal, Nonconformist families were much involved in temperance and philanthropic causes. In 1882 Sarah Ruth Wilson became the first woman to be elected to the Sheffield School Board and in 1894 Elizabeth Chappell was the first woman to be voted on to the board of one of the two Poor Law Unions.

The First World War brought the Victorian and Edwardian era to an abrupt end. Public enlistment of volunteers began on 10 September 1914, and by the end of the next day 900 men had been accepted into the Sheffield City Battalion. On 12 May 1915, having endured the rigours of a winter's camp at Redmires, the battalion left for Staffordshire. On 3 April 1916, after service on the Suez Canal, they reported for duty, together with 143 other battalions, at the front line on the Somme. After five days of heavy bombardment, on 1 July 1916 the Allied Forces attacked the German lines along a twenty-mile front. On that first day, 248 Sheffield men were killed, of whom 165 were never identified. The Hallamshire territorial battalion of the York and Lancaster regiment, formed in 1907, also fought on the Somme and at Passchendaele. Their headquarters in Glossop Road was subsequently re-named the Somme Barracks to commemorate their valour. Civilians also experienced the horrors of the war through a series of Zeppelin raids targeted at Sheffield's industry. Bombs dropped on Attercliffe and Burngreave from Zeppelins on 25 September 1916 killed 28 people and injured another 19. Altogether, 5,139 Sheffielders died during the First World War. A fine memorial stands in Weston Park to the 8,814 members of the York and Lancaster Regiment who were killed. The civic memorial was erected in Barker's Pool in 1925.

An aerial photograph, dating from 1945, of the lower Don valley, with east to the top. Brightside Lane (left) and the road through Attercliffe Common (right) frame Hadfield's and Vickers's steelworks, which were at full production as the Second World War drew to a close. The river Don winds its way through the centre. Rows of terraced houses lead off Brightside Lane.

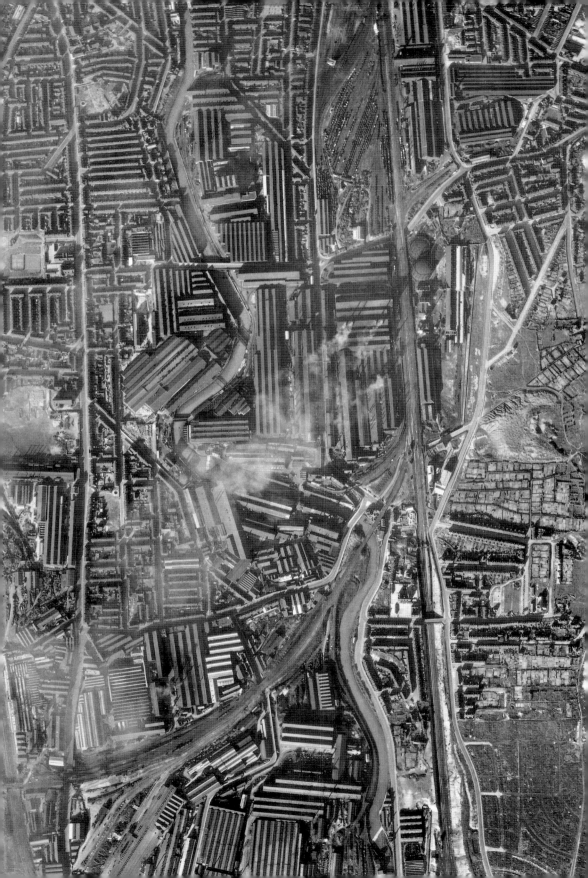

S.D.WILLIAMS

S.D. WILLIAMS
TAILORESS
→

CHAPTER 6

The modern city

Between the wars

In a famous passage in *The Road to Wigan Pier* (1937), George Orwell wrote:

> But even Wigan is beautiful compared with Sheffield. Sheffield, I suppose, could justly claim to be the ugliest town in the Old World: its inhabitants, who want it to be pre-eminent in everything, very likely do make that claim for it. It has a population of half a million and it contains fewer decent buildings than the average East Anglian village of five hundred. And the stench! If at rare moments you stop smelling sulphur it is because you have begun smelling gas. Even the shallow river that runs through the town is usually bright yellow with some chemical or other. Once I halted in the street and counted the factory chimneys I could see; there were thirty-three of them, but there would have been far more if the air had not been obscured by smoke.

The courtyard of Butcher's Wheel in 2004. The former greatness and subsequent decline of Sheffield's staple industries is captured by this image of the decay of William and Samuel Butcher's works near the heart of the town in Arundel Street. This proud firm once exported enormous quantities of high-quality metalware to America. The problem now is to find new uses for the most important parts of Sheffield's unique industrial heritage.
PHOTOGRAPH: CARNEGIE

There is plenty of other evidence to support Orwell's view. 'Smoky Sheffield', set amongst beautiful countryside, was the prevailing image of the city right through to the 1960s.

Industry

In 1918 the Sheffield steel industry was in a buoyant mood, but the danger signs were there for all to see. The market for armaments quickly vanished at the end of the war, and American and Continental competitors had caught up with Sheffield technology in special steels. The First World War had ruined many of Sheffield's best markets. American tariffs hit Sheffield exports hard, and Germany, Russia and France no longer bought Sheffield's tool steel. Sales were therefore directed towards Australia, Canada, South America, China, Japan and the British colonies, and to meet the home demand from the aircraft, car and motor cycle industries. Firms such as Edgar Allen's, Samuel Osborne's, and Arthur Balfour & Sons rose to the challenge, but others, such as Andrew's, Beardshaw's, Darwin's and Huntsman's failed to adapt.

When the post-war boom ended in 1921, the general recession hit Sheffield badly as both home and foreign demand for steel fell sharply. Unemployment in the city rose to 49,500 in 1921, i.e. 32.5 per cent of the registered work-force. By 1927 it had fallen to 23,000 (14 per cent), but in 1932 it reached a new peak of

58,100 (34.1 per cent) and did not fall below 26,000 again until the new rearmament programme got underway in the years leading up to the Second World War. Most of this unemployment was in the steel industry. By 1931 employment in the heavy trades had dropped to 47,000 from its level of 66,000 ten years earlier. For most of the inter-war period, Sheffield's steel firms struggled to recover their former confidence.

One response to the new economic difficulties was to merge the largest firms into huge combines. In 1918 Steel, Peech & Tozer, Samuel Fox, and several other firms joined to form the United Steel Companies, a formidable combination of heavy steelmaking and rolling capacity. Ten years later, the English Steel Corporation was created from the mergers of Vickers and Armstrong and then of Cammell-Laird. Cammell's Grimesthorpe Works and Vickers's River Don Works were retained and modernised. Finally, in 1930 Thomas Firth & Sons and John Brown, who had worked in close association since 1902, were formally amalgamated. By the Second World War the only giant steel firm in Sheffield not to have merged with another company was Hadfield's.

These big firms were publicly quoted companies, which employed thousands of workers. They concentrated on the manufacture of heavy forgings and castings, on the mass production of alloy steels for engineering, and on armaments. The smaller steelmaking firms, such as Huntsman's, Balfour's, Osborn's and Beardshaw's, were privately run, often family-operated businesses, employing fewer than 1,000 workers (and often fewer than 400). They concentrated on making tool steel and high-grade alloys and castings.

When Jessop's was purchased by the Birmingham Small Arms Co. in 1919, it was the first time that an outside firm had bought its way into the Sheffield steel industry. Two new steelmaking companies bucked the trend by prospering in the inter-war period. In the 1920s the Neepsend Steel & Tool Corporation was developed by (Sir) Stuart Goodwin (1886–1969), who was born at Upperthorpe and who had developed his family's steel merchandising business. Goodwin nearly died from diabetes in 1923, but responded to the new treatment offered by the discovery of insulin, and later became one of Sheffield's most noted philanthropists. In 1929 he bought the bankrupt firm of Jonas & Colver. The other newcomer was Tinsley Wire, founded in 1933 by Leon Bekaert, a Belgian, in co-operation with British Ropes Ltd and the United Steel Companies. Sales of their products rose from 3,000 tons in 1933 to 20,000 tons in 1939.

Production methods in the east-end steelworks were a curious combination of the old and the new, the latest technology from Sheffield's research and development departments alongside the traditional methods of crucible steel manufacture. The demand for crucible steel declined steadily during the inter-war period, but the process survived until the 1960s. Electric-arc furnaces had been introduced during the First World War, and in 1927 Edgar Allen's installed a high-frequency induction furnace which was specially designed for tool steel by the American designer Edwin F. Northrup. By the late 1930s, all the major tool steelmakers had abandoned crucibles in favour of electric induction melting. These investments helped Sheffield maintain its lead in special steel technology between the wars.

The tool industry had flourished during the First World War and continued to do so for a while afterwards. The trade was still characterised by a large number of small- or medium-sized firms making an enormous variety of high-quality products. Many of these businesses were still family-controlled, secretive and unco-operative. In outlook and organisation they were essentially Victorian. They made saws, hammers, files, and joiners', masons', engineers' and mining tools. Two of the largest firms were Stanley's and Neill's. Stanley Tools had long been established in Connecticut. They came to Woodside in north Sheffield in 1936 when they bought J. A. Chapman, makers of joiners' braces and planes. James Neill & Co. began as a small crucible steel business in Bailey Street. The founder, James Neill (1858–1930), was the son of a wealthy and successful Rotherham industrialist, George Neill (1831–99) of Tinsley Rolling Mills. In 1889 James launched his own steel business, moving outside the city to Napier Street in 1904. His firm made cast steel and hacksaws, and from 1926 until the Second World War razors as well. Re-armament increased the demand for tools, a demand that was sustained throughout the war.

The cutlery industry went through the same cycle of post-war boom, quickly followed by recession. The evaporation of the market for luxury goods in the First World War had hit the previously prosperous silver- and electro-plate firms: Walker & Hall, Dixon's, and Mappin & Webb. Their workers had either enlisted in the Army or had sought higher wages in the local steelworks. After the war, many of them did not return to their old jobs. Manufacturers of high-quality knives such as Rodgers's and Wostenholm's also found that sales had declined considerably, whereas the smaller firms had benefited from war-time demand. The basic structure of the knife industry was hardly affected by the war; the trade was still characterised by a high number of small firms. For example, in 1918 over 100 pocket- and sportsman's knife makers were listed in the directories.

In the 1920s and 1930s the signs that the Sheffield cutlery industry was in decline were there for all to see. Even Government tariffs (33.3 per cent in 1924, 50 per cent in 1932) aimed particularly against German exports did not stop the slide. Large firms such as Hutton's and Martin, Hall and many small businesses went bankrupt. Although employment levels in the cutlery industry stayed at about 10,000 throughout the inter-war period, output was no longer rising and Sheffield's share of the world market fell in face of competition from the more efficient German and American firms.

Rodgers's and Wostenholm's failed to modernise, and the small firms continued in their Victorian ways. Walter Tyzack of Needham, Veall & Tyzack was one of the few owners to install German machinery in his works and to advocate mechanisation. The most successful cutlery firm between the wars was founded by a large family of German Jewish immigrants, the Vieners (who eventually shortened their name to Viner). The firm grew from humble beginnings until they possessed the largest cutlery factory in Sheffield after the Second World War. The family had settled in Sheffield about 1900, and soon established a silver- and electro-plate business in Glossop Road and West Street. In 1912 they moved to Broomspring Works in Bath Street, where they became the first firm to produce

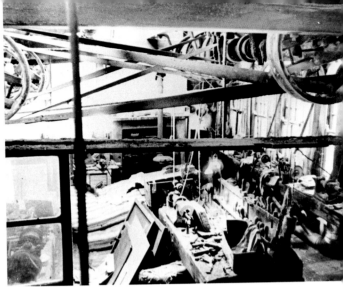

Horn Handle Works, Broom Close. The photographs of the exterior and interior of Hill Brothers' works, c. 1970, show a typical small-sized Sheffield business that specialised in a particular branch of the cutlery trades.
HAWLEY COLLECTION, UNIVERSITY OF SHEFFIELD

plated holloware in large quantities. They soon diversified into flatware (spoons and forks), and about 1934 became a public company. Their work-force numbered about 1,250 in 1945.

In the 1930s two other German families – Sippels and Richartz – set up cutlery businesses in Sheffield. The Sippel brothers settled in London in 1931 and moved to Sheffield two years later. By 1939 the Sipelia Works in Cadman Street employed 400 workers in a mechanised plated spoon and fork business. Two other brothers – Stephan and Paul Richartz – came from Solingen in 1932 to make pocket knives. They softened their name to Richards and by 1939 they, too, employed 400 workers, in Broomhall Street and Soho Street. Only one native Sheffield firm – Frank Cobb's Howard Works – expanded at a similar rate.

Buffer girls, shown on an early twentieth-century postcard. Every piece of cutlery and silverware received a high polish at the final stage of production in order to remove the dents and rough parts which were left on the blade after grinding. This hard job was traditionally women's work, and large numbers were employed.
HAWLEY COLLECTION, UNIVERSITY OF SHEFFIELD

Together, such firms showed that the decline of the Sheffield cutlery industry was not inevitable.

The firms that resisted mechanisation claimed that mass-production meant low-quality goods. They argued that Sheffield's reputation was firmly based on the high quality of its products, made of crucible and double-shear steel, even though the electric-arc and induction furnaces of the inter-war years were making the crucible process redundant. They were firm in their belief that hand-forging gave steel extra quality. They were also contemptuous of foreign competition, believing that their standards could never be matched. Marketing and design seemed small considerations to them. And so it was that the Sheffield cut-throat razor trade collapsed when Gillette entered the market with 'Safety' razors. The demand for many of the older styles of Sheffield knives fell steadily. On the other hand, Sheffield cutlers quickly recognised the potential of stainless steel, even though knife blades had to be forged by power because it was nearly impossible to do the work by the old hand methods. After the First World War, millions of knives marked 'Firth Stainless' were manufactured by mass-production techniques. They were punched out of cold-rolled stainless strip, then heat-treated and ground automatically. The hafting process was sometimes abolished because the whole knife could be made from stainless steel.

At the outbreak of the Second World War the basic structure of the Sheffield cutlery industry was similar to

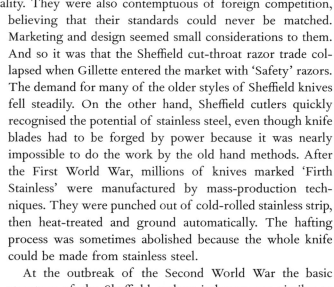

Stainless steel bell made by Hadfield's, engraved by James Dixon & Sons and presented to HMS *Sheffield* in 1937. The bell was returned to Hadfield's when the ship was decommissioned in 1961.
PHOTOGRAPH CARNEGIE: COURTESY OF SHEFFIELD INDUSTRIAL MUSEUMS TRUST

what it had been a century earlier. In 1940 nearly 200 firms still manufactured cutlery in the city. Some of the traditional features of the Hallamshire cutlery industry faded away in the inter-war years. The last of the water-powered grinding wheels ceased production, the hand-forging of forks in Shiregreen and the hand-cutting of files in Ecclesfield and other villages and hamlets came quietly to an end. Their passing was not mourned at the time. The later sentimental attachment to the memory of the 'little mesters' and the 'buffer girls' conflicts with the fact that many workers were glad to see the end of what had become a monotonous, dreary occupation.

The city

In the nineteenth century Sheffield had been slow to develop a civic conscious-ness. Its Town Hall, for example, had been erected almost 40 years after that in Leeds. But in the inter-war years the council made amends by extending the Town Hall (in the same style) and by commissioning a brand new City Hall in Darley Dale stone as a public works project to help reduce unemployment. E. Vincent Harris won the design competition in 1920, the foundation stone was laid in 1929, and the building was opened in September 1932. Built in a severe classical style, with eight grand Corinthian columns at the front and a large bow at the back, it soon became a popular concert hall and a welcome addition to Sheffield's limited range of dignified buildings. The roof was an advanced piece of structural engineering, for the two large reinforced concrete beams that supported it out of sight were the largest in any building at that time. The public face of the city was also improved by the Central Library and Graves Art Gallery (1929–34), designed by W. G. Davies in a modern 'Renaissance' style, with a steel frame hidden behind a veneer of Portland stone.

Political control of the Town Hall changed hands dramatically in 1926, when Ernest George Rowlinson led the Labour Party to victory. In 1918 the right to vote had been extended to all men and given to women over the age of 30. The potential support for the Labour Party had thereby been extended at the very time that the Liberals had split in two. A municipal electoral alliance between the Conservatives and the Liberals was effectively in existence from 1913, pre-dating the national Coalition of 1915. The huge rise in unemployment from 1921 increased the desire for change that the First World War had fostered. During the spring and summer of 1921 and 1922 demonstrations by the unemployed were vociferous and regular. The General Strike of May 1926 was well supported in Sheffield, whose east end had almost 10,000 miners, i.e. 5 per cent of the city's male work-force. In November of that year Sheffield became the first city council in Britain to elect a Labour majority. Since then, the Conservatives have been in power for only two terms, each lasting just a year. The Labour members who were elected in 1926 were moderate in their political stance; many of them were Nonconformists with a background of working-class self-help. They offered the electorate more houses and schools and were critical of the low-rates policy of the 'Citizens' Alliance' of Conservatives and Liberals. Sheffield was free of extremist politics in the inter-war period; it had no Fascists, and the Communists were never a serious force. The Conservatives held on to their Ecclesall and Hallam parliamentary constituencies, but except for a brief period in 1932–33, reflecting the downturn in their national fortunes, Labour was the dominant political party in the city.

J. A. MacDonald, writing in the *Toronto Globe* after a visit to Sheffield during the Imperial Press Conference of 1909, had reported his vivid impressions of a sullen, hopeless population:

> Sheffield staggered us all. We had never seen the like in any white country overseas or even imagined it possible within the limits of human nature ...
> What struck every observant delegate was the utter blankness of the faces that looked up at us from the pavement, or down on us from the windows ...
> Stooped shoulders, hollow chests, ash-coloured faces, lightless eyes, and

The city hall was designed by E. Vincent Harris in 1920, but work did not begin until 1929. It was completed in 1932. Originally intended as a memorial hall to those who had died in the First World War, it became the city's concert hall, with a Memorial Hall to the rear. The stones came from the quarries at Darley Dale.
PHOTOGRAPH: L. NUTTALL

ghastliest of all, loose-set mouths with bloodless gums and only here and there a useful tooth.

Too much should not be made of one man's observations on a fleeting visit, but the hardships of life were real enough. After the First World War, the improvement in the public health of the city was remarkable. The provision of council houses with proper sanitation played a large part in raising standards of living, though of course large numbers of people spent long periods 'on the dole'.

The City Council's main concern was to tackle the problem of the overcrowded and unhealthy houses in the central districts. In 1919 Patrick Abercrombie was appointed to direct a survey of the city's housing needs and to plan a programme of rebuilding. The report which he produced in 1924 was recognised as being of national importance in establishing the value of a detailed and systematic survey as the foundation for planning proposals. His recommended average density of 12 houses per acre, dispersed in the suburbs, was a far cry from the tightly packed rows of houses alongside the steelworks that had characterised the eastern and central parts of Victorian Sheffield.

The City Council, helped by central government subsidies, built 25,000 houses between the wars. Most of these were erected by the public works department that was created in 1926. The 'garden city' estate on the Manor was the most ambitious project in the 1920s. Here, on land which had once formed the huge hunting park of the lords of the manor, the council built houses to a high standard and a low density to a rigid geometrical pattern. Other major schemes, particularly in the 1930s, extended the Manor estate as far as Wybourn in the north and Arbourthorne in the south, and spread Sheffield in a northerly direction, over Woodside and the Brushes estate, and across Southey Green and Parson Cross. All these new houses were semi-detached, with gardens at both the front and the rear. After 1934 an average of 2,400 council houses were completed each year. A substantial rise in the number of people of a working age increased the demand for re-housing. By 1938 some 24,000 slums had been cleared, and 44 per cent of them had been replaced by new dwellings – the highest rate in England and Wales. But in 1938 almost three-quarters of the central area's housing was still condemned.

Between the wars the City Council built houses at twice the national rate. Meanwhile, the numbers of privately rented houses declined as the rise in real incomes of those in employment enabled many new owner-occupiers to take advantage of mortgages offered by building societies. Large numbers of privately owned dwellings were erected in the western parts of Sheffield, well away from the smoke and the grime of industry. The attractions of suburban life in Ecclesall, Beauchief, Fulwood and other western districts was increased by the availability of cheap land and by the trams and buses which provided reliable means of transport before the era of the family motor car. Between the wars, Sheffield became even more polarised between its east and west ends.

Demand for water on these new estates continued to rise. By 1920 the Sheffield area had a total daily supply of nearly 17 million gallons for trade and domestic

Court 5, High Street Lane, Park, 1926. The squalid housing conditions that were endured by the poorest sections of society in certain parts of Sheffield are captured in this photograph taken by the Medical Officer No. 2, up the steps was a single-room dwelling that was occupied by four people. The court was demolished shortly afterwards.

'What struck every observant delegate was the utter blankness of the faces ... Stooped shoulders, hollow chests, ash-coloured faces, lightless eyes, and ghastliest of all, loose-set mouths with bloodless gums and only here and there a useful tooth.

TORONTO GLOBE, 1909

A HISTORY OF SHEFFIELD

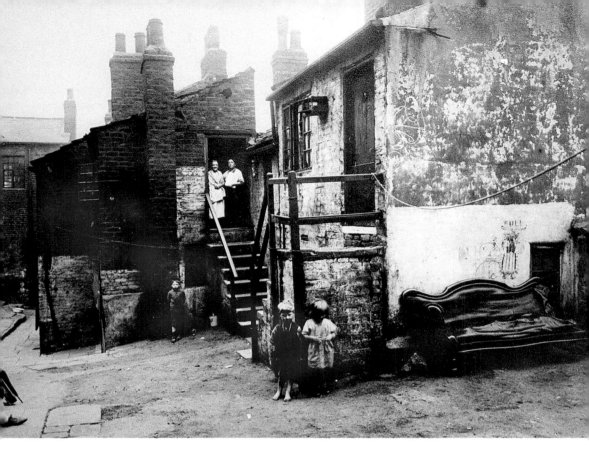

purposes. Major works at Langsett, Ewden and the Derwent Valley (whose water came to Sheffield through a tunnel) was renewed after the First World War. The major scheme at Ewden was completed in 1933. Work at Ladybower was allowed to go ahead during the Second World War. Sheffield then had to look further afield. By 1964 it was one of the authorities that were jointly drawing water from the Yorkshire Derwent.

The economic depression of the inter-war years meant that the council could not do all the things it wished. Housing was the priority, so economy was the word in education and Sheffield compared badly with other towns in the 1920s. Large classes and crowded schools were the norm, though a few new primary schools were built. Declining birth rates relieved some of the pressure. More secondary schools were essential if the demand for secondary education was to be met, though the majority of Sheffield children left school at the age of 14. The most important scheme was the re-siting of the Central Schools at High Storrs in 1933, when new premises were opened for 670 boys and 640 girls.

The appearance of the city centre was not radically altered after the upheaval of the late-Victorian period. Two of the new department stores were those of local co-operative societies. The Brightside and Carbrook Co-operative Society, founded in 1869, opened its City Store at the corner of Exchange Street and Waingate, and the Sheffield and Ecclesall Co-operative Society (founded in 1874) opened its new central premises at the junction of Cemetery Road and Ecclesall

Roads. Both stores have been demolished. C&A Modes Store (1932) and Montague Burton's (1930) added flair to the High Street until they were destroyed in the blitz. Woolworth's and Littlewood's also opened city-centre shops as Sheffield joined the trend in having large department stores that belonged to national or international companies. New shops were also built in the east end. Montague Burton built new premises on Staniforth Road in fashionable white faience, with the Astoria Ballroom on the top floor, and John Banner, whose family had been established several generations in Attercliffe, opened a new department store, built in the same material, in 1933; it had the distinction of being the first store in Sheffield with a moving staircase.

Sheffield's rise to city status was eventually matched in the ecclesiastical sphere. Sheffield had been an archdeaconry within the diocese of York since 1884, but it was not until 1 May 1914 that its ancient parish church was raised to cathedral status, with Lesley Hedley Burrows as the first bishop. In 1919 Sir Charles Nicholson designed a new cathedral incorporating the earlier church, but the plan was never fully implemented. A less grandiose scheme was carried out in the 1960s. The withdrawal of the population from the centre of the city meant that other churches became redundant. In 1936 it was decided that some had to be demolished. Sadly, these included St Paul's, the fine baroque church of the 1720s, whose site was converted after the war into the Peace Gardens. New churches were built in the suburbs, including Totley (1924), Millhouses (1936) and Arbourthorne (1939), and the Roman Catholic church at Hillsborough (1936).

The cinemas provided mass entertainment after the First World War. Several new ones were built in the suburbs. The finest were the Adelphi, Attercliffe (1920), the Abbeydale Cinema (1920), the Forum, Herries Road (1938), and the Rex,

Court No. 2, Doncaster Street, looking towards Court 2, Allen Street, 1937. Note that the Medical Officer has measured the heights of the building (18 ft 2ins) and the outhouse (6 ft 6 ins).

Intake (1939, demolished 1983). The Carlton, Arbourthorne (1938–39), has the distinction of being the first all-concrete cinema in Britain, for it was built when steel was not available for such purposes in the months before the Second World War. In the city centre, the ornate Regent (1927) was built opposite the Cinema House and next to the Albert Hall; it was later re-modelled as the Gaumont (1969) and then rebuilt as the multi-screen Odeon (1987). By 1931 the city had 45 cinemas, with a total seating capacity of 36,000. Meanwhile, in 1928, an amateur dramatics group had taken over the Temperance Hall in Townhead Street. When they turned professional in the 1930s, their theatre was re-named the Sheffield Playhouse and they became a popular rep company under Geoffrey Ost.

Football and cricket continued to attract huge support, as the Yorkshire County Cricket Club reigned supreme and both of Sheffield's professional football clubs did well. Sheffield United won the FA Cup in 1925 and were beaten 1–0 by Arsenal in the 1936 FA Cup Final. The Wednesday – who did not formally change their name to Sheffield Wednesday until 1927 – won the league championship in successive years in 1929 and 1930, finished in third place during the next three years, and won the FA Cup in 1935. A new attraction was the Owlerton Greyhound Racecourse, opened in 1932. Motorcycle speedway riding attracted large crowds at the same venue well into the 1950s.

Sheffielders were also active participants in sport clubs, choirs, amateur dramatic societies, and other such organisations, often attached to works or to churches and chapels. Rambling, cycling and fishing increased in popularity and when the open-air swimming pool at Millhouses was opened in 1929, it was hailed as the finest in the country. Less desirable outdoor activities were the pitch and toss rings, which were formed on derelict land, and which attracted protection rackets. In one of the most notorious gang exploits, in Princess Street in 1925, a man was stabbed to death outside his house in a brawl. Compared with other large cities, however, Sheffield was not a violent place.

Motor bus, December 1913. The bus is show crossing Heeley Green into Gleadless Road from Richards Road, in otherwise traffic-free conditions.

SHEFFIELD LIBRARIES, ARCHIVES AND INFORMATION: LOCAL STUDIES

The Second World War

When war was declared again in 1939, the Government took over the national direction of the steel industry. During the war, the English Steel Corporation was the United Kingdom's largest producer of alloy steels, gun forgings, and tank armour. The River Don Works's 15-ton steam hammer drop-forged crankshafts for Spitfire engines. Spectacular advances were made in the development of heat-resisting steels for

The medieval parish church had to be enlarged when it was made into a cathedral, but work did not begin until 1937 and was suspended during the Second World War. The extensions were completed in 1966. The view shows the new south-west entrance and the octagonal lantern above the west crossing.

PHOTOGRAPH: CARNEGIE

jet engines. Other firms adapted production to the numerous requirements of the armed forces. Tool steel firms like Osborn's and Sanderson Bros & Newbould were kept very busy. The steel industry in the Lower Don Valley was crucial to the war effort, yet, surprisingly, it suffered little from enemy attack. Brown Bayley's was the only steelworks that was seriously damaged by bombing.

Between August and October 1940 Sheffield suffered only seven minor air attacks, in which eight people were killed and 33 seriously injured. Air-raid

Old Totley Bus, c.1920. Johnson's bus ran between the Dore and Totley railway station and the village of Totley

SHEFFIELD LIBRARIES, ARCHIVES AND INFORMATION: LOCAL STUDIES

Sheffield Wednesday Football Club, 1929. The Wednesday Football Club were League Champions in 1928–29 and FA Cup Winners in 1935. The championship team shown here consisted of (standing) R.Brown (secretary), A.Strange, T.Walker, T.Leach, J.Brown, E.Blenkinsop, W.Marsden, F.Craig (trainer); (seated) M.Hooper, J.Seed (captain), J.Allen, R.Gregg, E.Rimmer.

precautions were well organised; anti-aircraft guns were positioned on high points, at Shirecliffe, Manor and Brinsworth; and 72 balloons were raised to force bombers to fly higher. The main attack came on the night of Thursday 12 / Friday 13 December 1940. A nearly full moon and a crisp frost ensured good visibility over most of the city, but ground fog shrouded Attercliffe and Rotherham and obscured the steelworks. The first of 336 German bombers flew in from the south at 7 p.m. They came down the Sheaf Valley, dropping incendiaries and small high-explosive bombs, to form a huge ring of fire. Between 10.38 p.m. and 2.15 a.m. the raid was intense. The blitz on the city centre began around 11 p.m. Terrible damage was inflicted on the Moor, then on High Street, Commercial Street, Haymarket, Exchange Street and Campo Lane. At 11.35 p.m.

The Edgar Allen Football Club, 1920, winners of the first Tinsley Charity Cup. Sheffield has a strong tradition of amateur football teams playing in local leagues. Some teams, such as this, were works teams, others were based at pubs, or at churches and chapels. Few enjoyed the luxury of playing on a level pitch in hilly Sheffield.

a large explosion announced the destruction of the Neepsend gasworks. Ten minutes later, the Marples Hotel was hit and 70 people were killed in the cellar, in what turned out to be the worst incident of the raid. The fracturing of water mains severely hampered the efforts of the firemen, so fires in the city centre quickly got out of control. Every building in Angel Street and King Street was either bombed or on fire. C&A's, Walsh's, Burton's, and Sheffield's other major shops in High Street and The Moor were devastated, but those in Fargate and Pinstone Street escaped. The last bomber departed at 3.50 a.m., and at 4.17 a.m. the all-clear was sounded. The Luftwaffe returned home without losses. They had destroyed much of the city centre and had inflicted heavy damage on an area bounded by Millhouses, Meersbrook, Heeley, Norfolk Park, Park Hill, Pitsmoor, Neepsend, Glossop Road, Broomhill, Sharrow and Nether Edge. Water, gas, electricity, and transport services were seriously disrupted, but the industrial east end had escaped.

German bombers returned three days later. This time their target was the steel-works. At 6.50 p.m. on Sunday 15 December the first of 94 aircraft reached the Prince of Wales Road. They dropped their bombs with considerable effect until 10.05 p.m. A rolling mill at Brown Bayley's was completely destroyed and two others were damaged. Other works suffered to a lesser degree. Incendiary bombs did a great deal of damage in Attercliffe. Ten people were killed in Coleford Road and many more were made homeless. Christ Church was burnt out and never rebuilt.

In these two raids, 2,906 houses and shops were destroyed or damaged beyond repair. Altogether, 82,413 buildings were affected in one way or another, though many of them merely suffered broken windows. Precise casualty figures are hard to establish because accounts vary. The Official History of Civil Defence (1955) records 589 killed and 488 seriously injured. Further attacks were feared, but the Germans began to blitz Manchester, Liverpool and Derby instead. After 1940, the only bombs dropped on Sheffield were those jettisoned by isolated aircraft. Weather conditions probably saved the city on two later occasions. Meanwhile, Sheffield soldiers were being killed at the war front, though not in the horrendous numbers of 1914–18. This time, Sheffielders fought in a wide variety of units, across the world.

Since the Second World War

The Second World War was not followed by a slump, as in 1921. Full employment continued throughout the 1950s and 1960s. The job market was different, however. By 1951 women formed 32 per cent of the gainfully employed labour force in Sheffield, and employment in the service sector of the economy had risen to 29.6 per cent. The proportion of the work-force at work in other jobs, such as transport and building, was about the same as in similar-sized cities, but Sheffield still had a lower proportion of higher managers and professionals. The city remained unusual in having 57.5 per cent of its work-force employed in manufacturing (44.4 per cent of them in the traditional 'heavy' and 'light' trades).

The Blitz. During the blitz on 12-13 December 1940 the Marples Hotel, on the corner of High Street and Fitzalan Square, was destroyed by a direct hit. At the sound of the sirens people in the hotel made their way to the cellars, but the building collapsed on top of them. Seventy people were suffocated and only seven came out alive. In the background of the photograph is C & A Modes, which was badly damaged at the same time.

A HISTORY OF SHEFFIELD

The city centre

The damage caused by the blitz in 1940 was on such a scale that the city centre had to be re-designed. The increasing amount of traffic, as shops had their goods delivered by lorries and more people drove private motor cars, also posed problems for the planners. The remaining slums needed to be cleared, and the post-war baby boom raised the demand for more houses. Improvements to the city centre slowly got under way in the early 1950s, as new shops and offices were built by private developers within the guidelines of the local authority's plans. During the next decade, the centre was gradually changed, all the way from the bottom of The Moor to Lady's Bridge, by the building of large new department stores, office blocks, multi-storey car parks, the College of Technology, and other large buildings clad in concrete and glass. Sheffield lost much of its individuality as its old buildings were torn down and new ones rose in styles that could be found all over Britain. The traffic problem was tackled by a ring road and, eventually, by broad new thoroughfares such as Arundel Gate, which brutally cut through the centre and forced pedestrians into gloomy, graffiti-sprayed underpasses. But the banning of traffic from the central streets slowly gathered pace in the 1970s and 1980s, making shopping safer and more pleasurable.

The city centre became a much more agreeable place once the amount of smoke was reduced dramatically by the vigorous application of powers granted under the Clean Air Act (1956). Government grants were used to wash or sand-blast important buildings. The Town Hall was washed in 1959, the old part of Cathedral was cleaned in 1964 (two years before the new part was opened), and the restoration of other buildings followed soon afterwards. It is now surprising to recall that at the time some people regretted the disappearance of blackened buildings which they thought gave Sheffield its distinctive character. St Mary's Church was the last to lose its layers of grime.

Sir Nikolaus Pevsner agreed with the common perception of outsiders (and of many natives) when he wrote in his *The Buildings of England: Yorkshire, the West Riding* (1959): 'Architecturally Sheffield is a miserable disappointment ... In walking through the main streets of Sheffield one never knows where one is or what is to follow next.' But he praised the modern buildings, especially those at the University. Since his visit, many more public buildings, department stores and office blocks have been erected in the city centre. Those whose designs have met with wide approval include the Central Division Police Station in West Bar, the interior of the Mappin Art Gallery (which was devastated by bombs), Cole Bros's department store in Barker's Pool (all from the early 1960s), and the South Yorkshire Police HQ in Snig Hill (1975). The extension to the Town Hall between 1973 and 1977 did not receive the same praise.

right Aerial view of the Cathedral (bottom right) and the district north-west of the city centre, 1966. West Street and Trippet Lane lead into Townhead (bottom left) and Campo Lane. Broad Lane cuts across the centre of the picture down to West Bar. Hollis Croft, White Croft, Pea Croft and Scotland Street preserve their early eighteenth-century lines over the former townfields. Gibraltar Street leaves the picture top right. This is an area of numerous small firms in Sheffield's distinctive trades.
MERIDIAN AIRMAPS LTD

The University of Sheffield. The University grew from the union of Firth College, the Sheffield School of Medicine, and the Sheffield Technical School to form a University College in 1897. Sheffield achieved full University status in 1905. The Mappin Building (shown here) housed the Department of Applied Science.
PHOTOGRAPH: CARNEGIE

Housing

In 1961, another distinguished and informed visitor, John Betjeman, found the best and worst of Victorian England in Sheffield's west and east ends. The City Council continued to make the clearance of slums its priority. Housing was the dominant issue in Sheffield until the 1970s, when the state of the local economy became the major concern. It also led to protracted controversy with neighbouring authorities, as Sheffield sought to acquire land on which to build.

Formal approval of a provisional green belt had been given in 1938. The City Council had been sympathetic to the viewpoint of the Sheffield and Peak District Branch of the Council for the Preservation of Rural England, which was influential in preserving the countryside around Sheffield. The council had acquired moorland for its reservoirs in 1928–33, and had bought the Longshaw Estate, which it presented to the National Trust in 1931. Two years later, Alderman J. G. Graves bought Blacka Moor and gave it to the council on condition that it remained an open space in perpetuity. The need for extra land for housing brought the council into conflict with the CPRE in the 1950s and 1960s, however. The CPRE advocated the creation of a distant new town as the answer to Sheffield's housing problems, and suggested Gainsborough as a likely site.

In 1945 the city published an ambitious rebuilding plan, which sought to remove housing from the Lower Don Valley and to replace it with industry. In 1947 local authorities were given new planning powers under the Town and Country Planning Act, which enabled such schemes to be put into effect. A draft plan was agreed by the council in 1952, and after public enquiry and modifications, it was approved in 1957 by the Minister of Housing and Local Government.

The scale of the housing problem is indicated by the 1951 census finding that 85,000 of Sheffield's households did not have a fixed bath. The council was unable to clear its slums and to build many new houses in the years immediately after

Housing in the Gleadless Valley. From the mid 1950s to the end of the 1960s the Council built a large estate of some 4,000 dwellings at Gleadless. This scheme is generally recognised as the most successful of the post-war housing developments. The architects and landscape designers took full advantage of the hilly nature of the terrain. This photograph was taken in June 1965, looking down the valley from Newfield Green to Rollestone.

the war, apart from 2,100 prefabricated bungalows and some rebuilding on bomb damaged sites. The 'Prefabs' were designed with a life expectancy of 10–15 years, but lasted much longer. The first new council houses were erected at Parson Cross, where the infrastructure had already been prepared by prisoners of war from Redmires camp. In 1951 the 26,500 applicants on the council's housing list still faced a wait of about six years. The first priority was to clear the slums in the central districts. The slum clearance of the east end did not get underway until the 1970s, except for a few small groups of back-to-backs.

The plan had identified an urgent need for 30,000 houses. The failure to secure land in neighbouring authorities, meant that the council had to build at relatively high densities on difficult and sloping sites. In 1952 the council began the process of seeking compulsory purchase orders for land within its boundaries at Gleadless, Stannington, Bradway, Totley and Foxhill. In 1953, when J. Lewis Womersley was appointed as city architect, work began on major slum-clearance schemes. At Park Hill, Woodside, Netherthorpe, Burngreave and Norfolk Park, previous houses were cleared for the new dwellings. At Gleadless, Greenhill, Norton and Woodhouse, buildings were erected on new sites. By the end of the decade, 12,500 dwellings had been completed. Private housing on the fringes of Sheffield also ate into the countryside.

In the 1950s, the central government's desire to rapidly increase the number of houses forced all local authorities to reduce building standards. The 'People's Houses' that were built at Greenhill-Bradway consisted of maisonettes and three 13-storey blocks of flats, with one or two bedrooms. They were followed from the mid-1950s to the mid-1960s by an estate of over 4,000 similar dwellings in the Gleadless Valley. This scheme was one of the most successful and popular, for it was carefully and imaginatively designed to fit the existing fine landscape, with mature trees and extensive views across the valleys.

The next scheme was more ambitious and more controversial. In the late 1950s

and early 1960s the council built 3,500 dwellings in high-rise blocks of reinforced concrete at Park Hill and Hyde Park, close to the city centre and places of work. Influenced by Le Corbusier's concept of 'street decks' or 'streets in the sky', and by the Quarry Hill Flats in Leeds, they made a dramatic contribution to the townscape. The flats were accessible not only by lifts and wide pedestrian walkways at the front, but from the hillside to the rear. Household refuse was burned in a central incinerator which heated the flats. Shops, schools and pubs were built nearby, and considerable efforts were made at Park Hill to re-house neighbours together so as to maintain a sense of community. Further inner-city estates were soon built on similar lines, notably the even higher Hyde Park flats nearby. The Hyde Park scheme (opened in 1966) differed from Park Hill in several ways, all to its detriment. Its 18 storeys could be reached only by lifts, fewer social facilities were provided, and most of the original tenants came from different parts of the city. These schemes actually cost two-thirds more than conventional two-storey housing on suburban estates, but the net cost to the council was lower because of government subsidies.

In the 1960s the Park Hill housing scheme attracted world-wide attention. The flats were praised for their innovative architectural grandeur by people who did not live in them, but the residents faced problems from the start. When the first tenants died or moved away, the sense of community was weakened, for the new occupants came from scattered parts of the city. Noise at unsocial hours, vandalism, and a high rate of unemployment ruined the dream. By the 1980s the Park Hill and Hyde Park flats had a poor reputation. They were finally emptied in 1989 and refurbished to house participants in the World Student Games two years later. After the games the highest blocks were demolished, but two of the lower blocks were refaced with aluminium panels and re-let; one block for council tenants, the other for a housing association.

By the mid-1960s some 2,500 dwellings a year were being erected. From the mid-1960s, system building and non-traditional materials were used to speed the housing programme, to reduce costs, and to solve the problem of shortage of skilled labour. Everything had to be done within tight government cost controls. More high-rise maisonettes and flats were erected in pre-cast concrete building systems at Broomhall and Kelvin in the late 1960s and early 1970s. They were soon recognised to have failed, both technically and socially. The 650 maisonettes and flats at Broomhall were demolished in 1988, the Kelvin Flats soon afterwards. The City Council returned to building low-level, compact estates, as at Darnall, in the hope of preserving traditional community links. Financial constraints also forced them to concentrate on maintenance and the refurbishment of whole streets of houses. Terraced housing for existing residents, for example in Highfield, and the 1920s' houses on the Manor estate were successfully refurbished.

This extensive housing programme was still not enough. Sheffield's planners had calculated that about 40,000 people needed to be housed beyond the city boundaries up to 1972. Mosborough was the choice of site for Sheffield's 'new town'. From 1967, the city boundaries were extended southwards to include most of the parish of Beighton, the Mosborough and Gleadless areas of the parish of

Aerial view of the Park Hill flats, 2004
© WEBBAVIATION.CO.U

A HISTORY OF SHEFFIELD

Eckington, and small parts of the parishes of Holmesfield and Killamarsh (all from Chesterfield Rural District Council), together with parts of the parish of Ecclesfield to the north. The planners acknowledged that growing numbers of car owners had to be accommodated by their scheme for Mosborough, so they proposed a cellular structure of townships defined by a grid of primary roads. Developers were selected in 1982, and six years later the first phase of the Crystal Peaks shopping centre was opened.

Between 1951 and 1973 the number of houses managed by the local authority grew from 40,000 to about 75,000. The creation of the South Yorkshire Metropolitan County Council on 1 April 1974 split planning functions, until this new council was abolished in 1986. The Sheffield Metropolitan District Council, which was also created on 1 April 1974, proved to be more lasting. It incorporated Stocksbridge Urban District Council and the civil parishes of Bradfield and Ecclesfield and thus covered most of the old lordship of Hallamshire. Sheffield failed to get Dronfield, Eckington and Killamarsh from Derbyshire. Old loyalties proved remarkably tenacious.

Between 1951 and 1991, while 100,900 new dwellings were built, over 55,000 old houses were demolished. In 1981 the council owned over 90,000 dwellings, comprising 45 per cent of the city's housing stock. This was a very high proportion, even for an industrial city. The Housing Act (1980) gave tenants the right to buy their council houses or flats, and by the end of 1990 just over 14,500 council dwellings had been sold, i.e. 16 per cent of the stock (against a national average of 20 per cent). During the 1980s housing associations emerged on the national and local scenes as significant providers of rented accommodation. Meanwhile, private development in Chapeltown, Stocksbridge and Mosborough accounted for 4,400 of the 6,800 new dwellings that were completed between 1981 and 1988. Very little development land was available outside these areas, but the large private estate at Dronfield and further private developments in Sheffield's western suburbs helped to cater for the expanding demand for home ownership.

The City Council can also claim credit for removing the smoke from Sheffield. No break with the past was so complete and so welcome. The amount of smoke from industrial chimneys was unique to Sheffield, but it was recognised that household fires played a large part in the dense smogs that occasionally enveloped the city. Despite the obvious advantages of clean air, many Sheffielders were reluctant to change their cheerful coal fires to smokeless fuels. The Clean Air Act (1956) provided generous government grants for industry to replace or recondition furnaces. The council's first smoke control order over domestic fires came into effect on 1 December 1959. It covered the city centre and the southern and western suburbs (the windward side of the city). The last order, covering Birley and Mosborough, came 13 years later. After the city's boundaries were extended in 1974, smoke control was extended throughout Stocksbridge (1976), Stannington (1978), Ecclesfield (1979) and Chapeltown (1982). Meanwhile, the closure of the Neepsend power station in 1976 and the Smithy Wood coking plant, near Chapeltown, in 1986, helped to make the air cleaner. The problem of pollution from car exhaust fumes remains.

Cutlery

During the war, increased orders for the cutlery trade's staple products were offset by serious disruptions. Sheffield's most ancient industry was again adapted to the supply of such things as fighting knives and helmets. Wostenholm's Washington Works and Thomas Turton's were bombed in December 1940. The shortage of materials, including stainless steel, continued after the war. When Australia put duties on imports in 1951, the Sheffield cutlery industry was badly affected. But the trade shared in the boom of the 1950s and its old firms revived.

In 1957 no fewer than 650 of the 700 cutlery firms in the United Kingdom were located in Sheffield. The ethos and structure of the industry remained Victorian. The trade was still characterised by small family firms, most of which had been in Sheffield for generations. Over 500 of the 700 firms in the UK had fewer than 11 workers; only 11 firms employed more than 200 workers. The small

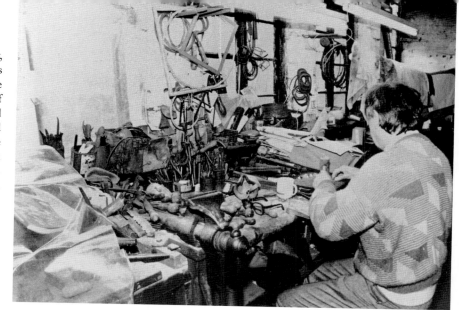

Philip Drury, silversmith. Leah's Yard. The traditional skills of the Sheffield craftsman are still being used to make beautiful objects in small workshops. This photograph was taken in December 1996.
HAWLEY COLLECTION, UNIVERSITY OF SHEFFIELD

firms generally lacked capital. Their management was complacent, parochial and amateurish. Marketing skills were unheard of.

The exceptional firms were the ones with German origins. In the 1950s, Richards employed over 500 workers in their new factory at the junction of Moore Street, Charter Row and Fitzwilliam Gate (demolished in 1985). They had become the leading pocket-knife makers in the country. Richards disregarded the old Sheffield insistence on high quality and concentrated on making cheap, mass-produced knives, whose blades were blanked out by machine and whose hafts were made of plastic. Viners became the largest cutlery firm of all, with 800 employees by 1965. In 1949 over 70 per cent of their business had been in stain-less-, silver- and electro-plated holloware; cutlery accounted for only a quarter

Sheffield is still the home of high-quality cutlery. These kitchen knives are made by modern methods at Richardson Sheffield Ltd, one of the city's leading firms.
BY COURTESY OF RICHARDSON SHEFFIELD LTD

Basil Walker, mark maker, at work shortly before the closure of his workshop in 1995. The making of marks is an old trade, going back in Sheffield to at least the sixteenth century, when cutlers' marks were issued by the manor court. Fine skill was required to file the end of a steel punch to an individual design, back to front when compared with the finished mark. The old hand skills have been replaced by modern technology. The Sheffield firm of Edward Pryor's is a leading name in this field.

Grinding a kitchen knife by hand. Grinding is still a manual skill, even though electricity has replaced water- and steam-power and the wheels are no longer obtained from local quarries.

of their trade. Viners expanded in the 1950s, taking over Thos Turner in 1953 and Harrison Bros & Howson in 1959. They then acquired factories in Ireland, Australia and France, and in 1968 prepared an ambitious five-year expansion plan, with investment in expensive capital equipment.

During the 1950s Sheffield cutlers had no fear of competition in the home market. Were not their products so much superior in quality to those which were then being made in the Far East? Japan was the first Asiatic country to use American methods and machinery; labour costs there were about a third of those in Sheffield, taxation levels were lower, and stainless steel was about half the Sheffield price. By the early 1960s Hong Kong and Taiwan had also entered the cutlery trade. Ten years later, South Korean firms made cutlery with labour costs one-seventh of those in Sheffield. The Far Eastern countries could sell cutlery at a lower price than Sheffielders could buy their raw materials. Foreign imports came flooding into Britain from the mid-1960s onwards.

Few Sheffield firms responded effectively. After a tour of the Far East in 1964, John Price re-named his firm (which had been founded in Birmingham in 1902) Arthur Price of England and launched a vigorous marketing campaign, selling exclusive patterns, particularly plated flatware and giftware, in his own shops within British department stores. Viners' response was the controversial one of importing cheap cutlery blanks from a Hong Kong subsidiary and stamping them with their mark. This desperate move did not save the firm, for in 1982 it went into receivership, and the factory was subsequently demolished. Many a famous firm ceased trading in the 1970s and 1980s. Wostenholm's was taken over by Rodgers in 1971, Sippel's closed in 1972. Richards took over Rodgers-Wostenholm in the mid-1970s, but by 1983 were bankrupt. Motorways and new buildings obliterated the sites of Mappin's Queen's Cutlery Works and Rodgers' Norfolk Street Works. The old silver- and electro-plate firms, hit by stainless steel, went a little earlier. Walker & Hall's great Electro Works was demolished in the early 1960s, Dixon's Cornish Place Works was largely derelict by the end of the 1980s, and Atkin Bros., Frank Cobb, and Cooper Bros. were among others who closed.

Knife and fork handles designed for a modern market by Harrison-Fisher Ltd, a long-established Sheffield firm occupying the old 'Eye Witness' works in Milton Street.

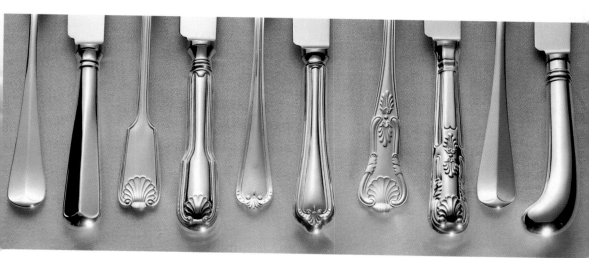

The number of Sheffielders employed in the cutlery trades quickly dropped from 10,000 to 2–3,000 by the early 1990s. Only a few firms survived at the quality end of the market. C.W. Fletcher's (founded 1894), for example, continued to sell hand-crafted cutlery and silverware to rich foreign customers. A few 'little mesters' can still be found in workshops in the decaying Victorian courtyards of the old cutlery area of Rockingham Street, Solly Street, Garden Street, Furnace Hill, Arundel Street and Milton Street. Harrison Fisher (founded 1896, and at the 'Eye Witness' works in Milton Street since 1975) is the only surviving example of the type of cutlery firm that flourished in the nineteenth century. The firm employs about 200 workers and makes a comprehensive range of knives.

The best-known Sheffield cutlery firm is now Richardson Ltd, makers of the famous 'Laser' knives. Westall Richardson began making table knives in Cavendish Street about 1879; by the 1890s he had moved to Brook Hill. In 1956 Regent, an American cutlery firm, bought a half-share of the business and invested in new machinery. By 1960 Regent was the sole owner. In 1986 they sold the business to McPherson's Ltd, the leading Australian manufacturer of kitchen knives and cutlery. Bryan Upton, who joined the company in 1959, became managing director in 1966 and chairman of Richardson-Sheffield in 1986. Under his leadership, the firm responded to the growing demand for kitchen knives, and in 1979–80 began to make 'Laser' knives, using the latest technology and marketing skills. They quickly acquired an international reputation for their products.

High-quality Sheffield cutlery that is well designed, well presented and produced by modern methods still sells well. The outstanding designer, David Mellor (born in Sheffield in 1930), lived and worked at Broom Hall from 1973, but in the 1990s moved to his new Round Building at Hathersage. His silver work and flatware are exhibited in the Victoria and Albert Museum and the Museum of Modern Art, New York.

The conservative family firms that had so long characterised the industry failed to invest in modern equipment and collapsed in face of foreign competition. The successful firms were nearly all outsiders. But, contrary to widespread belief beyond the city, the cutlery industry has not disappeared. Each year, millions of Sheffield knives are sold around the world. The formal dining market remains strong, particularly for established brands of silver or highly durable silver-plated cutlery. The total market in 1992 was worth £125 million, and the work-force numbered 2,888 people. The market has remained relatively static since 1982, with no significant growth or decline in the various market segments. Sheffield cutlery firms continue to do well, more than 700 years after the first documentary reference to a local cutler.

Tools

The tool industry has encountered similar problems to the cutlery trades. Many of the numerous small family firms have collapsed, the old hand skills have disappeared, and the work-force has been reduced drastically. Those businesses which were prepared to invest in modern plant and to market their goods in

Eight different kinds of anvils, from the Hawley Collection. Each trade has its own type of anvil ; only a few are shown here. From the top, they are classed as follows: engineer's tool; double arch; coach spring maker's; double bick; engineer's tool; pen and pocket knife maker's; blacksmith's; table knife forger's. Mousehole Forge, at the confluence of the rivers Rivelin and Loxley, had an international reputation for its anvils.

Marples' tools. A presentation tray of chisels, screwdrivers, plane, bradawls, gimlets, etc, now on display in the Hawley Building at the University of Sheffield. The firm of William Marples at Westfield Terrace were leading Sheffield toolmakers in the nineteenth and twentieth centuries.
HAWLEY COLLECTION, UNIVERSITY OF SHEFFIELD

attractive ways have maintained their position, however. On the whole, the tool trade has performed better than the cutlery industry. The production of hand tools soared in the 1950s and 1960s, when DIY retail stores opened throughout Britain. This trade has helped to offset the decline of industrial demand for tools.

Foreign competition became severe in the 1970s. It was countered by improved technology and marketing and by mergers. Research and development into new grades of engineering plastics has resulted in many new tools, particularly trimming knives and screwdrivers, and the almost unbreakable handles of chisels, saws and planes. The modern tool industry is highly mechanised.

By 1989 the work-force had declined to 3,650. Many tool firms closed in the 1980s, but Sheffield has remained the principal centre of the UK hand tool industry. In 1990 Sheffield-owned tool companies employed over 36 per cent of the national work-force and were responsible for approximately two-thirds of the country's output. The largest privately owned tool firm in Sheffield is Footprint Tools, re-named in 1948 by John Jewitt when he bought Thomas R. Ellen's Footprint Works in Hollis Croft. In the 1990s three of the largest UK hand tool companies – Stanley, James Neill, and Record – were based in Sheffield.

Stanley Tools (an American company) grew

vigorously in the 1950s. In 1990 they bought the firm of James Chesterman (founded 1820), which had been amalgamated in 1963 with John Rabone & Sons of Birmingham. James Neill & Co. also expanded. The firm acquired Hallamshire Steel & File, and by 1960 employed over 1,000 workers. Two years earlier, Neill's had been described by the *Sunday Times* as the largest family firm in the country, but they later went public and are now owned by an American finance company. Neill's bought other firms in Birmingham and the Black Country, and by the time that they purchased Spear & Jackson in 1985, they had become one of the largest tool-making businesses in the world. Sheffield's third large company was formed from amalgamations of firms whose history goes back into the nineteenth century. In 1965, half the old-established firm of William Marples (founded by 1833) was taken over by C. & J. Hampton (founded in 1898), who had used the Record trademark since 1909. The other half went to William Ridgeway (founded in 1878), who merged with Hampton's in 1972 to become Record Ridgeway. In 1988 the Oscar Works became the home of Record Marples (Woodworking Tools) Ltd under the group title of Record Holdings Ltd.

Steel

In 1949 the Labour government announced that the largest steel firms were to be nationalised. The policy was bitterly opposed by the Sheffield steel owners. In the end, even the biggest family businesses, notably Arthur Lee and Samuel Osborn, remained privately owned. The private sector included such old and well-known names as Balfour, Beardshaw, Bedford, Huntsman, Ibbotson, Jessop, Jonas & Colver, Kayser Ellison, Sanderson Bros & Newbould, Vessey, and Wardlow. A wide gap separated them from the giants of the industry.

In 1953 the Conservative government began to de-nationalise the steel industry, and within two years all had been returned to the private sector. Sheffield's traditional advantages of technical knowledge, a vast pool of human skill, and a unique clustering of metal-working and engineering industries continued to give the city a competitive edge. Sheffield remained a major centre for steel research and its firms quickly adopted new technology. The steel industry was in full production during the 1950s. By the end of the decade, Davy's employed 3,000 workers and Ward's, which had become one of the largest and most comprehensive contractor's plant departments in the country, employed another 3,000. United Steel's profits rose from £9 million in 1954 to £23 million in 1960. In the late 1950s the English Steel Corporation regularly achieved profits of £4–5 million. Firth-Brown's trading profits increased from £586,173 in 1949 to £2.2 million in 1960.

About £150 million was spent on the post-war modernisation of Sheffield steel. The contrast with the cutlery industry could not have been greater. The most spectacular developments were United Steel's new Templeborough Electric Melting Shop, which was opened in 1963 with a capacity of over 1.25 million tons per annum, and the ESC's new £26 million Tinsley Park Works, which was opened in the same year. Over £30 million was also invested in new electric-arc

  A HISTORY OF SHEFFIELD

A crucible steel works. This famous photograph of men teeming crucible steel was taken at Firth Brown's, where some crucible holes were re-opened during the Second World War, in order to make tool steel. The molten steel is being poured from a crucible into an ingot mould.

and oxygen steelmaking equipment at Tube Investments' Park Gate Works. In 1964 the English Steel Corporation employed 14,140 workers, Steel, Peech & Tozer 9,315, Samuel Fox 7,679, Firth-Brown 7,500, Park Gate 6,200, Hadfield's 4,000, Balfour Darwin 3,500, Brown Bayley's 3,500, Osborn 3,000, Arthur Lee 2,700, Jessop-Saville 2,550, Edgar Allen 2,000, and Sanderson Kayser 1,900. The smaller firms that had never been nationalised also prospered. For example, Richard W. Carr's work-force rose from about 40 in 1953 to about 400 by the mid-1970s. Sheffield firms had full order books, with customers having to wait up to two years for deliveries. About 3 million tons of ingots and castings were made in Sheffield in 1960. This was, admittedly, only one-eighth of the UK output, but Sheffield dominated alloy steel production by producing over 1 million out of the 1.6 million tons that were made nationally. The future looked rosy.

Since the 1950s, British standards of living have risen substantially. Sheffield became a prosperous industrial city. But the optimism of the 1950s and 1960s died as world steel demand collapsed in the 1970s. The UK steel industry was partly re-nationalised in 1967. Fourteen major British companies and their 200 subsidiaries were merged to form the British Steel Corporation, with Lord Melchett as chairman. From now on, decisions affecting the local steel industry were made at BSC's headquarters in London. In Sheffield, only the ESC, Park Gate and United Steel were nationalised; the remaining 50 or so companies were left in private ownership. Complicated arrangements, such as the common practice of hire-work (unique to Sheffield) blurred this neat division. As Britain's share of overseas trade declined and the UK demand for alloy steel in the engineering industry (ships, cars, aircraft) suffered from the recession, the BSC's ambitious plans for expansion were laid to rest. By the later 1970s Sheffield no longer produced as much alloy steel as did countries as diverse as Brazil, Italy, Spain and Sweden.

Drastic re-structuring was agreed upon. In 1976 British Steel Stainless was created and its Shepcote Lane site was developed into the biggest purpose-built stainless steel plant in Europe. The ESC's new Tinsley Park Works were closed by the mid-1980s, when production was concentrated at Stocksbridge. Meanwhile, well-known names in private industry disappeared in mergers. In the tool steel manufacturing sector, Balfour's were amalgamated with Darwin's, and Sanderson Bros & Newbould were merged with Kayser, Ellison. Under its chairman, (Sir) Robert Atkinson – a Tynesider in origin – Aurora quickly rose from a modest position as gear manufacturers to become the fifth largest engineering group in Sheffield by 1978. The company then turned its attention to tool steels. In 1978 Aurora took over Osborn's; in 1979 they acquired Edgar Allen Balfour. For a time, Aurora were making 60 per cent of the nation's tool steel, with a work-force of 4,000, but by 1983 they had huge debts and their steel business collapsed. The remaining tool steel firms – Barworth Flockton, Carlisle's, Carr's, Johnson & Firth Brown, Neepsend, and Sanderson Kayser – employed fewer than 5,000 workers. Worse was to come. In the tool steel sector, the number of workers fell from 20,000 in 1970 to 1,200 in 1991.

Until 1981 Sheffield's post-war unemployment level was continuously below the national average, but the city's work-force was seen to be dangerously dependent on the traditional industries. In 1979 Sheffield's manufacturing base began to shrink drastically. Both the British Steel Corporation and the private firms faced serious difficulties from foreign competition and the shrinking home market in engineering. During the 1970s, the BSC lost £2,836 million, its annual production of steel fell from 24.2 million to 14.1 million tonnes, and its national work-force was reduced from 252,400 to 166,400. Sheffield firms were forced to strive for even higher quality in their special steels. They had, however, to reduce labour costs and to make steel in sufficient bulk to justify investment.

The massive redundancies and the wholesale closures of steel and engineering works in the 1980s were unprecedented. Until the late 1960s Sheffield's unemployed numbered about 6,000, or 2 per cent of the work-force. Between January 1976 and January 1980 unemployment fluctuated between 12,000 and 14,000, or 4.3 to 5.1 per cent. The turning point came in 1980, with huge numbers of job losses. Unemployment in the city reached a peak of 47,500 (16.3 per cent) of the registered labour-force in 1987. Some estimates of the real number of unemployed go up by another 15,000. In parts of Sheffield, a very high proportion of the inhabitants were out of work. A natural response was to protest vociferously against the closures, but the national steel strike of 1981 ended in failure.

In 1980 the British Steel Corporation and the private sector launched a series of joint ventures under the name 'Phoenix'. Two years later, at a particularly bleak time for the industry, Sheffield Forgemasters was formed by combining several disparate firms, including those which had once traded under the names of Vickers, Cammell, Brown and Firth. The capacity for huge forgings at the River Don Works was increased, but the remaining part of John Brown's Atlas Works was closed in 1983, only ten years after it had been modernised. The collapse of the market for forgings, caused mainly by the high exchange rate and the virtual disappearance of British industries such as shipbuilding, brought the new company close to receivership by 1984. Sheffield Forgemasters slowly turned the corner under the forceful management of Peter Wright from 1985. Meanwhile, in 1983, the ESC's Templeborough site ceased production, and Lohnro, the owners of Dunford Hadfield, closed Brown Bayley's and Hadfield's East Hecla Works, which had been the scene of mass-picketing in the bitter strike of 1981.

Some of the old family firms in the private sector survived. The fortunes of William Cook, the steel castings firm, were transformed by Andrew Cook, the great-great-grandson of the founder. But, generally, the Sheffield steel industry was no longer dependent on local talent and capital. It was now characterised by large-scale businesses which were run as public companies, with professional managers and technologists.

Employment in the South Yorkshire steel industry (i.e. Rotherham as well as Sheffield) fell from 60,000 in 1971 to 43,000 in 1979 and to 16,000 in 1987. By the mid-1990s, the work-force had fallen below 10,000. About two-thirds of the total registered unemployment in the Sheffield district came from the loss of jobs in the steelworks. The cutlery and tool making industries were contracting rapidly at the same time. Within only a few years, Sheffield had lost much of its ancient and distinctive character as an industrial centre. The majority of the local labour-force were no longer employed in either the 'heavy' or the 'light' trades. A long era in the history of the city was coming to a close.

By 1981 all the metalworking trades together employed only 27.5 per cent of the Sheffield work-force, and all the other manufacturing activity employed only another 8 per cent. The trend, as in other parts of the country, was towards employment in services. Half the registered work-force in the city (50.8 per cent) now worked in services, and another 5.6 per cent found jobs in transport and communications. The steel industry accounted for only 9.9 per cent of the work-force in 1981, since when it has fallen by more than half. Many of the old jobs had been skilled and well paid. Many of the new jobs went to women, for less pay, and often on a part-time basis. By the mid-1990s, two-thirds of the jobs in Sheffield were in the service sector; only one-quarter of the work-force found employment in manufacturing. The leading employers were all in the service sector: the City Council, the Sheffield Health Authority, and the two universities.

The Meadowhall shopping mall, with 7,000 workers, employed more people than any of the local steel companies.

But the employment figures tell only part of the story. The local steel industry is still of international importance. At the beginning of the twenty-first century Sheffield and Rotherham have some of the most advanced and productive steel-melting facilities in the world. Almost all of Britain's special engineering and stainless steels are made here. Modern technology has destroyed jobs, but more steel is now made in Sheffield than during the Second World War.

Regeneration

The catastrophic fall in the numbers of people employed in Sheffield's industries occurred at a time when the Labour-controlled City Council was locked in combat with the Conservative central government. The 'new urban left' had become a political force in many of Britain's cities during the 1970s. In Sheffield, a group of left-wing councillors based in the Brightside parliamentary constituency gradually took over the leadership of the local Labour Party. By 1980 they were in control. David Blunkett was elected as the Labour group leader and others were chosen to chair the important committees. They soon came into conflict with the Conservative government. In 1981 they refused to make Sheffield one of the government's new enterprise zones. The red flag was flown from the Town Hall on May Day and the city was declared a nuclear-free zone. The steel strike of 1981 and the coal strike of 1984–85, when mass pickets demonstrated outside Hadfield's and the Orgreave coking plant, heightened the tension, for the Thatcher government was determined to curb the powers of both local government and the trade unions. The City Council lost business tax revenue when works closed, yet had to cope with increasing demand for its services from the unemployed. The central government were meanwhile reducing grants and trying to force local councils to reduce the levels of local taxation. 'Rate-capping' was introduced to limit the amount of revenue that local councils could raise from local rates.

For a time, it seemed that Sheffield was going the same way as Liverpool, but in the mid-1980s, faced by the realities of the deep recession, the City Council abandoned confrontational politics. The turning point came in 1985, when 20 Labour councillors refused to follow the party leadership and voted with the opposition to agree a legal maximum rate. The unity of the party was shattered. A few months later, a leading group of businessmen who were prominent in the Chamber of Commerce approached the Labour group on the council to establish a working relationship that would promote Sheffield and attract new jobs. A new mood of realism gradually replaced previous hostility, and in December 1986 the Sheffield Economic Regeneration Committee was born as a collaborative venture between the public and private sectors in order to regenerate the Lower Don Valley. The shift in council policy from an interventionist stance to a market-led approach was remarkable.

At first, the future of the Lower Don Valley dominated discussions. The City

Ponds Forge. Sheffield built some of the best sporting centres in Britain in order to host the World Student Games in 1991. The Olympic-standard swimming complex was named after the old Ponds Forge of George Senior & Sons, Ltd, whose former entrance has been re-positioned to good effect.

PHOTOGRAPH: L. NUTTALL

Council had cleared the slums, but had built no high-rise flats in the east end. Its plan had been to remove housing from the industrial zone. But the steelworks had not moved into the empty spaces left by the old terraces of Carbrook, Attercliffe and Brightside. Instead, many of the steelworks had gone too. Many parts of the east end now had neither housing nor industry. Between 1975 and 1988 the number of jobs in the east end had fallen from 40,000 to 13,000. By 1988 fewer than 300 people still lived there and 40 per cent of all the available land was vacant, derelict or under-used. Firth Brown's, Hadfield's and Brown Bayley's had all been flattened. The appearance of the district had also been changed by the measures taken under the Clean Air Act and by cleaner steelmaking technologies. Parts of the east end now looked green for the first time for well over a hundred years. A pleasant walk could be enjoyed along the canal towpath.

The Sheffield Economic Regeneration Committee launched a promotional campaign to attract new industry, investment and jobs. A city-centre Sheffield

Trams returned to Sheffield in the mid-1990s, but the sleek, smooth running Supertrams are a far cry from the trams that ceased running in 1960. The Supertrams were built at Siemens Duewag works in Dusseldorf.

PHOTOGRAPH: CARNEGIE

Built in 1998 as the ill-fated National Centre for Popular Music, this striking modern building is now used by the Students' Union of Sheffield Hallam University. Designed to a cruciform plan by the firm of Branson Coates, the building has two floors and a basement. The four drums are clad in stainless steel and tilt outwards.
PHOTOGRAPH: L. NUTTALL

Science Park, for high-technology industry, and a Cultural Industries Quarter, for media, design, and music were early developments. Sheffield was promoted as a tourist and conference centre, and as a pleasanter and cheaper place for London-based civil servants and the office staff of insurance companies and banks to work and live. The Manpower Services Commission (now the Employment Service) had led the way in 1980, when they moved into a huge new building at the bottom of The Moor. Leisure and sport were identified as key providers of future jobs and as an area where Sheffield could claim an important new role as a national centre of excellence. In the late 1980s the City Council committed itself to an ambitious, and controversial, £100 million programme to make Sheffield into a major sports and cultural centre, starting with the holding of the 1991 World Student Games. An Olympic-standard swimming pool and diving pool, with seating for over 3,000 spectators, and an associated sports complex were built in the city centre on the site of the old Ponds Forge, a basketball stadium and leisure centre was opened on Penistone Road, and the Don Valley Stadium, with covered seats for 10,000 spectators and room for many more on the open ter-races, was built for athletics. Ponds Forge has since then been the regular venue for national swimming events. The Don Valley Stadium has attracted major ath-letic competitions and has become the home of the Sheffield Eagles Rugby League team. The nearby 12,000-seat Arena was opened about the same time as an indoor entertainment centre, home to the Sheffield Steelers ice-hockey team, and a suit-able venue for Pavarotti, Carreras and a regular stream of famous pop singers.

The most dramatic change to the city came with the decision to build an American-style shopping mall on the site of Hadfield's East Hecla Works. The original Meadowhall was actually on the hilltop on the other side of the Blackburn

Valley, but the name was thought to be more attractive for a shopping centre than East Hecla. Eddie Healey and Paul Sykes got the project off the ground, with finance from private sources and an Urban Regeneration Grant. Meadowhall cost £250 million to build, and shopfitting and associated costs added another £200 million to the bill. When finished, it offered a totally enclosed shopping district, with free parking for 11,000 vehicles, and 1.2 million square feet of shops. Trains and (soon) trams stopped close by, and the proximity of the M1 motorway brought shoppers from far afield. Meadowhall was opened in September 1990. It has been a huge success.

The progress of the London Docklands scheme encouraged the central government to offer large sums of money for the regeneration of derelict areas elsewhere, provided that the responsible body was not the local council but an unelected Urban Development Corporation. Sheffield was offered £50 million if the council gave up its planning powers to such a body. The City Council wanted to do the job themselves, but the central government insisted on its terms. The new conciliatory mood won the day. The City Council and the Sheffield

Development Corporation, with Hugh Sykes as its chairman, agreed to a programme of close, practical co-operation. By December 1988 the SDC staff had been installed at Don Valley House, Savile Street East, at what had recently been the heart of the steelmaking district.

The SDC was given full control of planning for the area under its authority, stretching from the Wicker Arches and the old canal basin by the city centre as far as the M1 motorway. The SDC did not own any land at first, but had the power to make compulsory purchases. This naturally led to controversy when the SDC made the first proposals to use these powers so as to obtain land for a

Aerial view of the centre of Sheffield, 2004, showing work progressing on the Heart of the City Project, featuring the Peace Gardens, Winter Gardens, Millennium Gallery, and a new hotel.

© WEBBAVIATION.CO.UK

above Meadowhall Shopping Centre. Built on the site of Hadfield's East Hecla Works, as one of the largest shopping malls in Britain, Meadowhall has been hugely successful in attracting shoppers from near and far.
PHOTOGRAPH: CARNEGIE

proposed new road through the valley. After a long and bitter battle, the SDC agreed on more modest road proposals, which would not affect the companies which still traded successfully. The new Don Valley Link Road cost £30 million and was the SDC's biggest single item of expenditure. It provided quick access from the M1 or the city centre to purpose-built premises on attractive sites, with ample parking. The Carbrook Hall Business Park was soon filled with offices, notably the Abbey National share registry headquarters, which was opened in a new building in 1992. The Meadowhall retail park was the next to grow. Major infrastructure work was completed throughout the SDC's territory, much of it hidden from view. In particular, the Don Valley Intercepting Sewer was a necessary and massive engineering project. Much effort was also put into landscaping, and the River Don was re-stocked with fish; a mix of dace and chub. At the city centre end of the valley, the canal basin was transformed and re-named Victoria Quays. This scheme, involving a hotel, restaurant, offices, a design innovation centre, art gallery, craft market, heritage centre, and facilities for open-air events, was officially launched by the Prince of Wales in the winter of 1994. The effects of the national recession slowed down the expected progress, but the SDC's life was extended to 31 March 1997, after which the City Council resumed its authority in the Lower Don Valley. The SDC finished with a flourish with the opening of the long-projected business airport in Tinsley Park. This failed as a commercial venture, however, and has been replaced by the Robin Hood (Doncaster & Sheffield) Airport at Finningley.

The City Council's acceptance of the SDC typified the new realism that became increasingly evident after the re-election of the Conservative government in 1987. The departure of some prominent local councillors for new careers as Members of Parliament signalled the end of confrontational politics. During the following year, Sheffield City Council regained many of the powers that it had lost in 1974 to the new South Yorkshire County Council, whose headquarters were at Barnsley. The Labour-controlled SYCC had waged a long and ultimately unsuccessful battle against the central government over its policy of cheap bus fares. When it was abolished in 1988, together with the other metropolitan counties, its environmental and structural planning powers went to the four local district councils (Sheffield, Barnsley, Rotherham and Doncaster), and its powers over police, fire services and transport were transferred to joint boards of these four councils.

By the 1990s the co-operation between the City Council, the SDC and the Chamber of Commerce had been extended to include other institutions, such as the two universities, in a body known as the City Liaison Group. Individual representatives differed on many matters, but all were agreed that ways must be found to regenerate Sheffield's economy by clearly targeted public investment. Attention turned from the east end to the city centre, whose shops had been hit by the competition of Meadowhall and by the long disruption caused by the laying of tracks for Supertrams. Towards the end of 1994, a strategy for the future of the city centre was agreed by the City Liaison Group. Between 1990 and 1996 at least £300 million pounds was invested in the city centre, and another £200 million was projected for further developments by the end of the century. The main investments were: Supertram £100 million, the Universities £72 million, Ponds Forge £52 million, Sheff Heat and Power £14 million, Transport Interchange £10 million, and Victoria Quays £10 million, but numerous smaller projects helped in the general improvement. The city centre still has twice as many shops as Meadowhall, and more than £450 million a year was spent there compared with £325 million at the new shopping centre, but Sheffield clearly lags behind Leeds, Manchester and Nottingham as an attractive venue for the modern national pastime of shopping. Traffic congestion and inadequate parking remain headaches for planners and the public alike, though a northern ring road is under construction and some thoroughfares have been made safer and more attractive for pedestrians. A major scheme is under way to improve access to and from the railway station and huge investments have been made in modernising the City Hall and Weston Park Museum and Mappin Art Gallery.

Sheffield has obtained outside funding for its major development programmes, such as the regeneration of the Manor, Wybourn, Park Hill and Castle estates.

The Crucible, 1996. Opened in 1971 as the successor to the old Playhouse in Townhead Street, the Crucible's innovative thrust stage and the quality of its productions have attracted large audiences and critical acclaim. It recently won the National Theatre of the Year Award. The Crucible Studio is the home of the annual Music Festivals organised by The Lindsays.
PHOTOGRAPH: L. NUTTALL

A HISTORY OF SHEFFIELD

The National Lottery provided funds for the National Ice Centre and the striking building that was opened as the National Centre for Popular Music but is now the Sheffield Hallam University's Students' Union building. Other public money has funded the successful Heart of the City Project, which involved redesigning the Peace Gardens as a public space and building the Millennium Gallery and the Winter Gardens, which have become major attractions.

The World Student Games turned out to be a huge drain on the city's resources, but it was a psychological turning-point. The city at last started to look outwards rather than inwards. No serious cost-benefit analysis had been made before the event. The games themselves went well, but the huge costs of

The Yemeni Economic and Training Centre. The various immigrants from Commonwealth countries who have settled in the old industrial districts of Sheffield since the 1950s have often adapted old buildings to serve as mosques or as community centres. The Yemeni Economic and Training Centre, for example, has converted the Victorian vestry hall at Attercliffe.

PHOTOGRAPH: L. NUTTALL

The Lyceum. Built as the City Theatre in 1890 and remodelled as the Lyceum seven years later, the theatre closed in 1969 and for many years it appeared forlorn until it was fully restored in 1990. Its touring productions complement the repertory work at the Crucible.

providing facilities left the City Council with large debts. Other council services have suffered as a result. Deteriorating school buildings, closed libraries, and a general shortage of money for all services were a legacy of the games. Politically, Labour lost much of its local support in the following years. The disruption created by the Supertram installation increased the dissatisfaction, though the council was not directly responsible. The Liberals Democrats capitalised on this unrest, capturing seats in the Labour heartland as well as replacing the Conservatives as the main opposition party in the city. After the local elections in 1996 only one Conservative councillor retained his seat in the Town Hall. Between 1999 and 2002 the Liberal Democrats were the governing party, but Labour recovered after a change of leadership and new policies, and in 2003 secured a sound majority.

In 1993 well over half of Sheffield's top twenty companies were either in steel or related industries. The local economy is nevertheless more diversified now than before. In line with national trends, it has become increasingly dependent on small- and medium-sized companies with a turnover of between £5 million and £100 million. In 1995 Sheffield had over 3,200 small businesses, which employed between 10 and 200 people. Some of Sheffield's best-known businesses outside

A HISTORY OF SHEFFIELD

steel, cutlery and tools, have been around for a considerable time. Henry Boot (1851–1931) started as a builder, like his father and grandfather before him, then expanded into construction and civil engineering; his son, Charles, was largely responsible for the development of the firm and for moving the headquarters to Banner Cross Hall in 1932. The history of a similar firm, A. Monk & Co., goes back to 1868, that of R. J. Stokes, interior decorators, to 1889, and that of Arnold Laver, timber merchants, to 1920. Tuckwood's, Sheffield's oldest restaurant, was established in 1856 in Fargate, before moving to Surrey Street. Henderson's Relish has been made in Portobello for over a century. Their near neighbours, Harrison's, the steeplejacks, go back to 1854, and J. W. Northend's, the printers, to the late-Victorian period. J. W. Thornton's confectionery business was started in 1911. Some other firms have risen spectacularly since the Second World War, none more so than that of Ernest Adsetts, who was born in a terrace house in Grimesthorpe in 1905, the son of a steel worker. His ice-cream and catering businesses were going through a bad time in 1956, when he and his son Norman began the home-insulation business that became Sheffield Insulations. Local businesses therefore continue to play an important role in Sheffield's economy, but in recent decades the city has also followed national trends in the provision of supermarkets and other stores with household names, both in the city centre and in disused quarries in the suburbs.

Education, religion and recreation

The rapid growth of Sheffield's two universities since the 1960s has had an enormous impact on the landscape, economy and prestige of the city, and mixed social consequences for the residential districts that lie close to the two institutions. Sheffield University has become one of the best of the old civics; Sheffield Hallam University one of the best of the old polytechnics. In 1995–96 Sheffield University taught 13,506 undergraduates and 4,820 graduate students (2,588 of whom were classified as international students), as well as thousands of part-timers. Facilities were improved in the 1960s, with the building of the Library, the Arts Tower, University House, and other steel, glass and brick buildings. The expansion continued in the succeeding decades with a series of teaching buildings until the two old centres at Western Bank and Portobello had been joined and the University had spread to Crookesmoor. The huge growth in student numbers also led to the building of halls of residence in Endcliffe, Tapton and Ranmoor – the superior residential district of the mid-Victorian era – and the conversion of numerous houses into self-catering flats. Local residents, especially in and around Broomhill, have seen the character of their area altered in ways that they have often thought undesirable. For example, the side streets have become one vast car park. But as an employer of 5,393 people and an annual income of £159.6 million, Sheffield University makes a large contribution to the local economy. The collective purchasing power of students is also of great benefit to local traders. The University's significance lies not only in its international standing for its research and teaching, but in its role in the local community, providing expertise to local industry and public services and, through its Medical School, enhancing the skills and facilities offered by the Hallamshire and Northern General Hospitals.

The gradual merging of the College of Technology and the College of Art was completed in 1969 upon the creation of one of Britain's first three Polytechnics. The School of Art was housed in a new building in Psalter Lane in 1970, while the College of Technology grew on its old Pond Street site. As a Local Education Authority, the City of Sheffield had created its own Training College in 1905, followed by the Thornbridge Hall College, near Ashford-in-the-Water, in 1948, and Totley Hall College, for domestic science teachers, two years later. In 1976 these three colleges joined the new polytechnic, which was re-named the Sheffield City Polytechnic, with Dr George Tolley as principal. The Polytechnic quickly earned a reputation for its 'sandwich-degree' courses, and then for its courses leading to higher degrees. On 1 April 1989 it became independent of the City Council. When it achieved university status in October 1992, it was re-named Sheffield Hallam University, in a conscious attempt to retain the name of an old district.

Further Education expanded at the same time as the two Universities. Granville College was the only FE college in Sheffield until Richmond, Shirecliffe and Stannington Colleges were built. They catered principally for the 16–18 age group, but also became the homes for both practical and liberal adult education classes, alongside the academic courses provided by the Workers' Educational Association (in Sheffield since 1929) and the Department of Extramural Studies at the University of Sheffield (since 1947).

In the 1950s and 1960s Sheffield LEA built a lot of new schools, in the brighter, less formal styles that were being introduced all over the country. Tinsley Junior School, on Bawtry Road (1963–65), is a good example. The last all-age school was closed in 1965. The raising of the school-leaving age, first to 15 then to 16, meant that larger secondary schools were required. Examples include Hurlfield Secondary School (1952–56) and Silverdale Secondary Modern (1954–56). The school population reached 110,000 at its peak in the 1960s. Myers Grove, the first of the local comprehensive schools, was opened in 1960. Two years later, the City Council decided to implement comprehensive education by stages, throughout Sheffield. The last 11-plus examination was held in February 1968. This contentious policy was continued by the local Conservatives when they achieved a temporary majority in 1968–69. An HMI report in 1987 was broadly supportive of the policies of the LEA, whose schools were thought to be 'fundamentally sound and well'. That optimism was soon eroded by the severe financial problems faced by the City Council as a legacy of the World Student Games and the reduction in central government funding, by the problems of reorganisation to deal with falling enrolments, and by the increased pressures on teachers from the central government's National Curriculum and OFSTED inspections.

The Cathedral remained a focus for the life of the city, despite falling church attendance. St Marie's was also upgraded to cathedral status, when the Roman Catholic Diocese of Hallam was created in 1980, with Gerald Moverley as the first bishop. The rebuilding of the bombed church of St Mark's Broomhill, the remodelling of the nave of All Saints, Ecclesall (1964), and the construction of churches on new estates, e.g. Greenhill (1963), pointed to continued vitality as the Church of England sought a role in an industrial city. In 1970 the inter-denominational YMCA, whose Sheffield branch had been founded in 1855, moved from the building that they had occupied in Fargate from 1891 to 1967 into new premises at Broomhall. But from the 1960s churches and chapels throughout Britain experienced a steady reduction of membership. The reduced social role of churches and chapels in face of other attractions was part of the problem. The Whit Sings withered away. Sheffield was no longer a Methodist city. In 1989 an English Church Census discovered that church or chapel attendance in South Yorkshire amounted to only 5.8 per cent of the adult population, compared with a national average of 9.5 per cent. The Free Churches attracted 2.4 per cent, the Church of England 1.9 per cent, and the Roman Catholic Church 1.5 per cent. The evangelical congregations, who had sometimes taken over old buildings from failing denominations rather than erect new churches, were the only ones that bucked the trend. They included churches whose members came from an Afro-Caribbean background.

Late twentieth-century Sheffield also has its Moslems, Sikhs, Buddhists and Hindus. The first immigrants to settle in Sheffield after the war were 1,200 members of the Polish armed forces, who did not wish to return to Russian-occupied Poland. They gradually became integrated into local society. A major change came in the 1950s, when large numbers of workers arrived from distant parts of the British Commonwealth, particularly people who had been born in East and West Pakistan, the Yemen, or the West Indies. Men usually arrived without their families and took unskilled jobs in the east end steelworks or in the public services, particularly transport. The settlers came with different expectations and from different backgrounds. Many of them had no intention of staying permanently. The reality was hard work and long hours in jobs that other people did not want to do. The Bangladeshis who came from the Sylhet area of east Pakistan (a poor rural region) were unique amongst the immigrant groups in that many of them often knew each other well before emigrating. By 1972 an estimated 12,000 immigrants were living in Sheffield, including 5,000 from the West Indies and 5,000 from the combined areas of present-day Pakistan and Bangladesh. They faced considerable hostility from sections of the native population, though their numbers were relatively small compared with those of the Commonwealth immigrants in the West Riding textile towns. Most of these settlers moved into the old working-class districts around the steelworks, at Darnall, Attercliffe, Tinsley, Wincobank, Brightside, Grimesthorpe, Burngreave, Firvale and Firth Park. Later, the Abbeydale Road district became popular amongst immigrant groups, with communities in Highfield, Lowfield, Sharrow, and Heeley. When the steel industry declined, the unskilled jobs were the first to go; unemployment rates amongst the newcomers remain high. From 1962 to 1981 the British government passed increasingly severe measures to restrict entry into the country, but wives and children were allowed to join their menfolk and for much of the 1960s and 1970s the Indian sub-continent continued to send skilled and professional workers. The main group of Somalis came in the 1980s as political refugees, after escaping from civil war. Racial tensions have lessened in recent years, and the younger generation frequently choose partners from different ethnic origins. Islam has been a unifying force for many of the immigrant groups, though the various mosques are as 'denominational' in their outlook as are the Christian churches and chapels. Some old buildings in the east end, including some chapels, have been converted into mosques, and Industry Road, Darnall, has a purpose-built mosque, complete with minaret.

In the late twentieth century Sheffield has become an entertainment centre that attracts people from many parts of South Yorkshire and the north Midlands. The first attraction was the Crucible Theatre, which opened in 1971 with a thrust stage in the main auditorium and a smaller studio for experimental plays and special events. Its name had appropriate associations with Sheffield steel and, through Arthur Miller's play, with the world of theatre. No-one at the time imagined that the Crucible would become nationally famous as the home of the World Snooker Championship. The neighbouring Lyceum had been closed as a theatre in 1969, but survived as the occasional venue of bingo and pop concerts. In December 1990, after full restoration to its former glory, it was re-opened with a performance of *The Pirates of Penzance*. The Lyceum has attracted national touring productions, while The Crucible has been the home of a repertory company. The Millennium Gallery, Graves Art Gallery and Central Library complete a cultural centre in the heart of the city. Meanwhile, amateur dramatics has flourished round the corner at Montgomery Hall and at a church in Glossop Road that was converted into the University Drama Studio. The major musical events have been the weekly series of concerts by the Hallé and other famous orchestras at the City Hall, where the annual performance of 'The Messiah' by the Sheffield Philharmonic Society (founded 1935) became the most popular musical event of the year. More recently, performances by the Lindsay String Quartet and other small ensembles and soloists have attracted enthusiastic audiences at the Crucible Studio. The annual music festival has become nationally famous.

The arrival of television in Sheffield in 1954 reduced cinema audiences dramatically, but since the late 1980s cinema-going has revived. In 1988 a ten-screen cinema on American lines was opened at Crystal Peaks. Sheffield now has a wide choice of cinemas, in the city centre and at a major new complex in Broughton Lane. The most astonishing change in the Sheffield night scene, however, has been in the growth of clubs. The first post-war multi-entertainment centre was the Epic Building in Arundel Gate, which opened in 1968 with a night-club, ballroom, shops, cinema and car park. In the 1990s Sheffield began to rival Manchester and Leeds as a major centre for clubs which offer music and dancing throughout the night. In 1996, even the local magistrates eventually recognised that the granting of longer licences might not lead to disaster. Sheffield is on its way to becoming 'a twenty-four hour city' for entertainment. For young people, the most famous Sheffielders are Jarvis Cocker and Pulp, and Deff Leppard. Middle-aged Sheffielders might choose Joe Cocker, late of Crookes, now of Colorado.

The city is also a regular venue for national swimming and athletics tournaments and FA Cup semi-finals. At one such event, on 15 April 1989 Hillsborough was the scene of Britain's worst soccer disaster, when 95 Liverpool supporters were crushed to death and 766 injured; the causes of the disaster are still bitterly debated. The two grounds at Hillsborough and Bramall Lane have been substantially improved, but since the war neither soccer club had won a major honour until Wednesday won the Rumbelows (or League) Cup in 1991. In the city's centenary year in 1993 Wednesday reached both Cup Finals, after beating United at Wembley in the FA Cup, but lost both final matches to Arsenal. Cricket supporters have had less to cheer about since the Yorkshire County Cricket Club were triumphant in the 1960s. In 1973 the cricket pitch at Bramall Lane was torn up, and although Yorkshire CCC kept up a minimal presence at Abbeydale Park, by the end of the century they will have abandoned the place where they were founded. Meanwhile, numerous local football and cricket teams continue to play at an amateur level.

Sheffield has its share of sporting heroes outside football and cricket, the most famous being Sebastian Coe. Brendan Ingle's St Thomas's gym, at Wincobank, has produced the boxing champions Herrol Graham and Naseem Hamed. In recent years new games have attracted strong support. The Sheffield Eagles

Rugby League team beat Wigan in a memorable Cup Final in 1998. The Sheffield Steelers ice hockey team have fervent followers at the Arena. Enormous crowds cheered the 4,500 runners in the first Sheffield Marathon, on a hot and humid 6 June 1982; the race has become an annual event. The most unlikely of all these successful ventures is the Ski Village, which boasts the biggest artificial ski-slope in Europe. Increased leisure and the proximity of Sheffield and the Peak District's open spaces have encouraged rambling and climbing, at various levels of effort and expertise.

In the late 1990s Sheffield became internationally famous as the setting for *The Full Monty*, the most popular film ever made in Britain. Audiences throughout the world responded emotionally to the plight of a group of unemployed men, to their enterprise in dealing with their situation, and to their deadpan humour. The Sheffield experience struck a chord everywhere.

For most of its long history, Sheffield has been an inward-looking community, tucked into the Pennine edges and badly connected to other places until the M1 was built in the 1960s. The continuity of so many families over the generations is remarkable for such a large city. This insularity gives the place real strengths at times, but it can also lead to sentimentality and to an acceptance of the second best. Despite being the fifth city in England in terms of population, Sheffield still fits the old description of 'the biggest village in the world'. The city centre does not have the metropolitan feel of Manchester or Leeds, and the hills and valleys still give the suburbs a strong sense of being separate communities. Perhaps as a consequence of all this, Sheffield is a safer place than most large cities. This is not to deny that certain districts are notorious or that Sheffield does not have its share of social problems. The unemployment rate is well above the national average, and though the average standard of living is much higher than it was a generation ago many people have to struggle. There is, however, a general feeling that Sheffield is recovering from the hardships of the 1980s. At the beginning of the twenty-first century, a new air of confidence is apparent.

Select bibliography

Barraclough, K. C., *Sheffield Steel* (Hartington, 1976).

Barraclough, K. C., *Steelmaking Before Bessemer: Blister Steel; Crucible Steel*, 2 vols (London, 1984).

Binfield, C., Childs, R., Harper R., Hey, D., Martin, D., and Tweedale, G. (eds), *The History of the City of Sheffield, 1843–1993*, 3 vols (Sheffield, 1993).

Binfield, C. and Hey, D. (eds), *Mesters to Masters: A History of the Company of Cutlers in Hallamshire* (Oxford, 1997).

Bradbury, F., *History of Old Sheffield Plate* (Sheffield, 1968 reprint).

Crossley, D., Cass, N., Flavell, N., and Turner, C. (eds), *Water Power on the Sheffield Rivers* (Sheffield, 1989).

English Heritage, *'One Great Workshop': The Buildings of the Sheffield Metal Trades* (London, 2001).

Flavell, N., 'Urban allotment gardens in the eighteenth century: the case of Sheffield', *Agricultural History Review*, 51,1 (2003), pp. 95–106.

Harman, R. and Minnis, J., *Sheffield: Pevsner Architectural Guides* (New Haven and London, 2004).

Hey, D., *The Fiery Blades of Hallamshire: Sheffield and its Neighbourhood, 1660–1740* (Leicester, 1991).

Hey, D., 'Yorkshire's Southern Boundary', *Northern History*, xxxvii (December 2000), pp. 31–47.

Hey, D., *Historic Hallamshire: History in Sheffield's Countryside* (Ashbourne, 2002).

Hey, D., Olive, M. and Liddament, M., *The Forging of the Valley* (Sheffield, 1997).

Hunter, J., *Hallamshire: The History and Topography of the Parish of Sheffield in the County of York*, revised edition by A. Gatty (Sheffield, 1869).

Jones, M., *Sheffield's Woodland Heritage* (Sheffield, 2003).

Jones, M. (ed.), *Aspects of Sheffield, I: Discovering Local History* (Barnsley, 1997).

Leader, R. E., *Sheffield in the Eighteenth Century* (Sheffield, 1901).

Leader, R. E., *The History of the Company of Cutlers in Hallamshire*, 2 vols (Sheffield, 1905–6).

Leader, J. D. (ed.), *The Records of the Burgery of Sheffield* (Sheffield, 1897).

Lloyd, G. I. H., *The Cutlery Trades* (London, 1968 reprint).

Mathers, H., *Steel City Scholars: The Centenary History of the University of Sheffield* (London, 2005).

Nether Edge Neighbourhood Group, *They Lived in Sharrow and Nether Edge* (Sheffield, 1988).

Myers, S., *Cars from Sheffield: The Rise and Fall of the Sheffield Motor Industry, 1900–1930* (Sheffield, 1986).

Olive, M., *Central Sheffield* (Bath, 1994).

Pawson and Brailsford's *Illustrated Guide to Sheffield and Neighbourhood* (Sheffield, 1862, 1879).

Pollard, S., *A History of Labour in Sheffield* (Liverpool, 1959).

Pollard, S. (ed.), *The Sheffield Outrages* (Bath, 1971).

Pybus, S., *'Damned Bad Place, Sheffield'* (Sheffield, 1994).

Roach, J., *The Shrewsbury Hospital, Sheffield, 1616–1975* (York, 2003).

Smith, A. H. (ed.), *The Place Names of the West Riding of Yorkshire*, I (Cambridge, 1961).

Tweedale, G., *Sheffield Steel and America: A Century of Commercial and Technological Interdependence, 1830–1930* (Cambridge, 1987).

Tweedale, G., *Steel City: Entrepreneurship, Strategy, and Technology in Sheffield, 1743–1993* (Oxford, 1995).

Tweedale, G., *The Sheffield Knife Book* (Sheffield, 1996).

Unwin, J, 'The Smithy Hearths of Sheffield, 1672', *Transactions of the Hunter Archaeological Society*, 21 (2001), pp. 78–95.

Walton, M., *Sheffield: Its Story and Its Achievements* (Sheffield, 4th edition, 1968).

Numerous articles on the history of Sheffield have been published in the *Transactions of the Hunter Archaeological Society*, which has appeared annually since 1914. A complete collection of printed material relating to Sheffield can be consulted in the Local Studies Department in Sheffield Central Library.

The documentary sources which have been used for this book are housed in various local and national record offices. The collections in Sheffield Archives, in Shoreham Street, are particularly rich in local material and are far too numerous to list. The Cutlers' Company archives and the tools and catalogues of the Hawley Collection at the University of Sheffield are important sources for the history of local industry. Probate and church records are kept at the Borthwick Institute of Historical Research, York, and the Lichfield Joint Record Office. Other records are housed at the West Yorkshire Archive Service, Wakefield, the National Archives (formerly the Public Record Office), Kew, and the British Library, London.

Acknowledgements

I WOULD PARTICULARLY LIKE TO THANK past and present members of staff at the Local Studies Department in Sheffield Central Library; Sheffield Archives; Sheffield City Museums and Art Galleries; Sheffield Industrial Museums Trust; the Cutlers' Hall; and the Hawley Building, the University of Sheffield, for their friendly and professional assistance over the years and for supplying many of the illustrations. I also give my warm thanks to Alistair Hodge and Claire Walker for all their help with the illustrations and design of the book.

Index

Index entries in *italic* type refer to illustrations or to information given within illustration captions.